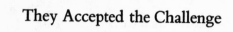

They Accepted the Challenge

Also by the author:

The Physical Fitness Encyclopedia
Activetics
Color Me Red!
Heartbeat
Rating the Exercises
The Exerciser's Handbook
The Complete Book of Walking
Consumer Guide to a Flatter Stomach
The Complete Book of Marathon Running
The Complete Guide to Figure Shaping
The Beat Goes On

DEDICATED TO

Mother and Daddy—
    who challenged me to do my best.
Al Erdosy and Bill Garrett—
    who challenged me physically.
Carol—
    who taught me self-confidence to face
    any challenge.
Beth—
    who walks with me in the challenge of life.
Debbie, John, Tom, Lisa, and Becky—
    who make the challenge of life worthwhile.

Contents

Acknowledgments

I have many people to thank who helped make this book come alive. Lyn Cryderman deserves a special accolade for helping me write this book. His writing, criticisms, suggestions, setting up of interviews, and follow-up were and are greatly appreciated. Without him this book would still be in the starting blocks.

I acknowledge the assistance of Dan Runyon and Lynette Van Alstine: Dan for editorial suggestions that were extremely helpful; Lynette for her patient typing.

Recognition is given to Marvin Fields, M.D., for his review of the medical aspects of the various disease conditions which appear in this book. His directions and advice kept us from straying too far from the proper medical descriptions, although we did take a great deal of liberty in the various explanations.

I'm particularly grateful for the aid and assistance of many others who provided leads on various stories, arranged interviews, and got me to connect with the right people. Thank you's go to Mike Bass; Jeff Boone; Halbe Brown; Thomas Creer, Ph.D.; Marlene Crisler; James Fixx; Terry Hagen, Ph.D.; Pat DeBoer; John Greist, M.D.; Dee Howell; John Huber; Bonnie Hyde; Terence Kavanagh, M.D.; John Kendell; Jo Kennedy; Anne Kufus; Michael Leaverson; Robert Lovell, M.D.; Pat Lundy; Tom Machalki; Roger Martin; Paul Perry; Deborah Pint; George Randt,

M.D.; Grace Reynolds, George Riggins; William Walker; Judy Wilcox; and Harry Welch.

There were several people I interviewed as potential stories for the book but did not include because of space limitations. They have excellent stories to tell, and I was touched by their sincerity and willingness to give of their time. These people are Jean Dubois, Natalie Cooper, Phyllis Friedman, James Goldwasser, Vince Godfrey, Larry Johnson, Bruce Light, James McGowan, Hale Seymour, and all the guys at Dr. Kavanagh's Rehabilitation Centre in Toronto. To all those whose stories I did not use, I apologize.

A special thank you is extended to Barbara Anderson, editor at St. Martin's Press, for her patience and understanding.

Love and kisses go to my wife Beth. Her loving support was magnificent. I am truly thankful for her many valuable criticisms and suggestions as well.

Finally, I want to thank all the people who appear in this book. They interrupted their busy schedules for me and provided kind hospitality. They corresponded via letter and phone frequently regarding the content of their stories. They patiently criticized my rendition of their lives and afflictions. Their candidness and willingness to cooperate were exemplary. I hope I have told their stories well. And trust that the readers will get a glimpse of them and their philosophies of life.

CTK

Introduction

Challenges. I like them. I like to hear about people who overcome insurmountable odds to achieve their goals. They are an inspiration to me in my work and play. A woman, man, or child who accepts challenges is my kind of person. They make me feel good about the human race.

When I see Rocky Bleier of the Pittsburgh Steelers score a touchdown, spring Franco Harris loose with a bone-crushing block, or catch a pass I get chills. The chills are not because Rocky Bleier has the moves of an O.J. or the bullish power of an Earl Campbell. I get excited about Rocky Bleier because of what he had to go through to get to play in the NFL. He had to overcome and rehabilitate himself from a 1969 Vietnam shrapnel wound that damaged his left leg and foot so badly that walking was difficult and running next to impossible. Yet he came back to help lead the Steelers to their shining decade of football.

I think other people like challenge stories as well. Movies, TV shows, and novels play on this theme. Who can forget the dramatic challenge of *Rocky* and the excitement the film generated. The plot was basic: bring a two-bit boxer from the pits to the top of the sports world.

And who could forget that magic moment in February 1980,

when the United States Olympic Hockey Team paraded around the rink at Lake Placid, enjoying that sweetness connected with upsets in sports. No one gave them a chance for the gold. Experts were saying they might be in line for a bronze medal. Few took that prediction as more than wishful thinking. Yet that brash bunch of youngsters forgot to listen to the experts and met the challenge against unbelievable odds.

The drama of a challenge is probably one of the reasons most of us champion the underdog—the one who doesn't seem to have a chance—the Cinderella team or player.

Pastors, politicians, teachers, coaches, athletes, and businessmen punctuate their speeches with stories of people who fought the odds and won. They know there is nothing like a good comeback story to stir people into action.

In my role as fitness consultant, writer, and teacher I also tell challenge stories. I think they're great motivators. I weave these stories into my lectures on the why and how of exercise and the techniques of how to return to a more healthful way of living.

My stories are always about people who exercise in spite of adversity. I use these stories on first-time exercisers or on people who are starting to waver during their first few tenuous weeks of commitment. I've even used them with the veterans.

People are filled with good intentions to exercise. But the good intentions usually last only a few weeks. They miss a day or two for some legitimate reason—a cold, travel, etc. Then they slip back into their old habits and drop their resolve to run, walk, bike, swim, or whatever. Soon they make excuses on why they stop exercising.

In the community where I live—Spring Arbor, Michigan—there's a beautiful college fieldhouse that is within walking distance of every person in town. The college has made this facility available to members of the faculty, students, staff, and community.

During the first week in January the place is packed. Everyone has made a New Year's resolution—a dedication to run laps, lift weights, hit tennis balls, and/or swim. You actually have a difficult time exercising because it's so crowded. During the second week, however, participation falls off appreciably. And by the third or fourth week, the number of participants is down to pre-January levels.

When I first observed this phenomenon, I asked several of the dropouts why they were no longer exercising. On the surface, their excuses seemed valid: It's too hot. It's too cold. I don't feel well. I feel good, so why should I? I can only run in the evening and then it's too dark. I can only run at noon and then it's too hot. I have too many kids at home. No one wants to exercise with me. I just had a heart attack. I've heard that exercising uses up extra heartbeats. My legs get sore when I walk. I'm too old. Young people don't need to exercise. Jogging has no purpose. Tennis is too competitive. Exercise is boring. I don't like to sweat. I don't like the hassle of changing my clothes. My hair gets frizzy. I'm too tired. I have enough energy. I'll get big muscles. I don't have the muscle power to do it. When I run I can't breathe. My wind is good, so I don't need exercise. I don't have time.

Sound familiar? They're the same excuses you've probably heard. Perhaps they're some of the ones you've even used. They're also the same rationalizations I've heard across the U.S. and Canada as a consultant to the National YMCA, Phillips Petroleum Company, and other corporations and schools on matters of health and fitness.

Many times, fitness directors and leaders have asked me, "How do you answer these excuses, Charlie? How do you convince people that you only take time to do the things you want to do?"

I tell them to tell stories—stories about people who exercise in spite of the fact that they may have perfectly legitimate excuses not to. People who swim or run even though they're blind. People who walk in spite of the fact that they are condemned to life in a wheelchair. People who view their handicap as a challenge, not as an excuse.

I tell these stories to everyone—friends, students, children, parents, and even myself. I've found these stories helpful any time my motivation has faltered. When many fitness leaders have taken my advice to heart, they report back that these stories really work. They found them an inspiration which helps many people over their "sticking points."

In 1978, I gave a speech on motivation for fitness at the Center for Disease Control in Atlanta, Georgia. There I talked about Don Klosterman, the general manager of the L.A. Rams. Don was once a fine quarterback in the Canadian professional football league. But a skiing injury paralyzed him from the waist down. Even though the experts told him that he would never walk again, Klosterman did come back. He came back to walk. Hesitantly perhaps, but he did walk.

I talked about Patty Wilson, the young high school (now college) student, who is subject to epileptic seizures. Yet she runs marathon distances. She and her dad have run from San Diego to Seattle, a distance of fourteen hundred miles, and are currently planning to run across the United States. They are running to educate people about epilepsy.

I mentioned Eula Weaver—an amazing woman who was down and out at the age of seventy-seven with a heart attack and hardening of the arteries. She was told that *the big one* was around the corner. She was to go home, take her pills, and try to be as comfortable as possible—in other words, live as an invalid. But another physician told her it was her job to improve her health. Eula liked this alternative better. She changed her diet and started walking and running. Now, at the young age of ninety-one, she holds the age group records for the half- and one-mile runs, and she looks forward to running with her grandson when she reaches one hundred.

I told them about Pete Strudwick, a marathon runner who was born without feet. I told them about Harry Cordellos, the blind physical educator from San Francisco who runs marathons. I also mentioned that in several races Pete Strudwick has led Harry Cordellos around the course serving as Cordellos's eyes.

After the talk one of the participants said to me, "You know, Charlie, those stories should be in a book. They were a real inspiration to me, and I'm sure a lot of other people would be challenged by those stories as well. I mean it. You've convinced me that I have no excuse. It's my job to take care of my health."

I made a mental note of what he said. Then a few days later I was talking to Barbara Anderson from St. Martin's Press in New York City. We had a discussion on some book ideas. I mentioned the idea of telling the story of people who exercised in spite of adversity. She liked the idea. I got excited. And the more we talked about the book, we decided it should not be about famous people.

With that as a backdrop I started out in earnest and wrote to several of my friends in the many YMCAs across the country. I asked them to forward me the names of people they thought would qualify for this book. I expected to receive a few names. I had a fear that there might be a struggle to get enough material. But I received over a hundred stories—all excellent. It seemed as though every city and town in America had a person with a super story to tell.

I scanned the one hundred names and stories and picked thirty personalities that intrigued me. My criteria was simple. First, the story had to make one want to get up and do something—anything—as long as it was acitve. In other words, I wanted "up" stories by "up" people. But the people had to be real, down-to-earth types—no stars, no pro's. Second, I looked for variety. I must admit, however, that I was partial to running and other cardiovascular-type exercises. The fifteen previous books I had written and the three National YMCA programs I developed reflected that bias. Furthermore, my doctorate in exercise physiology from Temple University had focused on heart-type exercises.

Then Lyn Cryderman, my associate, and I started to track down these stories. We interviewed many people: the actual "stars" and their significant others. Since we felt the book would be better if we met the people, we arranged to spend some time with them. Now over one year later, with more than fifteen thousand miles traveled, countless letters, and a phone bill that would excite Ma Bell, is the book *They Accepted the Challenge*.

When I started the interviewing process I had no idea what kind of people I would find. I wondered if they would have good-quality stories to tell. I wondered if they would really communicate their feelings to me. As the interviewing process began and continued, one thing became clear; their stories were better than I expected and were told by warm, caring people.

But the best thing for me was that I benefited tremendously from the interviews. What a treat it was to meet and listen to these wonderful people! During many an interview I was visibly shaken. Afterward, I would reevaluate my priorities and sensitivities to others. I became acutely aware of the talents and gifts I had taken for granted. For example, I have complained for years about running in the cold Michigan winters. The hassle of two layers of clothing, keeping my feet dry, and protecting my fingers, face, and ears from frostbite can be quite distracting. Then I met Randy Nelson who runs in a wheelchair. Like me, he has the problem of keeping himself warm in the cold weather. But he can run only at those places where he can take his chair. Most of the time it's only along isolated roads, parking lots, or on a track. And when it snows or when the roads are ice-covered, he must confine his efforts to a snow-cleared parking lot.

Then there is Bob Ables, a blind, deaf, and mute swimmer from Milwaukee. A man who swims ninety minutes nonstop along with from five to twenty minutes of diving. I communicated with Bob by writing on the palm of his hand or using a special typewriter—a difficult and frustrating experience, yet an experience that moved me to tears when I told it to friends.

I vividly recall, a couple of days after my interview with Bob, waking up early one cold December morning, thinking, "Gosh, I'm not sure I want to exercise." My wife apparently had similar feelings. She rolled over and said, "Let's not run this morning—it's too cold." Whereupon, I took her hand and wrote HI. We immediately got out of bed and ran our allotted distances for the day.

Something else emerged. A common theme or philosophy ran through the stories of all the people selected. Each one thought that his or her story was no big deal. But if I thought their story would help other people, they would consent to the interview and permit their stories to appear in print. Steve McKanic, a heart attack victim whose life hung in the balance for two weeks, said it best for all: "I'm not a hero, Charlie. Don't make me out to be something special; I'm not. I just want to help other people if I can."

Furthermore, these people felt that they had no handicap—just an inconvenience. Lori Markle is a fine eighteen-year-old softballer from Oklahoma. She plays with an intensity that mirrors Pete

Rose, despite the fact she was born with only one leg. Lori told me, "I can't see that I have a handicap. There are some things I can't do as well as others, but there are some things I can do better. Furthermore, I don't know why you're making such a big deal of this. I don't think I'm any different."

Perhaps Lori can think that way. But Lori and the others in this book are different. Although these people have had significant challenges in their lives—challenges that would defeat most people—they remain optimistic. I like optimistic people who are fighting the good fight and winning. They may not be winning medals, but they are winners because they've played the game of life and tried their best. This attitude made the writing and interviewing difficult at times. They had a hard time remembering their struggles, their hardships. They wanted only to talk about now and the future. They wanted to talk about life. They are excited about living and what life has to offer.

These are people who would not let the hardships of life get them down. No matter how much they bottom out, they respond. They try harder. Deanna McKenzie, a multiple sclerosis patient, told me she decided that if she was going to get better she had to have a positive attitude about life and start to pull herself up by her own bootstraps and do something herself about the disease. It's not enough to simply rely on the physician and the medical profession. "You must assume responsibility for your own health," she said.

These people are not quitters. No matter how much they have been clobbered, they come back for more. No matter how many times they have been told they can't do it, they try. Perhaps not with the grace and poise of an able-bodied athlete, but they try.

Bob Gilley personifies all of these people. He told me that as a child and even today his favorite story is "The Little Engine That Could." Too simplistic? I don't think so. These people are fighters. They overcome.

I think their stories will show you that. I hope that on the following pages you will get a glimpse of their personalities, the complexities of their problems, and their method of working through them.

Here are the stories of some pretty remarkable people. People who have legitimate excuses not to exercise, yet they do. People who have found joy and a love of life. Here are people who inspire me. Eighteen people who keep me going when my resolve to exercise slips. Eighteen people who challenge me. I hope they challenge you to understand that you can really become fit if you want to.

Susan Guild

Susan Guild

Everyone in the Omni Coliseum in Atlanta instinctively slid forward in their seats. The tempo of the music picked up. The spotlight, a giant wand of brightness, followed the dancing, twirling skater, sending flashes of brilliance reflecting off the silver blades. A long, graceful arc, to build up speed, as the end of the program drew near. Head back. Body arched. Arms gracefully moving as if underwater. Then suddenly a magnificent leap. The pretty, slim seventeen-year-old dared gravity for a moment, then reluctantly returned to the smooth, shimmering ice for her bow to the audience.

The arena resounded with an approving roar. Few in the audience realized a milestone had been reached in this skater's life. One person remained seated, her head bowed. Her prayer of thanksgiving was not for the performance. In the tumult of the moment, Mrs. Leta Guild whispered before joining the cheers:

"Thank you, Lord, for sparing her life."

When the final scores were tallied, Susan Guild emerged in fourth place at the 1980 National Figure Skating Championships. That called for even more cheers by Susan, her mother, and Norma Sahlin, her coach. It was a happy moment indeed.

I know what you're thinking. Why all the fuss about fourth place? First of all, being fourth in the nation in anything is no shabby achievement. To put that into perspective, consider the fact that there are literally thousands of young ladies competing in skating in the United States. Only the nine best girls in the nation are allowed to compete at Nationals. Just getting there is only a dream for most. For Susan, it looked impossible. Just eighteen months before the event, her doctor told her she had leukemia.

Tragic news, indeed, to a fifteen-year-old figure skater with tremendous potential. Her first shot at Nationals was just around the corner. She had spent over a year practicing five hours a day. Arrangements were complete for her to go to Littleton, Colorado, and train under one of the foremost coaches in the nation. With all this going for her, you'd think such a blow would literally destroy Susan's world. It would most people's. But I have since discovered Susan is one of a kind.

It all started with pigeon-toes. That's right, pigeon-toes. As Susan started walking, her mother noticed her toes pointed in slightly. Nothing serious, but enough to attract the attention of any concerned parent. Her physician assured her it wouldn't pose a problem, so Mrs. Guild forgot about it.

When Susan was two-and-a-half, Mrs. Guild discussed her concern with the nurse at the school where she was teaching.

"We were talking about it, and she said skating was good therapy for that kind of problem. She was talking about roller skating, but I knew the local university had a toddler ice skating program. So I enrolled her in it as therapy. I had no idea it would develop into this."

Little Susie took an immediate liking to the ice. So much so that by the time she was four she constantly begged her mother to take her skating. Mrs. Guild felt that the skating was as good as playing with dolls and probably better. She enrolled her in more classes.

When Susie was seven, she entered her first competition. It was the Tri-State Freestyle Competition in Bowling Green, Ohio.

"The older kids were all talking about going to Bowling Green, and naturally Susie wanted to go. I asked her coach what he thought about it and he said, 'Oh, I think she would have a ball!'"

Sue, as she prefers to be called, remembers that day well.

"I wasn't scared, but upset. The rink at home went east and west, while the one in Bowling Green faced just the opposite direction. I'm really conscious of directions, and it threw me a little."

After warming up, she skated back to her mom, walked off the ice, and announced defiantly, "I can't do it!"

Naturally her mom wanted to know why, and when Sue explained the situation her mother laughed and told her the red lines are still the same regardless of which way the arena is facing.

"Go back out there and skate," she encouraged.

Which is what she did. In her first competition, Sue finished third.

"That's when I really started to believe she had talent," recalled her mother. "Up to this point I approached it as a kind of a lark. You know, a cute thing for a little girl to do. But suddenly I realized I had a gal who was quite talented."

Susan started putting in longer hours of practice on the ice. Organized figure skating is a demanding sport requiring discipline and determination. The competition includes two categories: compulsory figures and free skating. During the compulsory section, judges draw six patterns by lot. There are forty-one patterns from which to choose, and the skaters must know every one. Once the six are chosen, the contestants must execute each of those figures on the ice in triple repetition as the judges examine each mark traced into the ice. When that is completed, the skaters must perform a three-and-a-half minute program of turns, jumps, spins, and dances.

In order to attend organized competition, a skater must have passed an appropriate test. There are eight tests, each more difficult than the previous. Beginning skaters work on the first test, while the most advanced aim for the eighth test. It's like proceeding from kindergarten to graduation.

"I remember in the fifth grade I entered my first qualifying competition. I didn't do too well—I placed really low, but I did pass the test. My coach, who at that time was Myrna Bodek, asked me if I'd like to start working on the next test. When I told her I didn't think I was good enough, she really got mad at me. She told me never to say that again—never to even *think* that. She really lit into me for having such a low opinion of my talent and I think that's when I decided to go for the best."

So the long climb to the top began, and, like anything worth achieving, the struggle demanded discipline. By the time Susan was in the seventh grade, she was putting in from one and a half to three hours of skating each day. The routine was rough, especially when lined up against the daily routines of her classmates. It meant that besides school, her only other activity was skating. Little TV. No fun and games with friends. No hobbies. There was little time for that. To some, that would seem like a great sacrifice. Susan doesn't look at it that way.

"I never felt I was being deprived of anything because skating filled all my desires. I met a lot of great people and had some really fantastic times. It was a tremendous learning experience, and I lived for those times when I was on the ice."

As she proceeded with her training, she became more proficient. She was doing well in competition and progressing nicely on her tests. In the fall of 1976 she won the Eastern Great Lakes Competition but did not make it to the national level. Her coach, Kris Myers, Mrs. Guild, and Susan mapped their strategy. She would defend her Eastern Great Lakes Title in 1978, hopefully place in the top three at Sectionals, which would qualify her for Nationals. If she qualified, she would go to Littleton, Colorado, for the summer and train in one of the most advanced and demanding training centers in the nation.

Now Sue's training really picked up. She packed her classes into the morning at her high school and arranged to take an extra class as an independent study. She had little difficulty obtaining permission since she was holding down a 4.0 GPA at the time. But she needed to get out of school early so she could spend more time on the ice. At 11:30 A.M. her mother would pick her up at school and take her to a private rink where she would practice until 3:30. Then, her coach would pick her up and take her to the ice rink at the university. She was putting in about six hours of skating a day in addition to taking a full load of classes.

With such a schedule, it is little wonder they ignored those first symptoms. Gradually, she fatigued more easily. When she competed she lacked that characteristic spark she was known for. For the first time in her skating career, skating was becoming a lot more work and a lot less fun.

"But we all felt it was normal," said Sue's mother. "After all, who wouldn't be tired with that kind of schedule? I talked with her coach and she said Susan was just feeling pressure from her upcoming title defense. So we just lived with it for a while."

Unfortunately, the problems continued. Susan's legs began to ache and she never seemed to have enough energy. Still, she pushed herself.

"I knew I was in pretty sad shape, but I wanted so badly to qualify for Nationals. I felt if I could just hold on until after the competition, I would catch up on my rest before going to Littleton to train."

In November of 1977 she entered the Great Lakes Competition. This was the first step to Nationals. She needed to place in order to make it into Sectionals. She skated well, but not well enough. To qualify for Sectionals she needed to be in the top three, but she finished fourth, just a few points away from her chance to attempt to qualify for Nationals. It was a terrible setback, the type that causes many skaters to retire early.

"She was terribly disappointed," her mother told me. "But it didn't stop her. She went ahead and kept skating. She told me, 'Well, I guess I just need to work harder.' So she went right ahead and started preparing for her eighth test."

Susan resumed her Spartan training schedule, putting in five to six hours a day on the ice. Occasionally she would skate in an ice show or enter a competition just to keep her skills sharp under pressure. It was tough, since Nationals were held in February without her. Yet she felt she could qualify for Nationals the following year, after going to Colorado to train for the summer. But those who saw her skate wondered. Her mother was one of them.

"Other coaches would come up to me and say, 'That's not Susie out there. Something's wrong.' Also, for the first time, Susie started to complain seriously about skating. I began to question whether she could handle the demands of training."

By now, Susan began showing signs of something more than ordinary fatigue. She was tired all the time and experienced a great deal of pain in her joints. Though it was a warm and sunny spring, her skin had an unhealthy pallor. "I took her to the doctor for a sore throat and he treated her," said her mother. "But six weeks later, she woke up one morning with a black eye, yet never remembered being struck or bumped by anything.

"Still, no one suspected anything more serious than fatigue. We were worried she might be pushing herself too hard, and I had decided to take her to her doctor for a checkup. I thought maybe it was mono, but those classic symptoms we were seeing just never registered."

Susan awoke on Memorial Day feeling her chipper old self. She bounced out of bed, glad to be up early and happy it was a holiday—she wouldn't have to skate. After greeting her mom in a cheery voice, she went to the refrigerator to get some orange juice.

"Mom, come quick! I think I'm . . ."

Her scream startled her mother who rushed into the kitchen and found her daughter sprawled on the floor, barely conscious.

"Babe, I don't care if it is a holiday, we're going to the hospital *now!*"

The doctors were alarmed when they saw the black eye and noted the results of the blood test. The peripheral blood count showed an alarmingly small number of red cells and practically no white cells. The bone marrow test was even more distressing. There were no discernible healthy cells. They had been replaced by leukemic cells, indicating what doctors had feared might be true. Sue was admitted to the hospital and a hematologist was called in to study the case. After a few more tests and going over the results, the hematologist, Dr. Roshni Kulkarni, summoned Mrs. Guild.

"Mrs. Guild, I'm relieved to tell you that your daughter has leukemia, because we can treat it. When I first saw the results, I was afraid it was a strain of the disease that is untreatable, but it's not that. It will be a rough fight, but we'll make it."

Mrs. Guild was numb. The very sound of the word frightened her. Just a few weeks earlier, a close friend in the skating club who had leukemia had died after a long struggle. She could not face the possibility of that happening to her daughter.

"I was really devastated by the news. I kept thinking it was a bad dream. Susan had so much going for her, and I just couldn't understand why she was the one to get knocked down."

She went in to try and give the news to Susan, but found she was unable to say much of anything. She fought to maintain control of herself. Susan was ready with lots of questions.

"I remember when Mom came in and the look on her face. I asked her if they found out what I had, and she couldn't say anything. She just nodded her head. Then I said, 'It's not mono, is it?' And again she just shook her head. The only other thing I knew that had anything to do with blood was leukemia. For some reason that word just popped into my mind. It wasn't a shock or anything. It was just a reality. So I asked her if it was leukemia and she just nodded her head. And I just said *oh*."

Neither of them had much to say, so it was probably a good thing that Dr. Kulkarni walked in at that time. Dr. Kulkarni is an amazing woman who has had a great deal of experience working with leukemia. She always approaches it positively and openly. She walked over to the edge of Susan's bed, sat down, and took hold of her hand. She knew about Susan's love for skating, and spoke enthusiastically.

"Susan, you have leukemia. Give me this summer and I'll have you back on the ice this fall."

That's all she said. But it was enough for Susan and her mother. In characteristic fashion, Susan was ready for the fight.

"I figured, let's get this over with. Let's get on with it, you know? The doctor was very positive from the very beginning. And I think if I had a doctor that was not quite so positive, I might not have approached it in the way I did. As I look back on the whole thing, I think a proper mental attitude is very important. In fact, I would say it's the most important thing."

So the fight began. Dr. Kulkarni warned them both that it would be a rough summer, but no one knew just how rough it would be. It's probably a good thing, for if they knew what was ahead of them, they might not have been so "up."

The first thing they had to do was start the chemotherapy. This slow poisoning process affects different people different ways. Fortunately, Susan escaped the nausea that usually accompanies the treatment. But she did have constant headaches, and after each treatment she had a different pain.

"After the second treatment I woke up the next morning and I hurt all over. It felt like every single muscle or bone in my body was torn or broken. And I can just remember being so mad that this had happened. So mad that I had to go through it that I made myself get up. I just had to get out of my bed. I thought, I know what's happened. Someone up there doesn't want me to get up and get out of bed so I'm going to show them. I'm going to show them that I can do it. No matter how hard it hurts I'm going to fight this thing. In fact, as the pain increased I got angrier. It just made me fight harder."

During the five weeks that Susan was in chemotherapy, she was placed in what is called protective isolation. That means she had to go to the hospital only for her treatment, but could come home as long as she stayed in her room. No one was allowed in her room except her mother and her sister because her white blood count was so low that she was very susceptible to any type of infection. Since no one could come in and see her, her friends decided to visit her in a somewhat unorthodox manner.

"One day I heard a tapping on my window and I looked out and there was one of my friends. The window was up high and I couldn't figure out how she got there until I went over and looked. My friends had brought a ladder over and leaned it up against the house. From then on they used to come over and sit on the ladder and talk to me to keep me company. It really made me feel good that my friends still cared about me."

Susan feels that such contact with the outside world is extremely important for the patient fighting leukemia.

"I know a lot of people are scared of leukemia, and don't know what to say to someone who has it. But it was really important to me. I was going stir-crazy because they wouldn't let people come visit me in the hospital. But really the best thing is to be surrounded by people who care."

Once the chemotherapy was finished, the real work began. Though the bone marrow indicated Sue was in remission at that point, she was to have cobalt treatments to the brain. This is given in case there are leukemia cells in the central nervous system. The chemotherapy is given through the veins and does not get into the central nervous system. So during the next two and a half weeks she had thirteen cobalt treatments and five spinal taps. Toward the end of the cobalt treatment she began having pains in her side. X-rays indicated that her spleen was beginning to enlarge, which is not unusual with leukemia cases. But finally hers got so big and so painful they decided to take another look at it with a spleen scan. The spleen looked like a sponge and was full of white spots. Dr. Kulkarni had never seen anything like it, so she consulted with several doctors throughout the country. No one seemed to know about a spleen that looked like that, so they determined they would have to remove it. The only problem was they couldn't remove it until the cobalt treatments were completed and these could not be stopped. Susan would just have to live with the pain.

"Susan was in excruciating pain at the time. I think more than any of us realized. She was virtually living on Tylenol. When the last cobalt treatment was administered, I called the doctor and told her something had to be done. Susan just couldn't tolerate the pain any more. So they readmitted her to the hospital and scheduled her for emergency surgery."

The results of the presurgery blood tests were shocking. Just when it looked like the chemotherapy and cobalt treatments had successfully turned the leukemia into a remission stage, Dr. Kulkarni saw indications of a return of leukemia. She called Mrs. Guild and told her that Susan's blood count had gone completely haywire and that there was a remote possibility that she had developed a second type of leukemia. She also mentioned that they would have to do a bone marrow the next morning.

"By the time I got to Susan's room, Dr. Kulkarni had already explained to her what could have happened and what they were going to do. And so there I was with a fifteen-year-old who was just told for the second time in her young life that she might have another form of leukemia."

It didn't take long before Susan had her mother calmed down. It's incredible, but Susan faced this unwanted dose of bad news with that same fighting spirit that drove her to practice five and six hours a day on the ice. With a note of defiance in her voice she told her mother, "Well, we got over the first one and we'll get over this one, too."

After spending a few minutes with her daughter, Mrs. Guild returned home to make arrangements for her other daughter to spend the evening at a friend's house. When she returned to the hospital, she couldn't believe what she saw.

"When I arrived back on pediatrics it looked like they were having a party. I never saw so many people on that floor in such a good mood. They had finally gotten a report from the lab that said Sue had a kidney infection, and that's why her blood count had gone haywire. The doctor called me and said, 'I've never been so relieved for one of my kids to have an infection in my whole life!' She said she was reasonably sure that the only problem was the kidney infection, but that they would still do a bone marrow in the morning."

The next morning they performed the bone marrow, and it indicated Susan was still in strong remission. So they sent her home with medication for the kidney infection, and two weeks later they removed the spleen. Once again, Susan and her family were in for a shock.

The surgery was to have taken only an hour, but after the first hour Sue's hematologist came out and told Mrs. Guild that when they opened Sue up, they discovered her spleen was covered with a mass of absesses. Since they had to be extremely careful not to break any of the absesses, it would take another hour and a half or more. The worst news was what might have caused the absesses to form. A short time after the surgery the pathology report declared that the absesses were caused by a fungus which is very rare and, when found in humans, is fatal. There are many autopsy records of leukemia patients who are found with this type of fungus in their bodies. There are no records of anybody surviving the fungus.

At this point, however, Susan refused to be discouraged. Her recovery was almost unbelievable. She was up and walking around even though she had a tube in her side, IVs in her arms, and a tube through her nose into her stomach. She just hauled her tubes and bottles along with her as she walked up and down the halls of pediatrics getting to know other patients. Within three days she was in absolutely fantastic shape. Her doctor just looked at her and shook her head and said she couldn't believe it.

But the fungus was another problem. The doctors weren't exactly sure what to do. Should they treat the fungus or should they hope they got it all when they removed the spleen? Once again Dr. Kulkarni consulted doctors around the United States to determine what to do. To add to their worries, Susan developed a fungus on her tongue. After several tests failed to identify the fungus, they finally decided to perform a tongue biopsy to see if it was the same rare type of fungus found in the spleen. The biopsy proved negative; it was just a common fungus causing what is often called "hairy tongue." And throughout all this they were considering treating the original fungus, a treatment that is worse than the chemotherapy and cobalt combined.

During this time Susan tried to maintain a somewhat normal life. School had started and Susan was taking driver's training at night after school. She was going to school full-time and taking a regular course load. After the tongue biopsy proved negative the doctor said they were just going to forget about treating the fungus. She returned to school the next day, but she called her mom at school at ten in the morning and said she didn't feel well.

So Sue went home from school with her mom's permission. She went to bed and slept the whole weekend. When she got up on Monday it was as if she had awakened and nothing had ever been wrong with her. It was like the end of a bad dream.

While Susan was grateful to have returned to good health, she wasn't satisfied. She wanted to get back on the ice. As soon as she got clearance from her doctors she visited the rink, but she wasn't prepared for what was to happen.

"I laced up my skates and went out on the ice. I went around about twice and I thought, Oh, this isn't too bad. Even though I was warned not to try it, I decided to go backward for a while. I tried to perform a simple turn to skate backward and I fell. It stunned me. I had just attempted one of the simplest moves in ice skating, and I'd failed. I realized how far out of shape I was, and I got worried. But then I started to laugh. I thought, you know, this is stupid. So I just decided I was going to have to take one day at a time and start all over again."

When Susan had first been diagnosed, she was preparing for her eighth test, the top step. Because of her weakened condition, her coach had to take her way back to the first level and virtually teach her all the preliminary moves over again. That meant going back and practicing the first test, successfully passing that test, and then preparing for the second test, etc. While it was discouraging for someone who had reached her level, Susan was diligent and patient. It took most of the winter, but she did extremely well.

By April, her coach felt she had advanced enough to try

returning to competition. They chose the Tri-State Freestyle Competition. It was a good place to begin anew. After all, that was the scene of her first attempt at competitive skating when she was seven years old. Furthermore, she had won the Senior competition two years before, just prior to learning about her disease.

Everyone in the audience knew of Susan's fight for life. They had followed her courageous battle and were overjoyed to see her skate out onto the ice. Some were in tears as she was introduced and took her spot at center ice. Many more reached for their handkerchiefs as the frail but smiling skater danced gracefully through her routine. Her skating was flawless. The "old" Susan Guild was back. It was little wonder that when the judges awarded her the first place trophy, everyone jumped to his or her feet and gave her a standing ovation.

"There wasn't a dry eye in the entire arena," said Mrs. Guild.

People just couldn't believe it. Even to this day, Mrs. Guild has a hard time believing her daughter's life was spared. But she believes that she and her family weren't alone in her struggle.

"I believe in prayer, and there were an awful lot of prayers from people all over the country—in fact, from all over the world. We received word from as far away as South America that people were praying for her. In talking with Susan about the entire ordeal, I was quite surprised to hear her reaction to it. After our interview, I told her I was sure she would just like to block that entire summer right out of her mind.

"No way!" she snapped.

"I couldn't drop that summer out of my life. I wouldn't want to because it made me grow up even faster than I was. The whole experience taught me a lot about life and it taught me to appreciate life even more. Skating has always been important to me and will continue to be so, but I think I see it in the proper perspective. Now, my favorite thing to do if I have the time is to get up before the sun rises and start walking or start jogging and just as it rises I think it's just so beautiful and great to be alive."

Eighteen months after her ordeal with leukemia, Susan went on to make it to Sectionals, and from there qualify for Nationals. She had finally made it to Denver to train with the best, and it was only a year later than she had planned. She received permission from her school to take part of her school year independently so that she could devote her full time to preparing for Nationals.

Sue attacked her skating with a new confidence and a renewed desire. And if there were ever any doubts about her regained strength, a look at her daily training schedule should dash those. For six days a week it was the same. She was up at ten minutes to four. That's right, 3:50 A.M.! After a shower and breakfast to start the day, she left for the rink and was on the ice at 5:30 A.M. From 5:30 in the morning until 6:00 at night, Susan was either on the ice, in an exercise room doing special exercises, back on the ice, or in the library for an hour to work on her studies. By 8:00 P.M. she was in bed.

It must have paid off, because no one really expected her to do as well as she did at Nationals. I spoke with her mother before the event, and she was wary of making any predictions.

"We're just glad that she made it. That means she's one of the nine best skaters in the United States, and right now we'll settle for that."

Evidently, Susan wasn't settling for that. She skated better than she'd ever skated in her life, and was proud to accept her fourth-place ranking.

"My one big goal was to make it to Nationals this year and now that I have done that I've set more goals. I just had a wonderful time competing there, you know. I'm planning to go to college and I may even go to med school. And of course, keep on skating. Things are going really great for me. In fact, it's getting more wonderful every day."

Dave Roberts

David N. Robert

In 1965 Dave Roberts had the world on a string. He was ranked fourth in the nation for high schoolers in the half-mile with a time of one minute, fifty-three and four-tenths of a second (1:53.4). He was one of the most popular young men in his community. Many colleges and universities sought Dave because of his excellent half-mile time. His number one position in the state of Michigan and his national standing also gave him a lot of media coverage. Yessir, Dave Roberts was at the top of the world.

As with some teenagers, however, Dave was trying to find his niche. His place in the sun. He and his parents had a few problems, and Dave wanted to do things his own way. Confused and rebellious, he felt that the best thing for him would be to get away from home and get his head together.

He chose Utah State in Logan, Utah, partly because it was two thousand miles from home and partly because he got a full scholarship to run track and cross-country.

During his freshman year Dave showed great promise. In cross-country he ran four miles in nineteen minutes and fifty-four seconds (19:54). In the spring, he turned a one minute, fifty and one-tenth seconds (1:50.1) in the half-mile—good enough to be ranked number three in the nation for college freshmen. All this was pretty heady stuff for a young man of eighteen.

In March 1966, as a freshman, Dave got married. Shortly thereafter his wife became pregnant. To support his wife, Dave took a job as a laborer. Suddenly, life was pretty much of a hassle. Sure, he had a national ranking. But to maintain that position he had to train hard. He also had to study to stay in school. Life had become a little bit more complex than it had been when he was a senior at Southgate High School in Southgate, a suburb of Detroit.

To help solve his problems, Dave started to drink. Not much, just enough to cope. Just enough to help him forget his problems and responsibilities. Besides, it was the thing to do—everyone was doing it. He even justified it by feeling that it was a good source of carbohydrates.

During the summer things didn't get any better. Dave and his wife were having marital problems, and while he didn't have to go to school he did have a job and family responsibilities. So he began drinking more heavily. The extra calories in the alcohol caused his weight to jump to 145 pounds—15 pounds over his normal weight of 130.

When he reported back to training camp in the fall, at the start of his sophomore yea, hs coach was furious. Angry at his coach, himself, and the world, Dave threw himself into more booze. He started drinking five days a week. In fact, he drank so much that he was thoroughly drunk five days a week.

Everything went downhill from then on. Dave was kicked off the track and cross-country teams since he was breaking training rules and was unfit to compete at the level expected. That meant no scholarship. And no scholarship meant no school. So in the fall of 1967 Dave left Utah State. He returned to Michigan and got a job as an apprentice with Detroit Edison.

Disillusioned, confused, and angry, he continued to drink. The added responsibilities of a son didn't help, either. To add to the problem, he was no longer running and soon his weight mushroomed to 205 pounds. His waistline jumped from a rock-hard 30 to a marshmallow 40. An entire case of beer at one sitting was standard fare.

But beer wasn't Dave's only thing. He consumed copious amounts of hard liquor, smoked three packs of cigarettes a day, and started doing drugs. "Call it what you will," he said, "I was a member of the Kent State generation."

At first Dave deluded himself into thinking he was active by occasionally playing softball and football. But the real reason he did these things, he admitted, was because he could party afterward. He even claimed to go out running. "But I'd take five dollars in my pocket and find that I could run just far enough to reach the closest tavern where I'd stop in for some 'refreshments.' I wound up spending the night, drinking my problems away."

During the next few years things got worse. Dave continued to drink more and more. His health deteriorated. He had to see a doctor every three months for counseling to help control his blood pressure, which had become dangerously high. He developed frequent nosebleeds. He also had severe bleeding hemorrhoids. His health got so bad that he vomited blood and had blood in the stools.

While Dave's health was terrible, his life with his family was horrendous. Although he fathered another son in 1969 and a daughter in 1973, his relationship with his wife deteriorated badly. His self-image was destroyed. He hated himself and many times had seriously considered suicide. By the time he was twenty-six he was so far down the ladder he couldn't stand to look at himself in the mirror to shave. He felt that the world and his young family would be better off without him. As with most alcoholics, his self-pity and depression dominated his life. He wanted to be the ideal father, but how can you be a good father when you're always at the bars? To soothe his guilt about avoiding his responsibilities to his family, he would take his children to the bar with him.

At first, Dave didn't get into too much trouble with the law, in spite of his barroom brawls and fights at home. In 1969, his charmed life with the police was over. After working thirty-eight straight hours on the line, he went to a bar and downed boilermakers for eight hours. After a while he staggered to his car and started to drive home. On the way he hit the chief of police head-on, right in front of city hall. But as Dave says, "I got out of that scrape because I knew all the politicians in that city, and my family had a lot of influence there, so I got off scot free."

In 1970, at his high school class's five year reunion, Dave was the brunt of many a joke. Everyone exclaimed, "Here comes Dave the drunk." At first he thought it was funny. But when he started hearing it from everyone, it got depressing. It devastated his ego even more. Dave hated himself.

During this time Dave could never keep a good-looking car. It was always dented, banged, and gouged because of his drunk driving. One night he put his car through his neighbor's cinderblock garage. Three times he was nailed for drunk driving. The first two times he had his license temporarily revoked. Each time his depression became even greater. The third time he was arrested, the lawyer warned him, "The only way the judge will let you off is if you go to Alcoholics Anonymous to show your desire to be rehabilitated. Otherwise your license will be permanently revoked."

At first Dave was offended by the suggestion. "I don't have a drinking problem," he told the lawyer. It was a typical alcoholic's response. But his lawyer insisted. He said it was the only way Dave could keep his license to drive. So Dave went.

He liked what he heard at Alcoholics Anonymous. In fact, it amazed him, but it bothered him that he was able to relate to everyone in the room. "I must be an alcoholic if I can associate with all these alcoholics," he thought. But what really concerned him was when they started talking about the God concept. "They didn't talk about God," Dave pointed out, "they just mentioned a higher power. That scared me. As a youngster and as a senior in high school I was very religious. I never missed church. But as with most alcoholics, once they start the downward slide they throw God and religion out the window. I did the same thing."

After the Alcoholics Anonymous meeting Dave tried to dry out. He went through excruciating withdrawal symptoms. He had the DT's, saw snakes, sweated profusely, had the shivers; you name it, he had it. At the same time he was seeing a marriage counselor. The counselor told Dave that she didn't think he was an alcoholic. She said he should try the two-beer-a-day method. "Boy," Dave thought, "this girl has it together more than AA." But the truth of the matter, according to Dave, was that he wasn't ready to go dry.

When Dave had his court appearance for drunk driving, he had been dry for fourteen days. Because of his apparent sincerity, the judge believed Dave was serious about his desire to rehabilitate himself and therefore did not suspend his license. Upon hearing this, Dave thought, "See, this proves I'm not an alcoholic. After all, the judge believes me and the marriage counselor believes me. I must be all right."

Since he had been off booze fourteen days and the counselor had suggested two beers a day, Dave felt that, mathematically speaking, that entitled him to twenty-eight beers. This thinking set off a drinking binge that lasted twenty days and included considerably more than twenty-eight beers. He had no food. Nothing but alcohol. "I couldn't get off the stuff," he remarked. "I just kept drinking, drinking, and drinking. When you've been sober for two weeks you get the feeling you just have to catch up. It was my worst bout of drinking ever. I also felt the worst I ever did. When I finally came home I was so upset I said to my wife, 'Honey, I'm gonna go to AA.' She said, 'Just leave us alone. Don't even talk to us.'"

Rejected, Dave looked at his six-year-old son. An alcoholic will try anything to get into the graces of his family. He said, "Come on, Michael, come talk to Dad." And Michael (a six-year-old whose experience belied his age) said, "No, Dad, you're nothing but a drunk." That did it. Dave had reached the bottom line. "I didn't hate Michael," he remembers. "I knew what he said was true. I knew for sure that I was an alcoholic. There was no doubt in my mind, but I just didn't know what to do. I was afraid I'd lose my drinking friends. I was more afraid of losing them than losing my family.

"But I didn't like myself. So I went to AA that night. I was afraid they would reject me, too. I walked into the session with my head bowed, but they welcomed me with open arms. That was reassuring."

At the meeting one woman received her one-year cake for staying dry. She was crying and telling everyone how happy she was to stay dry for 365 days. It impressed Dave immensely. He remarked to a friend who was there, "That's incredible. She must really feel good about that. That must be a most rewarding thing to get a year cake." To which his friend Earl replied, "Don't get your hopes up, pal. You'll never make'er."

Incensed, Dave went home vowing to stay dry. "The next several weeks were pure hell," he said. "I had the DT's all over again. It was miserable coming off that booze again. It was worse than the first time. I saw snakes. I sweated profusely. Many times I thought I woud die. I wanted to die. My family life wasn't any better, either, and that added to the agony. My family was confused. It was quite an adjustment for them to get used to seeing Dad sober. They weren't quite sure my rehabilitation was legitimate. My wife and I talked about divorce, separation—you name it. Plus my self-concept was very poor. I still weighed two hundred and five pounds and had a forty-inch gut. With my frame I don't think I could have weighed any more. All my weight was in my stomach. It stuck out so far I looked gross."

Three weeks after the AA meeting Dave went to a dope party. But he noticed that as soon as he got high, the first thing he wanted was some wine. He decided right then that dope was not for him. A week later, at AA, a speaker said, "My name is Dave Thomas, and I have not had a drop of alcohol or any mind-altering drug in ten years." Dave thought, "That's amazing for anybody in this society not to smoke anything or take anything or drink anything. I like that." So Dave vowed to swear off the drugs and the alcohol, but he still smoked three packs of cigarettes a day.

After six months at AA Dave determined he needed exercise, so as a New Year's resolution, he joined a health spa. That was in January of 1974. "I was upset with the way my upper body looked. So I started to lift weights. After about two weeks of lifting weights I saw someone running on a motorized treadmill at the spa. Intrigued, I decided to see if I could still run. I ran for one minute and almost died. My lungs burned. My chest hurt. My legs ached. It was horrible. I just wanted someone to take me downstairs and shoot me. My only thought was, save me all this aggravation and sweat. Let me die, now! I just couldn't believe how far I had fallen. I was crushed.

"Right then and there I resolved to quit smoking. The decision was painful. Very hard. I wanted a butt so bad I could almost cry. But I decided to stick with it. Coming off three packs of cigarettes was tough. But I did it."

When the weather broke in the spring Dave started to run. A mile at first and gradually more distance. Soon he was up to two miles three times a week. "The pain and agony of running was unbelievable," Dave said. "My health had been so poor it was like starting after an operation. But I had made up my mind to do it. I never missed. Even if I worked twenty-four hours straight I would go to the spa first, get my exercise in, and then go home to bed.

"Some of the guys were calling me chubby, so I wanted to get my weight down. I was lucky, because there were some other guys from AA who were there doing the same thing. Even some of my high school buddies were there. I kept looking at their physiques and was embarrassed with the way I looked. Getting into shape became an obsession with me. I did some dumb things. I fasted. I read a lot about diets. I talked to people who went to different kinds of weight clubs. I was obsessed with getting back down to a thirty-inch waist. One day I would eat nothing but carrots. Another day nothing but pickles. It was really suicidal, but I had this obsession for a flatter stomach. During the summer I challenged one of my shot putter buddies from high school to a mile run. And he beat me. I couldn't believe it. A shot putter beating a half-miler. I was humiliated."

But his running improved. The regularity of running enhanced his physical condition. At the end of the year Dave decided to enter his first race at Belle Isle. It was New Year's Eve. The wind chill was −55°. He felt it was one of the dumbest things he'd ever done. But he finished thirty-sixth and got a tenth-place trophy for his age group. Elated, he thought, "You know, the old boy has still got it in him."

After that Dave chucked the weights. He had gotten what he wanted out of them. His upper body looked pretty good. Instead he started running in earnest, just for the love of running. At the same time, his sons were getting involved in swimming. One day while he was sitting in the bleachers watching the boys compete, one of the mothers mentioned to him that they were looking for someone to coach the girls' track team in junior high. Dave said, "If I can't find you somebody, then I'll do it myself." That was a mistake. He got stuck with it. He became the girls' track coach for Riverview Junior High School. Later he followed the girls along and became the girls' track coach for the Senior High School. He also ended up acting as an assistant coach in the school's swimming program.

Now that Dave was running and coaching girls' track, things seemed to be falling into place. The girls had a super year. They lost only one meet, and that was by one point. It looked as if Dave had made his comeback.

Coaching the girls' team was really therapeutic. The relationships he developed with the kids helped him immensely. He learned more about himself and life in general. He also learned about helping other people. Many times the girls would challenge him. One time one of the girls got a little cocky after Dave was pushing them and said, "Well, if you think this is so easy why don't you get out there and do it yourself?" So Dave challenged her to do eight 220's in 32 seconds. He told her if she could do it, Dave would try to better her performance. And if he was able to do that she would be required to do another eight 220's. So the bet was on. The young girl did her eight 220's in 32 seconds. But Dave reciprocated by running eight 220's in 30 seconds or less. When he finished his last 220 she said, "You mean now I have to do eight more?" But Dave said, "No, but next time don't ever look at your competition and think you've got it made."

At this point, Dave was running about seven miles a day and decided to run his first marathon, 26.2 miles. He chose the Belle Isle Marathon in October 1977. He ran it in two hours and forty-eight minutes (2:48), an excellent time for a first marathon. What makes the time all the more impressive is the fact that he did this on only seven miles of running a day, six days a week. Most runners who turn in that kind of time log a minimum of ten miles a day. Regardless, the time qualified him for the Boston Marathon, which was to be held in April of 1978. Stimulated by the success of his first marathon, Dave started to do more reading. He read about the Lydiard method of training which advocated more speed work and increased mileage. Dave did both. He upped his mileage slowly to nine miles a day, of which 5 percent was devoted to speed work. He was back in the groove again. He felt good.

Unfortunately, Dave got sick in March, so he didn't get all the mileage he wanted. Still, he ran at Boston and ran a very respectable two hours and forty-six minutes (2:46).

Excited about his time and the knowledge that he could do better, he started training very seriously for the Detroit International Marathon to be held in October 1978. But his travel commitments around the country restricted his training. It wasn't until six weeks before the race that he took a cram course in preparing for a marathon. Again he upped his mileage, did more speed work. But six weeks is not enough to train adequately for the performance Dave was expecting. Yet he covered the 26.2 miles in two hours and forty-three minutes (2:43). But that wasn't good enough for Dave. He was upset with his performance. He had the feeling he hadn't trained properly. Now Dave decided to train all out. His family, business, friends, would all have to suffer. He took days off without pay. He was obsessed with doing a good job at the marathon.

All the work paid off. When he ran in Boston in April 1979 he finished with a time of two hours and thirty-four minutes (2:34). That placed him 435th out of 10,000 runners. According to Dave, the run was a piece of cake. I'm sure it was more than that. But the time and the place of finish certainly revealed that Dave had returned to his old running form.

In a span of six years Dave had risen from the depths. He had pulled himself up by his bootstraps. Now, he pictured himself as a winner. A successful runner, coach, and person. Quite a change from the time he could not bring himself to look at himself in the mirror because of a devastated ego. Dave was again ready to lick the world.

But all of this changed on June 25, 1979. One week after he competed in the Glass City Marathon in Toldeo, Dave was working as a lineman on a pole top switch, something he was not too familiar with. "It's really not my regular job," Dave explained. "I don't even know what happened. All I remember is I passed what we call a hot stick over to the guys that were in the bucket truck. I was on the pole along with my pole partner, Marcel. He was working on the east side of the pole and I was on the west. He said, 'Dave, I'm going to go on.' I said, 'Yeah, go ahead.'

"I was just there on the pole and then all of the sudden . . . I don't know what happened, but somehow it went to ground, around me I guess. The guys in the bucket dropped down, and the guy who was on the pole that was making it hot lifted the jumper off, and then I passed out."

Dave was on fire. He was strapped in his body belt, and there were flames all around him. The other guys hurried up and put out the fire around his face first. Then they started pulling off his sweatshirt.

Like most linemen, Dave does not wear a polyester shirt. But that day he did. And as they were trying to put the fire out, the polyester melted into his skin. So when they tried to pull it off, they pulled the skin off at the same time.

When they got Dave to the ground and he came to he screamed, "God, what happened? What did I do wrong? Tell me what I did wrong!" His friend told him not to worry about it. Another told him not to look at his body. But he did anyway. Dave said, "I glanced at my Levi's and they were all burnt. I could see my legs were charred. I asked how Marcel was doing. They said don't worry about Marcel. He's doing all right. Marcel came over and I grabbed his hand and I said the Lord's Prayer. I hurt bad."

When the ambulance came they put a saline (salt) solution on him. Dave says it best. "That just blew me away. All hell broke loose. I just flew. I went sky high. I never experienced a more excruciating pain. The DT's, the snakes, the shakes, were never like that. But they had to do it, see? My salts and water were just draining right out of me. So they put that on me and rushed me to the Ann Arbor Burn Center. I was fortunate. We were working at Haggerty on I-94. It's just a twenty-minute hop and I swear it took them only ten minutes to get there."

Dave was coherent this whole time. When they asked him how he felt he said he just wanted to cry, except that he figured if there were any salt left in him it would run down his burned face and intensify the pain. Once they got him to the Burn Center they put him in a big bathtub of saline solution to cleanse what was left of him. Dave experienced the horrible pain all over again.

Afterward, they tried to keep Dave as clean as possible. They put all kinds of tubes into him. "Wherever there was an open hole there was a tube. I just hated it. But what really bothered me was that they kept taking EKGs on me every two or three hours."

Dave had a heart murmur, and he has taken a log of EKGs, so he knew there was something drastically wrong with him. It bothered him, and after two days Dave's sister, who is a nurse, came to visit him. He asked her how he was doing. She told him everything was fine. He told her she always was a lousy liar. He wanted it straight out.

Dave's sister explained that the electric shock had affected his normal heartrate pattern, and the doctors were concerned that it would lose its ability to contract rhythmically and eventually stop. So for a few days it was touch and go whether Dave would make it or not.

Later, the attending doctor told Dave, "When you came in here I figured you were a goner. In fact, I'd have bet money on it. Your heart was terribly erratic, and forty-two percent of your body was burned. But after talking to you and finding out you were a runner and a vegetarian, (a diet Dave had adapted in '78) I just knew you were going to make it. I knew survival would not be a problem."

But there were problems. Not heart or burn problems, just indescribable depression and the constant, burning pain. "There were many days when I just sat there and cried," Dave recalls. "More than once I begged the nurse to just give me a shot that would end it all, but she always said, 'I can't, Dave.' I wanted to die. Despite all the things I went through as an alcoholic, the burn, the pain, and the depression at this time was the worst."

Of course, some of Dave's friends gave him excellent support. They came to visit him in the hospital, and he loved them for it. Whenever they came he forced himself to smile. But when they left it was worse than ever. "The worst of it," Dave said, "was sitting there and thinking, I'll never be back. I'll always be an invalid. I'll never be back running again. . . ."

Eight weeks after being admitted to the Burn Center, Dave was told he could go home. But Dave had other plans. He told the nurses he wasn't going home. He told them, "If you think I'm going home looking like this, you're crazy. I got a look at myself in the shower, and I look like Mahatma Gandhi with patches all over." To add to the problem Dave's weight had slipped to 126 pounds. He always wanted to get back down to 130 pounds, but never this way.

The nurse just sat there and looked straight at Dave and said, "You've got to go home, Dave. We're not going to keep you." But Dave was adamant. He was back into that poor ego status again. He was ashamed to look at himself. Fortunately the same day a woman from AA called. She wanted to know how Dave was doing.

"Oh, fine," I told her. But she read right through his remark. She told him he sounded down, like he needed help.

Dave then told her that he had to go home and he didn't want to because he didn't like the way he looked. But she shot right back, "Did you ever think that none of us care what you look like on the outside? You're still the same Dave on the inside. And we love you." When she said that Dave was physically shaken. He concluded that if his friends felt that way about him he'd go home and work things out.

But there were more hurdles ahead. When Dave got out of the hospital in late August, the doctor told him to do a lot of walking, that the exercise would do him some good. This infuriated Dave. "You two-bit punk," Dave thought. "I could run twenty-six miles before I went into this stupid hospital and now I can't even walk a mile." Dave went home depressed. He had slid from the mountaintop to the deepest valley. He was totally frustrated.

But good fortune was to smile on Dave again. His good friend, Dave Simmons, head swim coach at Riverview High School, talked to Dave one day. They planned to walk and swim each morning and then go for breakfast.

The plan sounded like a winner to Dave. Especially the breakfast. "When it came to eating, the doctors had wanted me to just stuff myself," Dave said. "So I did. When I was in the hospital I went off my vegetarian diet. I ate all kinds of meat. I ate everything. And I continued to do this when I came home. I wanted to gain my weight back in a very short period of time. I got back to one-fifty in three weeks, and I started pumping in my vitamins again. I even rubbed vitamin E into my burns. It seemed to help."

But when he walked with his coaching buddy, Dave tired

quickly. Walking a mile was excruciating. This led to more depression and greater feelings of self-pity.

Then, five days after getting out of the hospital, Dave started running. But it wasn't his idea. His wife and two sons were doing a little running and they had just gotten home from seeing *Rocky II*. Michael, Dave's oldest boy, looked at his mom and said, "Mom, are we going to run?" She didn't want to. Then Mike looked at Dave and said, "Dad don't want to run. He's too old." That was all it took. Dave told his son to get his shoes. Both Mike and he ran a mile that evening. The running was not easy, but the die was cast.

Dave approached Simmons the next day and suggested they start running. Running with Dave Simmons was a killer at first. As Dave says, "Simmons was always laughing at me and saying, 'Come on, wimpy!' I used to just murder him out on the track, and now I could hardly make a mile. But he got me out there every day, rain or shine. We kept running. And gradually we increased the mileage from one to two. From two to three, three to four, and finally five miles."

When Dave went to see the doctor he asked Dave how much he was walking. Dave told him he wasn't walking, but that he was up to four miles of running in the morning and five miles of running at night. The doctor almost fell out of the chair. He still has a hard time believing the change. Maybe Dave will revolutionize medicine for burn victims.

Of course, Dave must still undergo some additional skin graft operations, but his recovery has been exceptionally swift and good, despite the fact that his body is scarred.

But the injury has left more than just scars on Dave's body. "To this day my feelings about myself are real bad. I don't like to walk around without anything other than a long-sleeved shirt," he explained. "People just look at me like I'm some kind of weirdo. When I'm in the pool with my swim kids I wear a short-sleeved shirt, because they know the whole story. But one time at a swim meet down in Atlanta, Georgia, I took off my sweatshirt and this one little girl looked at me and said, 'Oh gross, look at those arms!' That really freaked me out."

When that happened Dave went back to where his swimmers were and put his sweatshirt back on. But one of the swimmers said, "Would it make any difference if we told you that we all love you?" Dave just looked at her. And she responded, "Well, we do, so don't worry about it." I talked to Dave only a few weeks after that incident. Dave told me he thought that he had gotten a better attitude about his body but he still reflected, "I can deal with it better if I have a long-sleeved shirt on."

When Dave and I had our first conversation in December 1979 it was only three months after his being released from the hospital. So the reality of the burns was still deep. In fact, as we talked we both knew that the next day he was going in for a skin graft operation on his arm. He hoped it would be his last operation.

As we talked I could see that Dave's attitude about life had improved over the years. As he puts it, "I've been successful because I'm a firm believer in physical fitness. Exercise just makes you turn around and makes you feel good about yourself. I feel good that I've already gotten out and done my running this morning, even though it's five degrees outside and everyone looks at me like I'm crazy. The cold weather does bother me. And I have to dress real warm. But I still feel good.

"My problem now is that I'm awfully weak. I can't accept that. I ran fifteen miles last Sunday. That's my longest run since I've been out of the hospital. And I'm only back up to seven miles a day. But I'm going to keep trying."

Dave keeps himself pretty busy. He still goes to five AA meetings a week. He's still coaching. And again he's training for the Boston Marathon. His friends tell him, "You want everything yesterday; don't cramp your style. You'll come back."

But Dave is impatient. "I want Boston this year," he told me. "I'm in a hurry. My goal is to run the Boston Marathon in two hours and thirty minutes." If I was a betting man I would put money on him.

Mike Levine

Michael D. Levine

"Get him on his feet!" barked a short, bulldog-type man with a bullhorn.

"What's a guy like him runnin' in this for, anyway, dammit? Next thing you know he'll tell us he can walk on water. Hey, what's yer name?"

Mike Levine knew the question was directed to him, but for some reason, he couldn't answer. His insides were on fire, his legs felt battered and heavy, he couldn't seem to get enough air, though he was gasping heavily. His lips were parched and bleeding, and though he knew he was being asked a question, all he could think of was Coca-Cola.

"I . . . uh . . . name . . . argh!"

He heaved, but nothing was there. To accommodate the contraction, his body slumped forward, leaving Mike a grotesque heap of spent muscles and bones. The harsh pavement offered no solace. His cheek lay against the hot asphalt while his arms struggled to push his aching body up off the cruel bed that offered little comfort. Again, his stomach rebelled and again, the retching felt as if it were going to tear him inside out.

"Ungh . . . wa-water . . . pul . . . pulease!"

A couple of college students acting as attendants rushed to his aid, one carrying a squirt bottle of water.

"Take it easy, buddy. You'll be okay."

The one with the bottle sprayed a cool stream of the precious liquid over Mike's head and shoulders. Mike lifted his head and opened his mouth to receive a few drops to quench his thirst.

"Easy does it, fella. Not yet. We gotta get you up first before you get a drink. Get his other arm, Jim. Here we go."

Just like that, the two attendants had Mike on his feet and were trying to walk him around the finish area. However, Mike wasn't being too cooperative. As hot and dirty as the pavement was, it looked awfully tempting to him. He just wanted to lay down, but the attendants kept walking him around. One of them noticed a pronounced limp.

"Hey, buddy . . . you all right? Looks like you're limpin' a little. Didja cramp up?"

Mike was just starting to come to his senses, just beginning to realize he had finished his first marathon. The question about the limping annoyed him.

"Naw, it's nothin' . . . how'd I . . . uh . . . finish?"

"Never mind about that. Let's get you over to the medical truck and have a look at that leg. Looks like you really messed it up."

"You're damn right I messed it up," returned Mike. He had never been known for diplomacy, and this first marathon seemed to give him even more license to speak his mind.

"But I didn't do it in this race. I was born this way. I have cerebral palsy."

The two attendants almost dropped him.

"Uh . . . well . . . uh . . . come on, Jim, let's get this guy to the truck—fast!"

"Relax!"

Now it was Mike's turn to administer aid.

"Unless you got a cure for CP in that truck, I don't need anything. Just help me to my car so I can drive back to the hotel and die."

Mike got back to the hotel with his girlfriend and started drinking Coke. His stomach had calmed down a bit, and the dark, sweet liquid seemed like heaven to him. He finished the first bottle, then popped open a second. Within an hour or so, he had gone through an entire six-pack. Finally, he became curious about the results of the race and called race headquarters.

"Tom Johnson won the senior men's division, Loren Harvey won the masters division, and a Mike Levine won the college division," droned the mechanical voice at the other end of the phone.

"Are you kidding?" Mike screamed.

"About what, sir?"

"About that Mike Levine guy."

"No, sir. Is there anything wrong?"

"Absolutely not!" answered Mike, throwing the phone back onto the hook. Had he possessed the energy, he would have jumped off the bed and danced around the room in celebration of his victory. Instead, he pounded the bed, wept, and laughed, while his girlfriend looked on incredulously.

"For Pete's sake, Mike, what's wrong?"

"You're not going to believe this, but I just won the first marathon I've ever entered. I just beat all the other college runners in that lousy race. I'm number one."

By now, he was shouting and holding the victorious first finger high in the air as he had seen his idols on the Oklahoma football team do many times when they had won.

"I'm number one!"

Nearly a thousand miles to the south, Dr. Jack Levine was sitting by the pool of an Acapulco hotel, enjoying the warm morning sun of Mexico. His orthopedic practice in New York was far from his mind as he settled comfortably in his lounge chair, anticipating a relaxing morning around the pool, with, perhaps, an occasional dip in the water. His reverie was interrupted by a shapely attendant approaching with a note.

"Dr. Levine?"

"Yes, what is it?"

"You have a person-to-person phone call from Artesia, New Mexico. You can take the call at the bar."

Dr. Levine was a bit annoyed, but thanked the girl, then got up to answer the call. "Who the hell could be calling me from Artesia, New Mexico?" he thought. He hadn't even heard of the place. He reached for the phone, not really sure what to expect.

"Hello?" he mumbled.

"Hey, Dad, how's it goin'?"

Dr. Levine was both pleased and curious.

"Well, good morning, Mike. Would you please tell me what you're doing in Artesia, New Mexico."

"You're never going to believe me, but I just ran my first marathon and—"

"You what?"

"I said, I just ran a marathon and I won my division."

The elder Levine was stunned. He muttered a few words of congratulations, listened to Mike's account of the event, then said good-bye and hung up. By the time he returned to his chair by the pool, the news finally hit him and he was beside himself with pride.

"You know, at first I just didn't believe it. That crazy guy never told us he was training for a marathon. We knew he was running, but you don't just go out and run twenty-six miles without really training. I'll tell you, I'm about as proud as a parent can be. He's always been number one in my book."

Mike Levine had never been number one before in his entire life. Born with crippling cerebral palsy, he had always been a step behind his playmates when it came to sports.

"When the kids on my block chose up sides for stickball or basketball, I was always picked last," he says.

Throughout his early years as a youngster growing up in Brooklyn, New York, Mike struggled to show everyone he was just as capable as the other kids. The struggle was enormous, and sometimes his body just wouldn't cooperate. Cerebral palsy is a disease that interferes with the messages the brain sends to various parts of the body. The brain may tell the leg to move forward, but the leg may just sit there until it feels like moving. Or, for no apparent reason, an arm may jerk uncontrollably. Consequently, sports are almost an impossibility for CP victims, and Mike was one of its victims.

Naturally, the disease was tough for Mike, but his parents were also involved in the struggle. Dr. Levine recalls the heartache upon learning that his son would be different from other, healthy boys. He agonized over the difficult life ahead of Mike and wondered if it would adversely affect his son's chances of having a regular, normal childhood. He still recalls having to hide his tears from Mike when his son approached with miserably contorted hands and legs. The question was always the same.

"Daddy, why did this happen to me?"

There was never any suitable answer for Mike or for his father.

However, neither Dr. Levine nor Mike felt the disease should stop him from doing the things he wanted to do, and, like most kids his age, Mike wanted to be active. He saw the games of stickball in the streets and wanted to join in. In the fall, the games of football played on a vacant lot beckoned, and Mike always gave it a try.

Because of his desire to give Mike a chance at an active life, Dr. Levine arranged for a series of operations to try and regain a little more mobility and flexibility for his son. First, physicians worked to open Mike's hands and allow him to manipulate them more freely. The operations failed. Next, they tried to lengthen the heel cord, hoping to give Mike a chance to run more easily. Again, the attempts met with failure.

"I finally decided to forget about any more operations and just let Mike do what he wanted to do," recalls Dr. Levine.

Once, when he was eleven years old, Mike tore his right heel cord. He was sent to the hospital, by then a familiar place to him. This time the tear was repaired, and he was put in a cast and told to take it easy for a while. He took it easy for as long as it took one of his friends to stop by and ask if he wanted to play handball. Mike agreed, and played a couple of games with the reckless abandon of a prizefighter in the fifteenth round of a title bout.

Crack! He looked down and much to his chagrin, noticed the plaster cast had shattered. He was especially worried, not so much because of his leg, but because of the fact that his father was an orthopedic surgeon. How was he going to explain this to his dad?

He thought up a good excuse, then walked home to break the news.

His father must have fallen for the story, because in no time, Mike was patched up and back outside playing. It didn't take his dad long to learn what really happened, because in the course of his convalescence, Mike broke the cast three more times.

"One of the nice things about having an orthopedic surgeon for a father is that we always had a lot of plaster around. My dad would just shake his head, then slap some plaster on the cast. I'd be back in action in no time."

Mike's parents were helpful throughout his childhood, and like most parents of handicapped people, they seldom pampered their son. They knew of Mike's drive and understood his desire to be normal. For this reason, they insisted on sending Mike to a public rather than a private school.

"One of the hardest things for us to do was to avoid pampering him. It's only natural for a parent to want to protect his child, and we were no different. Emotionally, we felt a private school could offer Mike more special attention, but realistically, we knew Mike needed to get used to fending for himself. Looking back, I think it would have been devastating if we had treated Mike with kid gloves."

Mike, too, wanted to be like everyone else, but he knew it was impossible. He saw his friends run to first base on a line drive, while the same hit would be a sure out for him. He always watched fast breaks develop on the basketball court, never being able to lead the charge himself. And he soon tired of always being the center when football was in season. He wanted more than anything else to run, jump, slide, and throw just like all his friends did.

"Mike always loved athletics. He read about them. Watched games on TV. Tried to participate as much as his body would let him. But because he couldn't perform as well as the other kids, he developed a pretty low concept of himself. We could just watch his personality change as he progressively became more withdrawn and shy."

Mike, too, sensed what was happening to him, but he felt powerless to do anything about it.

"It's a terrible feeling to be young and see all your friends doing things with ease that you can't even dream of doing. I think at that early age I decided I would just do my best and maybe, some day, show everyone I can do things they can't do."

So with that early determination, Mike Levine set about to show his detractors that a handicap is mostly mental. His first obstacle was to leave the comfortable environment of his home. There was nothing rebellious about this. Mike just felt that in order to reach his goals, he would have to avoid the security of knowing there was always someone around to pick him up if he fell. Through high school, he had never once been away from home.

"I hadn't even been to summer camp," he says.

He moved to Oklahoma to go to college, but he didn't stay long.

"It actually took me three attempts to move out. I mean, when you've been so used to being home all the time, it's very difficult to move away. But I knew I had to get out on my own if I was going to amount to anything."

Finally, he hit the campus of Oklahoma to stay, and began working toward a degree in education. He felt comfortable once he realized that he could blend in with the large, diverse student body. He noticed that people seldom stared at him as they had done back in the public high school he attended. He was still shy, but there were plenty of diversions for him. Like most students on the campus, Mike fell in love with the legendary Oklahoma football program. Saturday became his favorite day, especially when the Sooners were playing in the home stadium. He was their most rabid fan, devouring information about the team, memorizing statistics from the past, and offering keen, analytic comments about each game to anyone who would listen. As he watched coach Barry Switzer lead his charges onto the field, he mentally pictured himself excelling in the sport he loved so well.

Even though the campus was large and the student body numbered into the thousands, Mike ran into an acquaintance from back East. He was a member of the cross-country team and encouraged Mike to attend one of the meets. As far as Mike was concerned, a group of skinny guys running around the countryside in their shorts just didn't hold a candle to Sooner football. Yet a friendship developed, and Mike began going to the meets and learning more about the sport.

One day, his friend suggested he start running.

"I thought he was crazy. And when he said I could be a marathoner, I really thought he was nuts. My mom talked me into running once because she thought I was getting fat. That lasted about two days. But coming from an experienced runner, the idea fascinated me."

What seemed to fascinate him most was the idea that maybe he could excell at something that few people at that time were capable of doing. In recent years, marathon running has become increasingly popular, with more and more people running the 26-mile, 385-yard distance. Hardly a weekend passes without a marathon being conducted somewhere in the nation. But in 1970 the sport was rare indeed. Few people even knew what one was, and, frankly, Mike liked it that way. He decided it would become "his" sport.

So he began training. Every day he would drag himself out of bed at 4:30 in the morning, wipe the sleep from his eyes, struggle into an old pair of gray sweatpants, and pull on a sweatshirt.

"For me, just getting ready to run is an ordeal. My fingers don't always do what I tell them to do, and there is always the temptation to say 'nuts' and go back to bed. Don't get me wrong, though. The trouble was physical, not mental. I have NEVER not wanted to run!"

Mike never yielded to that temptation—never gave in to that urge to take the easy way out. He was driven by a desire to finish the twenty-six-mile race that relatively few, compared to today, had done.

"I was scared stiff about the whole thing because I didn't want to fail and I didn't know what would happen to me. I didn't know whether I could stay with it. Would I be able to stay in the race or would I have to quit? I just didn't know what it would feel like."

At first, his running only proved the impossibility of a marathon. Because of his disability, Mike lacked the flexibility needed to maintain a strong, relaxed stride. Instead, he ran in a jerky, uncomfortable manner, expending far more energy than would an able-bodied runner. After barely a mile, he would begin to cramp up, forcing him to go even slower. Discouraged, he would turn around and head home. The next day, however, Mike would be right back on the road, fighting the battle against fatigue and pain. He wanted to quit this silly idea and probably would have several times had he not been so stubborn.

"I just don't quit, that's all. I guess you could call it a positive attitude, but really it's more stubbornness than anything."

As he trained, he began to realize his goal was not that far-fetched. His confidence grew daily as he added miles and lowered times. He proceeded from four or five miles a day to six or seven. Occasionally, he would hit the roads for a ten-mile run. It was still a struggle, but he began to feel better about his running. He pushed himself hard, but at the end of his runs he felt a sense of accomplishment. While it wasn't Billy Simms breaking into the end zone for an Oklahoma touchdown, the feeling of exhilaration was great.

One day, Mike realized he hadn't even thought to look for a marathon. This was in 1970, and the marathon was a fairly rare occurrence. And since he didn't subscribe to any running magazine, his sources were limited. He started looking around, and with the help of his friend on the cross-country team, he found one that was being run in New Mexico at about the time he thought he would be ready.

With a real goal to work toward, Mike's training picked up. He knew that six miles a day with an occasional long run was not enough, so he increased his mileage. Naturally, it would take longer for him to complete his run, so he began getting up even earlier. Though 4:00 A.M. was still a tough time to get up and run, he approached the hour with the anxious attitude of a thoroughbred in the paddock. For once, his chance to prove himself was coming.

Finally, the day arrived. Mike and his girlfriend had driven to New Mexico and were a bit alarmed to discover the high temperatures (it was in the high 70s on the day of the race). Mike had never really enjoyed running in warm weather and wondered what effect it would have on him for the entire distance. He began to have doubts and wondered if he was just putting himself into the position of making one grand fool of himself.

When he approached the starting line, he noticed that most of the spectators and other contestants were looking at him in bewilderment. He had been through that many times before and was used to it.

"Actually, when I run, I look like the wrath of God. With my limp and my somewhat spastic movements, I guess I look pretty scary."

Once again, seeing those looks snapped Mike back to his gutsy stubbornness and provoked within him a desire to get started. He met the stares with a cool, yet defiant look as if to say, "I'll see you later on the road."

There were only about fifty runners in this marathon, but for those days, that was a sizeable crowd. Mike had signed up in the collegiate division, one that had about thirty contestants. When he looked over the names in his division, he noticed the name of a runner who was training for the Olympics. Mike hoped to stay with him long enough to watch his powerful stride and maybe learn something from him, so he moved up toward the line with that in mind.

The brief moments prior to the start of an athletic event are electric with tension, and this event was no different. Each runner has a different method of relieving the tension. Some jump up and down. Some shadowbox. Some jog in short, aimless circles. With the flurry of activity surrounding him, Mike simply stood and stared off into the direction the race would follow. Already, the pavement was rippling with heat waves, ominously inviting the runners to the challenge. Calmly, Mike went over his race plan, trying to anticipate how he would handle "the wall." Would he quit? Would he be forced to stop and walk the rest of the way? Would he even make it that far?

The gun went off, jarring Mike back to the reality of his first marathon, and a cheer arose into the hot, humid air. Each runner starting the race expressed an outward bravado to cover the inward doubts about his ability to finish. Mike was one of them.

Mike was careful not to go out too fast. He had heard enough stories about the wall, that point in the marathon race where everything hurts, where your body's sugar stores are depleted, where many a runner is forced to stop. It usually occurs some-where between eighteen and twenty-two miles. Mike wanted to avoid making the mistake of expending too much energy too soon, or hitting the wall and having to drop out. He comfortably settled into about a ten-and-one-half-minute-per-mile pace, and covered the first three miles without difficulty.

At the five-mile mark, Mike encountered the first runners' aid station. There, on a long table, were several glasses of cool, fresh water. By now, the hot New Mexico sun was climbing toward its zenith, and a drink of water sounded pretty good to Mike. Yet his pre-race plan was to avoid any water at all. He was concerned about stomach cramps and thought that if anything would stop him it would be a cramp from drinking too much water. For some reason, he gave little thought to dehydration exhaustion. So he waved away the attendant who was handing him a paper cup of water and plodded on.

At the six-mile mark, Mike began to panic. From what little he had read about the race, he felt he was hitting the dreaded "wall." That wasn't supposed to happen until the twenty-mile mark, but here it was. His legs were heavy, his breath was short, and his mouth was bone-dry. Had he gone out too fast? Was the weather too much? Was he really insane for trying something that, to date, only twelve thousand other Americans had done? He was certain the answer to these questions was a resounding "yes." Yet he was just as certain he would not quit. It was just not his style. Mike slowed up a bit, but plodded on.

Along the way, the temptation to drink was nearly overwhelming. He began thinking about drinking with every step he took. When he passed the aid stations, it took every bit of self-discipline to wave the attendants away. In addition, he refused to let people spray water on him, fearing it would cause his legs to cramp up. The course was a straight 26.2-mile stretch of hot New Mexico blacktop spanning the distance between two towns. Whenever he passed a house or gas station, someone would always have a hose ready. He wanted desperately to run under the cool spray, but fought back the urge and struggled on.

For several miles, Mike had merely trudged on in a kind of pain-induced stupor. The other runners, the aid stations, the trees, the houses—all blended into a foggy backdrop slowly passing by. His legs, stiffened by his disease and now punished by the distance, screamed for relief. He saw other runners running by him, and he yearned for two healthy legs. If he just had more flexibility, he thought, he wouldn't have to work so hard. He could stride easily and efficiently instead of pushing, pulling, and pounding those two uncooperative limbs along the highway. Still, he trudged on. Step by step. Yard by yard. Mile by mile.

Gradually, however, Mike began to notice his surroundings more acutely. He wasn't certain, but he thought he saw runners ahead of him who were walking. He turned, and thought he noticed a few runners sitting along the side of the road. Then he realized what was happening. The heat and pace were beginning to claim victims who moments before were running with apparent ease. Runners of all ages and abilities were calling it quits. Seeing this happen strengthened Mike's resolve to continue, and his pace picked up a bit. With just five miles to go, Mike was actually jubilant despite the pain that racked his body.

"The only way I'll *not* finish is if someone tackles me and holds me down," he thought to himself.

Mike finished, but not before agonizing through the final miles in dreadful pain. He was alarmed at the difficulty he had breathing. He was gasping, yet he didn't seem to be getting any air. He felt like he was suffocating, yet he knew all he had to do was to stop and the problem would be solved. In addition, his stomach muscles were cramping, sending sharp pains up and down both sides of his body. The pain from this was so intense it caused him to double over to gain some relief. This in turn made breathing more difficult and added more stress to his weak, crippled legs. It was the ultimate torture: whenever he tried to escape the pain, he only produced more torment.

"Throughout almost the entire race, I felt like dying. The pain was more intense than I thought possible, and when I finished, I couldn't walk. I just wanted to die, even though I was thrilled at finishing."

Yet Mike never once entertained the idea of quitting.

Being that way led Mike to tackle achievements that many able-bodied people would never attempt. However, he credits running with opening up an entire new world for him. The effect was more psychological than physical.

"My life really changed after that first attempt. In March, I ran my first marathon. In April, I ran the Boston Marathon. In July, I met a new girl and fell in love. In December I married her. Up to this point I had been somewhat shy and withdrawn, and never dated much. I credit running to turning that year into one incredible year."

When I talked with Mike, I sensed that his running was more than just something he did for his health. In fact, he once made the statement that he would continue running even if it could be proven harmful. I asked him about this.

"Even if running would shorten my life, I would still do it. I mean, it's something I enjoy doing because of the fact I can do something a lot of other people can't do. That makes me feel good about myself."

In fact, one day I called him during the work day and was surprised to catch him at home. He told me he had pneumonia and the doctor advised him to lay off work for a week or two. However, he was still running and was concerned about having great difficulty covering his normal distance. He asked me what I would recommend, and I told him he should probably stop running until he recovered from pneumonia. Then I asked him if his doctor knew he was still running.

"Yeah, I told him this morning," he answered.

"And what did he say?" I asked.

"Oh, he told me if I kept running it would kill me. But it's very hard for me to go through a day without running."

Running hasn't killed Mike Levine. Instead, it has made his life richer. As a freshman, Mike entered Oklahoma University shy, withdrawn, and frightened. All his life he wanted to be normal, to be accepted, perhaps to excel. He watched the football heroes come and go, and wondered what such adulation felt like. He knew such praise was reserved for the able-bodied, but his gritty determination drove him to dreams he felt far exceeded his grasp. With perhaps an overdose of the Walter Mitty complex, Mike often imagined himself taking a handoff from the quarterback, breaking through a scant hole in the defensive line, stiff-arming one tackler, and deftly sidestepping another as he pranced away for a touchdown, spiking the ball and basking in the tumultuous roar of the home crowd. Dreams?

At the end of the football season in 1972, Mike Levine was one of several honored guests at the university's sports awards banquet. To his right and left were football players, cross-country runners, and coaches. Each was called to the dais to receive an award. Mike waited, more nervous than he was at the start of the marathon.

"And now ladies and gentlemen, we will present one of the most treasured athletic awards to a very special young athlete. The 1972 Sports Headliner of the Year . . . Mr. Mike Levine!"

Milly Smith

Milly Smith

Y ou okay, Gramma?"
The voice belonged to fourteen-year-old Kurtis Smith. He was a little concerned because his grandmother, Mrs. Milly Smith, seemed to be having a little difficulty on the trail. As far as he was concerned, he was totally responsible for whatever happened to his grandmother. Sure, it had been her idea all along, but any fourteen-year-old knew you just didn't let seventy-five-year-old grandmas backpack around the countryside. He was going to make sure nothing happened to his grandmother.

"Aw, it's okay, Kurtis. I just needed to catch my breath a little."

She was exhausted, her feet were sore, and her breath was coming in quick gulps instead of regular, steady lungfuls. It had never occurred to her that keeping up with three boys sixty-one years younger would be a problem. She secretly hoped they were turned around a bit so she could catch her breath.

"Where are we, anyway?"

Kurtis was afraid she would ask. "Darn it!" he thought. "They told me back at Scouts that these trails were well marked. Then why are we at a fork in a place where the map shows a straight trail? Which way do we go?"

"Um, looks like we're right on course, Gramma," he replied in an uncertain voice. Grandmothers were great ones for reading faces and voices, and Milly was, perhaps, better than most.

"Well, if you're not sure, maybe we ought to work together on this. What d'ya say?"

So Milly Smith, her grandson Kurtis, and his two friends sat down on a log, somewhere in southern Michigan's Waterloo Recreation Area, propped their feet up on their backpacks, and tried to decide how to proceed with their fifty-mile backpacking trip without having it turn into a seventy- or eighty-mile excursion.

For Milly, walking had always been a pleasant activity, but this backpacking was something else. As a young girl growing up in northern Indiana, walking was a way of life. Her family lived out in the country on a farm, and every Sunday, when the weather was nice, the entire clan walked the mile and a half to church. For diversion, Milly would take daily walks ranging from one to three miles along the country roads near her home.

"I guess I walked because it was so pleasant," she recalls.

It wasn't long before the family moved to Detroit, Michigan, where Milly attended high school and prepared for a career of teaching. Upon completion of her degree, Milly was given a job teaching in a one-room school with forty children spanning kindergarten through eighth grade. She soon discovered she enjoyed the little ones best, and from that time on, spent her time teaching the elementary grades.

In 1968, Milly turned sixty-five, a fact that upset her only because it meant she couldn't teach anymore. She looked good, felt good, and loved her job. But thirty-one years is a long time at any career, so Milly accepted her retirement reluctantly, and set about on an adventure she hoped would help her avoid the rocking chair.

Initially, her retirement was similar to most retirement periods. While she had plenty of family willing to care for her, she wanted to keep her independence. So, she took up residence in a retirement home where she has her own room and her own time schedule.

When I arrived at the home to meet Milly, I was a bit disappointed to see the old, sprawling, hospitallike buildings. They just seemed inappropriate for someone of Milly's youthful spirit. I approached the desk, wondering if Milly might be in the lobby waiting for me. I had never met her before, and didn't quite know what to look for. Sitting next to the receptionist's desk was a lady who appeared to be in her late fifties—perhaps another visitor waiting to see a resident.

"Hello, I'm here to visit Mrs. Milly Smith," I said to the receptionist.

Before she could answer, Mrs. Fifty-Year-Old hopped up with a smile and said, "I'm Milly."

With that she said, "Come along, it's too noisy down here," and ushered me toward the stairway, passing the elevator along the way. Three flights of stairs later we were in her small but comfortable room, and she was explaining how she got started in her unique retirement.

"I enjoyed the extra time I had to be with my grandchildren, and it was nice to have the time to read a book or work on a quilt. But something was missing, and I wasn't quite sure what it was."

One day, in 1976, Milly's daughter suggested she go see the Grand Canyon for some diversion.

"She told me I just had to see it before I got one year older, then went ahead and made reservations, so I was kind of stuck."

Not only was Milly stuck in the middle of a trip to the Grand Canyon, she was stuck on a mule. Her daughter, fearing that her mother might not be able to get around too well along the rough, steep trail, arranged for her to ride a mule down into the deep canyon. While the mule was tame, and quite cooperative, it just wasn't Milly's cup of tea.

"Pauline [that was her mule's name] was a good mule, but all the time I was on her, I was scared stiff. She did her work all right, but when we got to the bottom to a little place called Phantom Ranch, I just wanted the owners to turn it into a retirement home and leave me there. I didn't even take any pictures throughout the whole trip because I was too scared to let go of Pauline's neck."

One thing Milly noticed on that initial mule trip was the number of backpackers she saw. To her, it seemed like a nifty way to travel, but she wasn't sure it was for her.

"Those backpackers sure looked like they were having fun, but I was kind of ashamed to go into a store and buy one. I didn't know anything about it, and at my age, you raise some eyebrows when you go shopping for things like that."

So Milly did what many Americans do. She pulled out her trusty catalog, and ordered one from a department store chain. With the sneaky excitement of a teenage girl who had ordered her first pair of nylon hose, Milly stealthily hid the plain brown package in her car, and drove quickly away from the retirement center. She turned down a country lane, then stopped the car near the start of a short trail. She cautiously scanned the road in both directions, then slipped the pack out of its box. Nervously, she filled it with books she had brought along just for this occasion, then slipped the pack on her back and hurried off into the woods.

Milly was hooked. She walked about a mile and marveled at how easily she was able to sustain the weight. As she strolled in the lush, wooded countryside, her mind raced. How far could she go without getting tired? How much weight could she carry? Could she carry a sleeping bag, too? Is it possible to be too old to sleep on the ground? Would everyone think she was crazy?

Milly decided there was only one way to find out. She hurried back to the car and, after making sure no motorists were approaching, placed her pack in the backseat and hopped in the car for the ride back to the retirement center.

"What was that package you got in the mail today, Milly?" asked one of her friends who was rocking in the lobby of the main residence building.

"Oh, nothing special," she smiled mischievously, hoping the Good Lord would forgive her this one white lie.

Once in her room, she dialed her daughter-in-law's number.

"Hello Luene, is Kurtis home? This is Mom . . . hello Kurtis . . . I'm fine, thanks . . . how would you like to go camping!"

The afternoon sun cast lazy shadows over the four hikers as they pondered their situation. Milly kept silent, preferring to listen to the boys bicker congenially over the right path to take. The birds chirped a melodious accompaniment to the earnest, youthful voices, while the breeze tossed puffs of milkweed in carefree patterns about their heads. Milly knew they were lost, but she wasn't alarmed. She reasoned if you had to be lost, what better way than doing something exciting with people you like. Besides, she welcomed the rest.

They finally decided it would be best to stick together, and their little strategy session dictated they should take the trail to the left. With packs strapped back on, the quartet of adventurers trudged on, only to discover an hour later that the decision to go left was wrong. It was a little problem, however. They retraced their steps and soon were on their way to complete a fifty-mile, four-day backpacking trip.

At night, Milly found herself in the best of care. She thought of her friends back at the retirement home and how they would laugh if they could see her now. The tents were pitched in a circle, and the boys had built a fire in the middle. They wouldn't think of making Gramma cook, but prepared a delicious meal with all the trimmings. When it was time to go to sleep, everyone got into his sleeping bag, and drifted off to a delightful chorus of crickets and frogs.

"At first I wasn't sure I'd be able to sleep on the ground. But when you're dead tired, you can sleep anywhere. And the night's sleep can really refresh you."

All too soon, Milly's first backpacking trip was over. She was proud of the boys because they received a 50 Mile Award from the Boy Scout troop they belonged to. She was somewhat proud of herself, too.

"I felt like I had accomplished something. That I had lived through it. It was tough. Sure it was tough. There were times when I got really tired, but when it's over you really feel great."

Most important, Milly proved to herself that she didn't have to spend the rest of her life in a rocking chair. That first fifty-mile jaunt with three fourteen-year-old boys launched Milly Smith on an incredible journey with life. She decided, while on that trip, that the next time she shouldered her pack, it would be at the edge of the Grand Canyon.

In the winter of 1976 Milly called her daughter-in-law and announced her intentions. The announcement brought no surprise reaction from her daughter-in-law. She knew the risks involved when a seventy-five-year-old grandmother embarks on a wilderness backpacking journey. She knew the difference between a hike in the comfortable, flat woods of southern Michigan, and the harsh, steep face of the Grand Canyon's walls. But she also knew her mother-in-law well enough to know it was little use trying to talk her out of it.

"When are you going?" she responded.

"I think I'll go in April. Tell Kurtis I'm planning on him and his friends to come along to keep me company."

Milly immediately set about preparing for the trip. She knew this excursion would present a stiffer challenge compared to her trek around the lake in southern Michigan. She was worried about the weight of the pack and carefully pruned her list of supplies so that she took only what was necessary. She bought a new pair of shoes well in advance so they would be comfortably broken in by the time she reached the canyon. And almost daily, she thought how nice it would be to descend into the canyon without Pauline.

The Michigan winter slowly gave way to spring, and the departure date for the trip soon arrived. Milly could hardly contain her excitement. When they got to the edge of the canyon, the air was clear and bright, allowing an unbroken, panoramic view across to the other side. After supper, they checked into their motel for one final night of luxury before the trek to the bottom of the canyon.

Milly jumped up at the alarm and threw back the drapes. She could hardly believe what she saw. A six-inch blanket of snow covered everything. Before she had time to reconsider, a knock came at her door, followed by a call from Kurtis.

"Come on, Gramma. Let's get going."

She smiled at the eagerness of youth, then realized she was just as excited to get going herself. She quickly dressed, then double-checked to make sure her pack was in order. With a sigh and a quick prayer, Milly slipped out of the comfort of the motel room and into the crisp, refreshing atmosphere of the Arizona morning. The trip was underway.

It's eleven miles from the edge of the canyon to the bottom, but the trip down took them two days.

The footing was treacherous, forcing the hikers to remain

constantly alert. Milly encountered for the first time the difficulty of constantly walking down an incline. New muscles in her thighs were called upon to transport the spry old grandmother and her forty-pound pack into the depths of the canyon. Those muscles at times felt heavy and lifeless as the party inched down the trail. By the evening of the first day, the snow had all melted, and the hikers were tired but in good spirits.

Milly welcomed the approaching darkness with a tired sigh. She gingerly slouched against a rock while the boys set up camp. Dusk in the canyon is both eerie and beautiful, the walls changing colors by degrees as the sun sinks slowly to its resting place over the horizon. The calm, cool air was invigorating and despite her exhaustion, Milly was glad to be right there against the walls of one of the celebrated wonders of Nature. After a delicious meal and some convivial talk, all four hikers crawled into their downy cocoons and fell fast asleep.

The next day proved even more arduous. The trail was strewn with knee-high boulders and passage was slow and difficult. Many times, the hikers had to climb over the obstacles. The boys were careful not to go too fast, but Milly was determined to show them she could keep up with any pace. As they approached each boulder, she inwardly groaned at the effort she knew it would take to pass. Occasionally, when she put one foot up on a large boulder, she wasn't sure she had the strength to push up and over it. But she never let up.

"I just kept putting one foot in front of the other," she smiles.

When they reached the bottom, there was little time to celebrate. They pitched their tents at Phantom Ranch, and the next morning, the boys left Milly behind for their ascent of the north rim. They wanted to be able to say they had hiked from rim to rim to rim, and thus earn a special Scout award. Milly decided she didn't need that award, but took the opportunity to rest for the trip back up the south rim.

The boys made it back to Milly and were ecstatic with success. The award they would be receiving is quite unique and they were glad to have had such an opportunity. Now the four were ready to tackle the south rim.

Milly wasn't quite sure what to expect. She knew it would be a little harder than the descent, but she wasn't prepared for what was to follow.

"It was unbelievable. Imagine, every step you take going just a little bit higher. Climbing, climbing, all the time, with no flat areas or downhills. It was really exhausting."

Still, Milly pressed on. Her younger companions were struggling, too, and Milly wondered if she had made a wise decision to try and keep up with a group of teenagers. Her legs ached. Her lungs burned. Indeed, her entire body was feeling the effects of each forward step. Walk ten steps. Rest for a few breaths. Walk a dozen more. Rest. The forty-pound pack grew to fifty, sixty, could it be eighty pounds? To Milly, it sure felt like it.

And then, that most beautiful of sights. Just a few more steps and the rugged trip would be over. Milly almost ran those final yards, and soon her mountain was conquered! She slipped off her pack, sat down by the edge of the canyon, and looked back over the distance she had covered. She could hardly believe she had done it. She felt good. Tired, sore, and hungry. But good.

"You just feel so good when you do something that everyone, even yourself, thinks is impossible."

It felt so good that almost before she had her boots off for this trip, Milly was planning her next. She went again the following year. And again the next.

"You see, I have all these grandchildren and they all wanted to go hiking with Gramma. So, I guess I've become a sort of family tour guide for the Grand Canyon."

One year, Milly led a group down the Wilderness Trail of the Grand Canyon, which is reserved for experienced climbers.

"That was the toughest trip," she laughs.

Milly's approach to her active life is refreshingly simple. She feels the retired person shouldn't consider him or herself too old for anything.

"I've taken my pack down to the community room of my retirement home and shown them how it works, but they just shake their heads. They don't think they could do it gracefully. They worry about how they might look trying to get up in the morning after sleeping on the ground. Well, I don't do it gracefully, either. I'm sure I look pretty ridiculous at times, but who cares, really?"

It's obvious Milly doesn't let little things like that bother her. She takes advantage of every opportunity to remain active, and it doesn't always place her in the company of other senior citizens. In fact, all of her backpacking trips have been taken with teenagers, and she intends to keep it that way.

"Kids today are marvelous! They've got the energy problem all solved, and they always go about singing and having fun. They're a great bunch to be around."

To keep in shape for her seasonal jaunts, Milly enrolled in a local gym class at the high school. It's a night class that meets every Thursday, and every Thursday Milly is there. The evening begins with exercises on padded mats, then proceeds to the pool where everyone swims. Milly enjoys the swimming so much, she now attends three nights a week.

"I try to swim a quarter-mile each time. It takes me twenty-five minutes. My grandson can do it in five minutes, but I can do mine in twenty-five."

There are times when she feels like staying in her room and rocking the evening away in front of the television.

"Once, when the new schedule was about to start in the fall, I was sitting in my rocking chair, very relaxed and comfortable. And you know, I just didn't feel like getting up and going across town to go swimming. I almost had to beat myself out of that chair to get up and go. But you know, you feel so much better and more refreshed and not nearly as tired as before. I just can't miss it!"

So three times a week, Milly hikes across town and does her twenty laps while the rest of the residents play checkers and watch television. That's something Milly just doesn't want to let herself do.

"I fell into that trap once. I got addicted to soap operas. I'd sit in that rocker and watch them every day. But I can't do that. I have arthritis, and if I don't walk or swim each day, my joints begin to ache. I have to stay active just to feel good."

Other than her arthritis, Milly is amazingly healthy. As a youngster, she was never sick, and in her thirty-one years of teaching, she seldom missed a day. She's careful about her health, and has annual checkups. On one of those checkups, a doctor noticed an abnormal heart rhythm. He referred Milly to another physician for a special series of tests. Milly felt great, but she was more than a little concerned at the fuss everyone was making about it. She went to the specialist and nervously watched the electrical pickups being placed on her head and arms. The machine spit out a peculiar graph paper with jagged blue lines darting across and Milly wondered what it all meant. The doctor tore the tape from the machine, and, with a serious look, studied the lines. Slowly, a smile spread across her face and she turned to Milly, who by now wasn't sure whether to call a minister or a mortician.

"Go climb your mountain, Milly!"

Milly breathed a joyful sigh. And then she was out the door, making plans to do just what the doctor said. "Why not?" she thought. "If I can climb the steep trails of the Grand Canyon, I ought to be able to climb a mountain."

Her daughter groaned at the news.

"You're going to what?"

"Climb a mountain, silly. Want to come along?"

Before she had time to answer, Milly had already spread a map out on the kitchen table and was poring over it with the expertise of a forest ranger.

"There, that looks like a good one. Not too high, not too small. Get your gear ready."

The mountain they had chosen was Flat Top Mountain, a part of the Rocky Mountain range in Colorado. I've climbed that mountain, and it's no beginner's molehill. Milly and her daughter, Sue Lockwood, packed the car and drove to Colorado. They took a look at the mountain looming before them, then started the climb. They made it with little trouble to the last camping spot, which was just below the timberline. They camped for the night, then set out the next morning for the most difficult leg of the trip. Since there were no camping spots above the timberline, they had to make it all the way across the peak and over to the timberline on the other side. They saw about three signposts that stretched up toward the peak, and estimated there were three posts to the peak, then three on the other side to the timberline. Just six or seven markers, they thought. It shouldn't be too difficult.

The climb was rough, and the thin, mountain air didn't help any. They made it to the first marker, though, and were surprised at the progress they were making. Soon they were at the second, then the third one was just ahead. Their spirits soared as they approached the sign.

For some reason, however, they were still climbing instead of descending. They pressed on, soon passing three more signposts and still climbing. Milly and her daughter didn't know what to think. It was getting late in the morning, and they still hadn't reached the halfway point. Their breathing was labored and their pace was slowing.

Milly was beginning to worry about her daughter. The altitude seemed to be bothering her more than it affected Milly. Sue was beginning to lag behind and show signs of depression. Once, she stopped and sobbed, frustrated at being on the side of a mountain in the middle of nowhere, far from a camping site, with no sign of reaching the top.

"I think she just reached a point where physically and emotionally she couldn't take it anymore. We stopped and I just told her she could, and it seemed to pick her up a bit."

Just as they thought they might be reaching the top, they met a ranger approaching. They asked how many more of the signposts they had before reaching the timberline on the other side, thinking at most they would have a dozen.

"Oh, you've only got about a hundred more," he told them.

Their hearts sank. They were tired, cold, and out of breath, and there was no way for them to camp until they reached the timberline. For the first time, Milly thought she wouldn't be able to make it.

"We had reached a place where we could see the trail ahead of us. It was heartbreaking. Back and forth, back and forth. It just kept winding on as far as we could see. And there was no way we could cut across and leave the trail because there were huge boulders in our way. My entire body was just plain tuckered-out and I didn't think I had any energy left. You just can't imagine how worn-out I felt. I just looked at that and told my daughter, 'I can't do it!'"

By that time, her daughter was feeling chipper and encouraged her mother to get up and keep moving.

"You climbed farther than this in the Grand Canyon, and you made it this far. You can make it."

Milly thought she could never do it, but she got up and started walking. Back and forth. Little by little.

"I wanted to quit in the worst way, but I just couldn't. I kept thinking that I didn't want to be left sitting up there in those hills, and decided it would be best to go as far as I could. You just have to have a positive attitude. I started feeling better as soon as I decided I was going to make it."

They rounded a hairpin turn, and just ahead they saw trees. Once again, Milly Smith had conquered her limitations. This time, she was too tired to run, but dragged herself to the campsite, quickly set up her tent, unrolled her sleeping bag, and fell into a deep, well-deserved sleep.

Milly's activities didn't stop at climbing mountains or canyons. In the summer of 1979, her daughter, knowing Milly's weakness for saying yes to adventures, invited her to accompany a group of teenagers on a wilderness canoe trip in northern Canada. Naturally, Milly's answer was yes.

Nine teenagers, two adults, and, of course, Milly, climbed aboard a yellow school bus and made the long trip to Sault St. Marie, Canada. They transferred all their gear, including six canoes, onto a train, and continued north for two hundred miles. When the train reached the end of the line, everyone hopped out, put the canoes in the water, and started paddling.

"It was really interesting and fun. Everyone had a backpack with food, utensils, and sleeping gear. When we got to rapids, the boys would hoist those canoes up on their shoulders and we would follow with the supplies. On the second day, we got a nice breeze, so one of the boys pulled out a tent and, using the paddles for a mast, made a sail. Before I knew it, I was getting my tent out, and we all sailed that day. Such ingenuity."

Milly, who has had her share of excitement, almost had more than she bargained for on this trip. At one point, the group reached a rapids and were unable to find the trail that would take them around it. So they decided to walk the canoes up the rapids. Milly was in one of the canoes as the kids pushed and pulled it through the white water of the rapids.

"That was horrible. I was scared to death. And to make matters worse, it was pouring down rain."

They passed through the rapids, though, and after a campfire to dry things out, they were back on their way. For the next ten days, the routine was much the same, and as the canoers progressed, so did the weariness of constantly paddling. There could be no let-up if they were to reach their destination in time.

Blisters formed on the palms of Milly's hands, and her shoulders ached constantly from the relentless paddling. Her plucky spirit prevailed, however, and two weeks after the start, they glided into the bank at Mile Marker 206, the end of their journey. They were all tired, wet, but happy. And the fact that some sixty-odd years separated most of them from Milly only made them all the happier.

"There doesn't have to be a generation gap. I just accept them and try not to be critical. I just love being with them."

Milly's love of life has had a contagious effect on those she meets. While not everyone in the retirement home cares to attempt her way of life, several middle-aged people have followed her example. She tells of receiving a letter from a forty-year-old mother who said she had spent the first forty years of her life never once sleeping on the ground in a sleeping bag. After hearing about Milly, she began camping with her husband and three sons.

"She just loves it now!" exclaims Milly.

Then there was the time she got a letter from the Calgary Hiking Club in Canada that invited her to come hiking with them anytime she's in Calgary.

"You meet the nicest people on the trail," she says.

Milly has also met some nice people on the tennis court, but she has had to be a bit devious to do so.

"It's hard to get people to play an old lady. Once a lady I knew asked me to tutor her son who was having some reading difficulties. I worked with him and he made a little progress. His mother was so pleased, she offered to pay me. I said, 'Fine, that will cost you two hours on the tennis court.'"

Milly says she needs two courts because the ball doesn't always go where she wants it to, and she thinks the builders of tennis courts need some assistance.

"I sure wish they would build those fences higher. I'm always hitting the ball over the fences, then we have to go and chase it down," she laughs.

Her influence is also felt in the senior citizens' bowling league in her hometown.

"When it first started, I thought it was a good opportunity to exercise, so I joined. When I showed up the first day, there were just two men and myself. But I talked to a few people and the next time we had six. And then it grew to eight, and now it's hard to find an open alley. I've been bowling there for seven years now, steadily getting worse, but I'm having fun!"

Milly never thinks of exercise as anything but fun. Indeed, the key to her active life is having a good time doing whatever you please. About her only difficulty in maintaining her active way of life has been blisters, but she is now recognized as one of the world's premier "blister fixers."

"Whenever we are hiking and anybody gets a blister, I'm the one they come to. I just put a little foam around them for protection and keep them clean, and they never bother you. I hiked for six days on Isle Royal and had blisters the entire time, but they never hurt me."

When it comes to shoes, Milly has the same practical approach.

"I've tried many different kinds of hiking boots, but I like these the best," she explains, pointing to a simple, suede, casual loafer, one that might be found in any shoe store.

"Even the lightweight boots were too heavy and cumbersome for my weak legs to lift," she laughs.

Other than that, she offers no special secrets, no exotic equipment, no magic formula. To her, everyone has a choice: they can either sit around all day and worry about getting old, or they can get up and do things that make life enjoyable at any age.

Sometimes, she admits, the choice to be active may not always bring about the desired result. Once, she decided to join a group on a hike in the Adirondacks. It was led by a young, eager naturalist who was a bit insensitive to the abilities of the group.

"It was just awful. Although I was the oldest one in the group, everybody was complaining about the pace. The leader was a nineteen-year-old farm boy with long, long legs. Why, it took three of my steps to equal one of his. At one point I just couldn't go on. The trail was rough, and I was afraid if I continued I might fall and break my hip or something. So I just sat down. Everyone else did, too. I apologized to some people near me who were in their fifties, but they thanked me. They said it was too much for them, too."

Milly Smith is now seventy-seven years old, though most of the time she claims to be no older than "forty-five or so." There is a mischievous twinkle in her eye and a sly twist to her smile that makes people wonder what special secret she is enjoying. That secret could be summed up in the words of the forty-year-old mother who started camping after hearing about Milly:

"My only worry about growing older is that the day will come when I won't be able to hike anymore. Thanks to you, Milly, I won't give it another thought."

Steve McKanic

Steve W. McKanic

"I'm sorry, honey, but I just can't stand to see you suffer anymore. I'm calling the doctor."

With that, Kate McKanic dialed her family physician while her husband slouched on the sofa looking pale and haggard. He had been bothered by pains for several years, but this time the sharp knifelike feeling in his chest wouldn't go away. Instead, it seemed to grow worse by the minute, and none of his limitless supply of tolerance was enough to turn back the throbbing tide of agony. He relented.

"Maybe he can call in a prescription," he muttered to his wife, who was now talking to the doctor.

While he was waiting for her to get off the phone, his mind raced. His first worry was the business. He was afraid he would have to go in for a checkup, which would interfere with his work as owner of a fuel oil delivery company. Then he thought of the expense. An office call. A prescription. Missing a few hours work. The whole thing would be a terrible inconvenience. As had happened many times before, Steve decided to stay home and try to weather the storm. He was about to tell his wife, when she hung up the phone.

"Dr. ——— says to take you to emergency right away." Her voice had an urgency to it that was uncharacteristic. She had lived with Steve long enough to know that he could never be seriously ill. It just wasn't his style. But this time she sensed something more crucial was in the offing.

Kate had little trouble coaxing her husband into the car for the ride to the emergency room of the small community hospital about fifteen miles from their house. The drive was quiet—neither wanted to talk. At the hospital, Kate pulled up to the emergency entrance, and Steve got out of the car and walked in. He felt a little strange walking into the emergency room, but his doctor had called ahead and the emergency room personnel were expecting him.

"Why don't you just sit up here on this table, Mr. McKanic, and we'll see what's wrong with you," said a nurse, leading him into a small examination room. Almost before he reached the table, she stuck a thermometer in his mouth and strapped a blood pressure unit around his right arm. She went through the usual routine of pumping the pressure bag, slipping her stethoscope under it, and then releasing the pressure valve slowly. A funny look crossed her face.

"Must be something wrong with this unit," she said, and left to get another one. Soon she was back with another unit and wound it around his arm again.

"Hmmm," she said in that professional voice that indicated something wasn't exactly the way it should be. She looked at her watch, then reached for the thermometer, looked at it, shook it, then shook her head.

"Looks like nothing works around here!"

"Maybe it's me," Steve joked.

The nurse smiled and walked over to the head nurse who was just outside the door. They were facing away from Steve, but as they talked they would sneak peeks over their shoulders at him. He felt a little like a lab specimen being examined for a biology class. One nurse said his color looked bad. The other disagreed. A third nurse, one of Steve's customers, came by and took a peek.

"I know that man, and that's not his normal color. Whatever he's got, it's bad. Let's call his doctor."

Under doctors orders, Steve was rushed up to intensive care. His wife was allowed to step into the room for just a few minutes. She was relieved to see Steve resting. Neither knew that just moments before, his blood pressure barely registered and his temperature was far below normal.

"You just go on home, honey," he said. "I don't want you to miss work tomorrow. I'll be just fine."

Kate kissed her husband and left. About the time she was in her car and on her way home, a red light began flashing at the nurse's station indicating trouble in Steve's room. Immediately, several attendants were at his bedside.

"Ventricular fibrillation, Doctor," said the head nurse to the physician on duty who had just rushed into the room.

He spoke briefly but with the controlled tone of a professional. "Defibrillator, please."

An orderly guided a portable CPR—Cardiac Pulmonary Re-scusitation—unit to the side of the bed and awaited further instructions. Another orderly placed the defibrillator next to the patient, while the physician grabbed the two stainless steel discs and placed them against Steve's chest.

"Stand clear," he said, then braced himself as the current shot through Steve's body.

In unison, the crew of attendants turned toward the monitor, only to see an erratic blue line indicating that the patient's heart was still not functioning properly. The doctor sighed, then tensely commanded, "Give one amp of sodium bicarbonate."

This was done by one of the nurses as the CPR provided vital support for Steve's circulation and respiration. Then the doctor placed the discs back against Steve's flesh.

"Let's try it again—clear."

Again, every head turned, but this time the blue line jumped, ever so faintly, to a normal beat. Moments after the first ripple, a second followed, slightly stronger. Soon, the blips on the monitor screen were racing each other across the electronic expanse as color returned to the patient.

"Let's hook him up and keep an eye on the monitor. Get stat blood gases, electrolytes, CBL, and cardiac enzymes. Please call me the results."

The doctor was obviously concerned and added, "I'm not sure we can save him, but let's give him our best."

Steve McKanic had always been healthy. In fact, he felt his greatest attribute was his body. As a youngster growing up in Detroit, McKanic was outside most of the time, romping through the neighborhood, always finding something active to do. After an eighteen-month stint in the army during WWII, Steve moved to Concord, a small town in rural southern Michigan, and got a job with his father, who had opened up a farm implement dealership. He worked hard and helped his father build up the business. He was a heavy man, thanks largely to the delicious home-cooking of his mother. Indeed, the dinner table was always a pleasant place in the McKanic home, and Steve took advantage of those bountiful meals.

Shortly after moving to Concord, he was married and began to raise a family. Soon, Steve's father sold the business and moved back to Detroit. Steve opted to stay and try his hand at business by owning and operating a gas station in the small town.

Steve gave the business everything he had and soon developed it into a bulk oil delivery enterprise. He prided himself in his physical strength, knowing that he could put in those long hours day after day, and never tire. The work was tough and demanding, but Steve was accustomed to such a lifestyle. He got up every day before dawn, gulped down a couple of cups of coffee, and was soon on the road. At each delivery he would haul the long, heavy hose, fill the tank, and haul the hose back. Because he needed to make as many deliveries as possible in order to satisfy his customers, he seldom stopped for lunch, but grabbed a quick snack and a cup of coffee. The three packs of cigarettes and several cups of coffee kept him going until late in the evening when he pulled into his driveway and walked into the kitchen for supper. After a large supper, and because it was usually late when he got home, it was off to bed for a few hours sleep before the next day would begin.

And so the routine continued for close to twenty-five years before Steve's way of life began to catch up with him. First he thought it was indigestion, then muscle spasms. Whatever it was, it was painful, but like the headaches, the backaches, and other aches he had experienced over the years, Steve thought it would go away. It didn't.

Soon, the pain grew to be almost intolerable. Every day for thirteen months, Steve experienced everything from spasms of pain in his midsection to severe cramps in his lower left side until he could walk only a few steps before he had to stop and rest, making his deliveries a tremendous burden. At night, he could sleep only a couple of hours before he had to get up and pace the floor until the pain finally subsided. But Steve kept on working. He always felt there was little difference whether you were sick at home or at work. In most cases if he went to work he felt better after he got into the fight and forgot his problems.

Throughout this thirteen-month ordeal, nobody knew about his pain but Steve himself. Not once did he admit to his wife Kate, or to their three children, Nannette, Tim, and Mary, that he was hurting. It wasn't long, however, before they found out.

Steve, along with Nannette and Tim, drove up to a cottage in northern Michigan to close a deal on a car he was selling. When they arrived, Steve felt awful and sent his kids into town to complete the transaction and deliver the car. After their car rumbled away down the gravel road, the pain intensified. Had they been there, he would have asked them to take him to the hospital, a place he had never been—and never hoped to be—in his entire life. But they were gone, and he had little choice but to slump on a cot and ride out the storm. By the time they returned, he had recovered somewhat. After having made it through the ordeal once, he figured he could keep on making it and overcome this problem.

Kate had known for some time that her husband wasn't feeling well. She had noticed the exhaustion, and worried about him constantly. He was seldom his chipper old self, and there were times when she was certain he was about to collapse.

"At night he would have those pains and would get up and go downstairs and I would go downstairs, too, and he would say, 'You go on back to bed, Kate.' Never once did he ever accept sympathy. He just wanted to suffer by himself, but I reached a point where I could take it no longer."

Finally, she confronted Steve with his physical ailments and tried to convince him to make an appointment with her family physician.

"I just kept nagging him until I finally got through. I just said, 'Steve, you know you've got to go. Let's just make an appointment and go see what the doctor has to say.' After saying that over and over he finally relented."

The appointment was scheduled for a date two weeks away on a Thursday but on the Wednesday before the appointment, the pain got so bad that Kate packed her husband into their family car and rushed off to the hospital. There was a gnawing fear inside of her that whatever it was that had been bothering her husband, it was serious.

"Doctor, I think he's starting to help us a little."

It was the nurse standing next to the monitor scope. She was on the phone talking to the doctor. The weak, erratic activity on the scope was gradually getting stronger and more regular. On hearing this report from the nurse, the doctor instructed her to keep Steve on oxygen and to report any further progress.

"I think we've turned the corner, but he's still not as stable as I would like. I'm going home. You can reach me there if anything else comes up."

His words seemed to reassure the nurse as she sensed the first crucial step toward restoration had been accomplished. But for Steve McKanic, the hope of recovery was a long way off. He was wheeled into intensive care where he remained for two weeks never fully realizing where he was, or even *if* he was.

Those two weeks were critical times for Steve as he hung between life and death. They were critical for Kate, too. She visited his bedside daily, yet still maintained her full-time job to try to stay ahead of the bills. Occasionally Steve would regain a state of semi-consciousness, and, true to form, tried to reassure Kate that everything was going to be all right.

"Even while struggling for his life Steve was more concerned about the rest of us. He kept telling me to go on home and that he would be all right. I guess because of his attitude, I never really seriously questioned whether he would come home or not. I just knew he was going to get better some day. The doctors were telling me there was very little chance of his recovery, yet Steve was telling me not to worry. But that's just like him, though."

When he finally woke up, Steve couldn't quite believe what he saw. Protruding at a slight angle from his left arm were two needles, attached to transparent, liquid-filled tubes that snaked ominously alongside him, then crept up into two bottles of clear, sterile-looking liquid. He watched for a moment at the slow but deliberate drip of the fluid at a juncture in the tube that looked something like a valve and wondered just what it was he was so involuntarily consuming. Then his eyes passed across his lifeless body to his other arm where he noticed the same configuration of needles, valves, tubes, and bottles. He had lots of questions and as soon as his doctor came in he got his answers.

The doctor informed him that they needed to take a few more tests, but that he was certain about a few things. One, Steve had a nonfunctioning gall bladder. Next, he had an ulcer. Finally, as if that wasn't enough, he had a heart that "wasn't worth a damn." The only consolation was that the doctor felt his brain hadn't been damaged by the attack.

There was nothing the hospital could do that couldn't be done at home, so once he was out of danger, Steve was discharged from the hospital. In two weeks he was sent to another hospital for more tests. As they hooked him up to the angiogram, Steve was in a good mood. He joked with the doctor and after the test, asked what the tapes meant. The doctor gravely answered that he could find out the results from his own physician.

So, Steve waited at home until his family physician called and said he had the results. When he got to the office the doctor was busy, but handed Steve a stack of papers and told him he could read the reports himself. He led Steve to a small treatment room and told him he would be back in a few minutes.

Though the terminology was unfamiliar, Steve understood enough of it to know what it meant. The doctor's conclusion was:

I had the pleasure of seeing Mr. McKanic, but unfortunately the workup in this gentleman showed almost terminal coronary heart disease. He had reached the stage that is now being called "ischemic cardiomyopathy" of a severe degree and I believe we are not going to be able to help him through surgical bypass of his stenosis. The right coronary artery and the left anterior descending coronary artery are 100% occluded and he has already undergone extensive anterior and posterior myocardial damage. I believe that the treatment at present should include Digitalis preparation, diuretic therapy, a low salt diet, and long periods of absolute rest. He may have to lose weight to achieve a more normal pattern and vasodilator drugs could be of some benefit. In this regard I would use Isoserbide Dinitrate 5 mg. q 3 h while awake and Nitrobid 6.5 mg. b. i. d.

I'm very sorry that I'm unable to give you better news regarding his future, but perhaps it may be possible to keep this patient comfortable for some time to come with the preceding therapy.

I hope this information can be of some assistance to you in the future management of this pleasant gentleman, and if you have any questions, please do not hesitate in letting me know. Thank you very much for your kind attention.

"I read it through once, and kind of laughed. I just didn't think it was true, I guess. So I read it again, and I don't think I really believed it."

What Steve had read was grave news indeed, and his doctor didn't mince any words when he went over the report with him. The report, in essence, told Steve to go home, settle his affairs, sell his business, and, in short, get ready to die. To add insult to injury, he was also told not to do anything physical.

"I guess I just couldn't accept that fact," recounts Steve.

As a result of the tests at another city, Steve was placed on one hundred percent disability. For a man who had worked so hard all his life and prided himself on his physical achievements, this was bad news indeed. But it wasn't the last. The Veteran's Hospital in Ann Arbor asked Steve to report for more tests to make sure they agreed with the other tests. Their testing was thorough, but the word was virtually the same. The chief physician called Steve into his office after the tests and gave him the news straight. He was told to go home, bide his time, take his medicine, and not engage in any physical activity—sex included. At this point Steve had taken all he could take. He defiantly said to the doctor, "I'm going to outlive you." His defiance was more vocal than felt, for the depression was still there.

The reality of his condition was finally beginning to sink in, and Steve felt the despair of a man sentenced to death but not being given an execution date. Preparing to die brought with it thoughts about the future—his family, his business, his friends. After a particularly trying day of dealing with Social Security and the VA, his mind was heavy with a sense of guilt and despair.

"I went to bed that night, and I guess this thing had just built up to where I couldn't take it anymore. I thought of my wife. I thought of my lovely children. I thought of myself. And I cried. I think some of it was fear, but I think mainly I was dealing with self-pity. Anyway, I shed a few tears and that was it . . . I think that was a real turning point for me."

It was at this point that Steve made a decision. His choices seemed both limited and undesirable. He could follow his doctor's advice of total rest and inactivity, coupled with strong medication. Or, he could fight. The first choice was totally out of the question. Even though the doctors told him any activity would be the equivalent of suicide, Steve knew he couldn't live that way.

"God made our bodies to move and I felt that was the thing I had to do with mine," he declares.

However, the second choice was frightening. How do you fight when you are in such a precarious position? Steve wasn't sure just how he would go about it, but he was certain he was going to fight for his life.

Ironically, Steve began his fight by reading. He scoured the library and practically bought out every bookstore's collection of books on health, nutrition, and heart disease. He devoured this material to see if there was an answer to his condition.

"All my life I had relied entirely on my body. I was always proud of my strength and figured I could muscle my way out of any predicament. I just never really thought I had much upstairs. But now my body offered no help so I had to use my mind."

What he discovered from his reading was a pattern indicating exercise and nutrition. It made sense to him, but he thought for sure he was too far gone to do anything in the area of exercise. After all, his doctors had told him to remain totally inactive. They had suggested even a walk around the block could be fatal. And yet he had already decided that if he had to live that way, life just wasn't worth it.

"I figured if I was going to die, I'd rather do it with my shoes on while doing something." Steve spent eight hours a day getting his health back. It was to be his full-time job for the next two years.

Steve threw his medicine away and decided he had had enough of doctors' negative thinking. He also sold his five businesses, stopped smoking four packs of cigarettes a day, started to lose weight, changed his diet drastically, and began to megadose on vitamins.

Many of the books he had read suggested walking for heart patients. At first, that seemed silly to Steve. He recalled the little old ladies he used to see walking around town, and he laughed when he thought of himself joining their ranks. Then he realized he had to start somewhere so he decided to try it.

One night, after his family had already gone to bed, he sneaked downstairs and put on a pair of shoes. He felt a little ridiculous, thinking back to the days in Detroit when he would sneak out of the house on a warm summer night to play with the guys from his block. He opened the front door slightly and looked up and down the street to make sure no one was out. He was fairly certain the streets would be empty because the little town seldom stayed up beyond the late news. Satisfied that "the coast was clear," Steve McKanic took his first step toward recovery.

"When I think back on it, I laugh, because I realize how stupid it was. But I don't think I'm unique, especially among men. With my heart problem, I felt like some kind of a freak. I was just embarrassed to meet anybody and have them say 'How are ya' doin'?' or something like that. Besides, I had sort of a tough-guy image and didn't want anyone thinking I was reduced to taking walks. So I started out by sneaking around town late at night, trying to get some exercise."

That first walk wasn't very encouraging. He started out with thoughts of perhaps a mile or two. After all, he used to cover several times that distance during a normal day of work. Now, however, he was only able to cover less than half a block before he began to feel pains in his chest. He turned around, discouraged, and headed home. But he kept at it and the next night, went about ten yards farther down the block. His plan was simple. He walked until he felt even the slightest twinge of pain, then he turned around, paused a bit to catch his breath, then returned home.

Kate meanwhile was uneasy about the whole thing. She vividly recalled the words in the medical report that suggested Steve avoid any physical activity. She also knew how hard it was for Steve to walk and how much he pushed himself.

"Every time he left the house for a while I was frightened. I was on pins and needles until he came back through that front door. It took a lot of convincing on his part to get me not to worry about him having another heart attack while walking. And then finally he said something that really put my mind at ease. One day after I was badgering him about not walking he just turned to me and said, 'Kate, I don't want to die, so I'm not going to do anything that will kill me.' I always look back on that statement as being the time when I started to accept his new lifestyle."

Even though he wasn't able to go very far in his early walks, Steve noticed some things happening that pleased him. First, he was able to see some progress in his physical condition. Each time he was able to go past his previous distance gave him a sense of accomplishment. He began to look forward to his walks because they gave him a chance to prove to himself that he was improving.

Another effect, and perhaps more significant, was the change in attitude. Gradually, he began to see things in a more positive light. Instead of thinking about dying, he found himself thinking about the future and planning activities for himself and his family. While his walking was making noticeable improvements in his body, it was also convincing his mind that hope was more than a dream.

"I firmly believe that mental attitude is number one. It's where everything begins for everyone. My walking helped develop the positive mental attitude in me that said I was not finished no matter who else might think so."

Steve had plenty of others who did think he was finished, his doctors among them.

"When I told my doctors what I was doing, they said I was

'crazy in the head.' Their advice was to take a pill for this and take a pill for that and sit in a rocking chair until I died."

But Steve had other ideas, so he kept on walking. And walking. And walking. Slowly, the distances began to increase. The day he walked his first complete mile was a day of celebration, but it was only the beginning. There were still many battles ahead, and one of them was with depression.

"I guess I was just in too much of a hurry to do a whole lot more."

His reading suggested that stress plays an important part in the health of an individual, and Steve thought this might be an area to work on to counteract the depression. He heard about a stress reduction/relaxation course taught at a local community college by my wife, Beth. This course taught him how to walk in a more systematic way, and soon his distances were increasing rapidly. Faster than recommended. In a matter of weeks he was up to ten to twelve miles a day.

At about this time Steve decided he wanted a little variety in his workouts. So he joined a local health spa that had an indoor track. He visited the spa a couple of days a week, and began doing a little running. First he would walk a little bit to get warmed up, then run a little bit at a slow pace. At the stress reduction class one night, he told Beth about his new program of running. She advised him on his intensity of exercise, suggesting that jogging might be a little bit too much for him. At this point Steve put his arm around Beth and said, "Little lady, don't worry about me. I know how to listen to my body."

"Whatever I felt like doing, I did," he says.

In the mornings, Steve would walk down the block to the local high school and do his walking on the track. He was no longer ashamed of his walking, but walked each day openly and proudly.

"Now I walk around town dressed like a young kid. People come walk with me and I have a chance to tell them what walking has done for me."

When he tires of the track and the streets around town, he heads for the rolling countryside surrounding the town. His particular favorite walk takes him through a beautiful woods and along a secluded lakeshore. Other times he walks to a local golf course, and in the morning walks around the plush green fairways, watching the flaming red summer sun rise in the east.

For a man who had little time to live, Steve was rapidly proving the folly of that prognosis. But he still felt the need to do more. Never before in his life had he felt such a vitality about life itself.

"Before, my job was my life. I gave it everything I had. I never gave much thought to what I was getting out of life. Only what I was putting into it. Now, I see life in an entirely different light. I enjoy it."

To supplement his walking, Steve works out at the spa in a neighboring city. He usually attends twice a week and walks/runs about seven miles each time, depending on how he feels.

At the same time, he began learning about the importance of nutrition. Not only did he pay more attention to his eating habits, but also he began taking vitamins to supplement his diet. Then, just as he felt he was in perfect health, his doctors discovered a hernia the size of an orange. In itself, the hernia posed little threat. It had been four years since his heart attack, and he was in the best shape of his life. His doctor tried to convince him that surgery would be relatively simple, with quick recovery. That wasn't quick enough for Steve. He remembered his days in the hospital and all he could recall was the inactivity, the tubes, and the bed. For a man who walked ten to twelve miles a day, the prospect of a week in the hospital was frightening.

In his reading, he had run across a story about a hospital in Toronto that allowed its patients to walk to the operating room, have a local anesthetic, and walk back to the room. He found a couple of men who had been there and confirmed this fact. Now that was the kind of hospital Steve could relate to, so he arranged to have his hernia operation in Toronto.

Steve, his wife, and their daughter Nannette drove to Toronto and checked into the hospital on a Thursday. True to form, he walked to the operating room on Friday, had the operation, and walked back to his room. He was on his back in bed for about an hour during which time he was so exhilarated that he started doing exercises such as leg raises and arm lifts. Then, after that, he got up and spent the rest of the day walking through the hospital. At

10:00 P.M. he finally went back to his room for a good night's sleep. The next day, Saturday, he walked all day, visiting patients, and exploring the hospital grounds, and on Sunday he returned outdoors and spent most of the day walking around the lush, green landscape. Steve was released on Monday, and he and Kate and Nannette walked all over downtown Toronto. On Tuesday they headed home. Steve drove, ready to resume his now active lifestyle.

Today, Steve actually credits his heart attack for opening up a brand new and exciting life for him.

"The toughest part to overcome is the depression. The feeling of losing your manhood if you're a man. The feeling of losing all that seemed so important to you. But I had to realize there was a lot more to life than what I had thought. To me, life had always been my tank truck, my gas station, and motorcycles. Now, I'm doing things I never thought I could do before. I've got a new business in sales that gives me the opportunity to speak in front of large groups, something I would have never been able to do before. I've been married for thirty-two years, but the years of our marriage since the heart attack have been absolutely the best."

Just to make sure the heart attack didn't cause any brain damage, Steve enrolled in several classes at the community college. Where he once had "a heckuva time getting grades in high school," Steve has made the dean's list every semester. He is taking human service classes and loves the companionship and challenge of college life.

Actually, the college was part of his rehabilitation program. He was contacted by the State Department of Education and asked if he was interested in attending school as part of his rehabilitation. Since he was considered handicapped, the state would pay for his schooling. After a counseling session and some testing, Steve enrolled in college.

Now, after just two years, Steve told the Department of Education he was ready to go it alone.

"I told them I was going into business for myself and that they could close their file on me and classify me as employable. My friends think I'm crazy for closing the door on Social Security payments, but for me it's a goal achieved. Taking that risk makes me feel more alive than ever."

"Positive attitude, regular exercise, and good nutrition. That's what has kept me alive, I firmly believe."

He also credits his lovely family, though he's quick to point out it wasn't always that way.

"At first, it was difficult for both them *and* me. The last thing I wanted was sympathy, yet everywhere I turned, there was the family waiting to do something for me. Out of genuine love and concern, they would try to keep me from doing things. So when I heard them say, 'You shouldn't do that in your condition,' I felt I had to prove I could. I interpreted their concern to mean they didn't think I was good enough anymore. But we got that worked out, and they've been really great."

Now Steve spends a great deal of his time traveling and telling other heart attack victims his story of recovery. He likes to talk with the entire family since he believes they are each responsible.

"I tell them not to smother the patient, but to support him. He's got to be allowed to do some things for himself, yet it's hard for his loved ones to sit idly by and let him do those things. Most men don't want to kill themselves, but they do want to function as much as they can. And when they are challenged by someone saying 'be careful,' they usually try to do too much and then run into trouble. I know it's dumb, but that's human nature."

Kate agrees. One of the biggest difficulties for her to overcome was always trying to do everything for Steve.

"It was hard not to pamper him. After all, we're all conditioned to thinking a heart attack is the end of the line. At first I did a lot of pampering. He didn't like this but I continued. I would always say things like, 'Let me do it, Steve,' or 'Are you sure you ought to do that?' While it's natural to want to pamper your husband if he's had a heart attack, looking back I don't think it's the best thing to do."

In retrospect, Steve now feels the biggest problem was attitude.

"Somehow, you have to realize you're not a freak. When people are stricken with a debilitating disease, they look at themselves as being unique, different. Believe me, we're not alone.

The leading cause of death today is heart disease. Just because you had that heart attack, you're not a freak."

Once Steve was able to recognize that, he was able to develop that positive mental attitude he feels is so important.

"Then the responsibility is up to the individual. Nobody else can do it for you."

Nobody did it for Steve McKanic. The struggle he faced seemed insurmountable. After that first, short, discouraging walk, the rocking chair and pills looked awfully appealing. The pension check was embarrassing to a man of his make-up. The inquiries of concern from family, friends, and neighbors seemed to emphasize his fallen stature as a man. Even today, there are times when lying in bed instead of walking seems attractive. But the struggle has changed to a challenge. And meeting that challenge one day at a time has become an adventure of priceless value.

"That long, lonely night several years ago keeps coming back to me. After I had shed my tears of self-pity, I started my recovery. I made up my mind right there that life was going to be a struggle, but I was going to put up a battle. As a Christian, I look forward to meeting my heavenly father in heaven, but I didn't think I was ready for it just then."

Apparently, He didn't think so either.

On July 17, 1980, Steve McKanic died at his home.

Lori Markle

Lori Markle

I read about her in the Bartlesville *Morning American*. "Her first time up she lashed a single to left field; stole second; went to third on a fielder's choice; then scored on an infield hit, beating the throw home.

"The second time on base, she sped around from second after a teammate singled, scoring with a head–first slide into home."

After reading this account my eyes flashed to the accompanying picture to the story. There stood Lori, ready at the plate, bat held high, jaw set and eyes focused narrowly at the pitcher. She seemed to be thinking: "I dare you to put one in the strike zone."

The only giveaway was what appeared to be an Ace bandage wrapped around her knee. Those who knew Lori well realized the "Ace bandage" was really her artificial leg. Lori

Markle, third baseman for the Masonic Lodge (Little League), the Sooner High School, and American Legion Bullets teams in Bartlesville, Oklahoma, was born without part of her right leg and only one toe on her left foot. Lori is classified as legally handicapped. But it was apparent to me that someone forgot to tell Lori.

I arranged to meet with this amazing young woman and her parents, Bruce and Marilyn Markle, at their home in Bartlesville. When I arrived I found an attractive teenage girl sitting in a chair. At first she seemed shy. Embarrassed. Probably wondering why anyone would want to interview her.

I sat down and exchanged some chit-chat with Lori and her parents. I found that she has lots of friends, is active in student government, is a member of the National Honor Society, a member of the Latin Club, carries a 3.98 average, and is listed in Who's Who Among American High School Students.

As we talked, Lori didn't move from her chair. This perplexed me. For I remembered the newspaper article. I wondered how she walked, ran, or moved. At this point her father suggested that Lori sit next to me so the tape recorder I was using would pick up her voice a bit better.

What happened in the next few seconds really rocked me in my socks. Lori got up, walked across the room without the slightest limp or hesitation—a walk as graceful and as athletic as any I've ever seen. I could see her heading for home—flat out. Here was a person who had *accepted the challenge*.

In talking with the family, I discovered that sports are a way of life for Lori. For enjoyment, she bowls and plays tennis. Prior to that she swam competitively. But recently she took up water-skiing, a skill her dad feels is her most remarkable physical achievement. "The first time she tried it she got up," he says. "But it took a good two summers for her to perfect the skill. She has to be perfectly balanced, you know."

But, of course, her real love is softball. She eats, drinks, and sleeps it. In a mere seventeen years Lori Markle has packed more physical activity into her life than most people do in a lifetime.

To Lori, however, there's nothing special about this.

"It always seemed kind of natural to just do anything I felt like doing." Because of this attitude, telling her story is difficult. For it's like Lori said: "I can do just about anything."

On August 13, 1962, Bruce and Marilyn Markle reacted to Mrs. Markle's first labor contractions like most young couples awaiting the arrival of their first child. They grabbed whatever was handy and rushed to the hospital. After the usual period of labor, Mrs. Markle was ushered into delivery. A few minutes later, the doctor appeared in the doorway of the fathers' waiting room and asked Bruce to go with him to Mrs. Markle's bedside.

Immediately, Bruce sensed something was wrong, but didn't want to seem too apprehensive.

"How'd she do, Doc?" he asked, trying to sound nonchalant. The good doctor must have sensed his concern.

"She did just fine, and she's resting comfortably. You have a beautiful daughter in the nursery meeting our wonderful nurses, but there *is* one thing I'd like to talk with you about her."

They approached the recovery room, and Bruce was relieved to see that his wife was, indeed, all right. In fact, to him she looked just great. He gave her a congratulatory peck on the cheek, then told her the doctor had something to say to them. He saw the look of fear cross his wife's face and comforted her, saying, "Don't worry. It's nothing serious."

"Well, Mr. Markle," began the doctor, "it could be serious, but it doesn't have to be."

"What do you mean, Doc? Give it to us straight."

"Unfortunately, your daughter was born with a deformed right leg, and is also missing some toes on her left foot. The deformed leg has no bones in the lower leg. So the foot is attached to her knee. In time, surgery will need to be performed. We probably will remove the rudiment of the foot and knee and leave a stump so a special prosthesis will be made for her leg."

Bruce was heartsick, yet tried bravely not to show any emotion. His wife began to sob.

"Now, as I said before, this doesn't have to be considered serious. As far as we can tell, all other functions, both physical and mental, seem to be perfect. Unless you decide to treat her otherwise, she can live a normal, active life."

Those words began to make some sense about eight months

later. The Markles had been told that a prosthesis could be made as soon as Lori could stand by herself. At first they were skeptical. How could an infant with only one leg possibly learn to stand alone? Certainly it would take longer than a "normal" child. That was the first of many myths that Lori would break, for like most children eight months old, Lori pulled herself up and stood.

They decided it was time to take her to the specialist and have her fitted with her first artificial limb. It was a rather primitive device with no hinge action to allow mobility. The physicians felt that she wouldn't be able to use the hinge at such a young age, but Lori showed everyone that she would have no part of anything that restricted her action. She took it off as soon as her parents weren't looking.

"She had been crawling all over the place and climbing on the furniture with one leg, but with that first limb, she couldn't even crawl. As soon as our backs were turned, she managed to slip out of it. We tried to get her to keep it on, but it was no use. She took it off every time. Finally, we decided to let her do what she wanted and took it back."

The specialist hadn't anticipated such an active girl, so they revised her limb with a hinge. That was all Lori needed. Even though the doctors told the Markles that physical therapy might be necessary to teach Lori how to walk, Lori jumped the gun and taught herself. Two days after her first birthday, Lori took those precious first steps on her own.

"We were ecstatic. Although she had crawled and sat up and done everything else normally, seeing her walk, run, and do as any normal child that age made us know that all would be okay. We knew then that Lori would make it."

Since then, the only problem has been trying to slow her down. Shortly after she learned to walk, the Markle family moved to Bartlesville. One thing they noticed was that all the small children on their block had tricycles. Even though Lori was only a year and a half, they decided to get her a tricycle. Sure enough, Lori hopped on and with a few preliminary attempts, pedaled down the sidewalk, her parents chasing along behind.

It was about this time that the Markles had some decisions to make. Up to this point, Lori's handicap had seemed rather minor. Other than interfering slightly with her efforts to get into little-girl mischief, the absence of a limb offered few difficulties. Now that she was beginning to gain some independence and venture beyond the backyard, the Markles were plagued with fear and worry for her own well-being. The temptation to constantly follow her around and protect her was constantly nagging away in the backs of their minds. And yet they didn't want to spoil their daughter.

"We just decided that Lori was normal and we would treat her like any parents would treat a normal child. The doctors and specialists had told us from the start that the worst thing we could do would be to baby her. So we just let her do her own thing. If she needed help in something, we gave it to her. If she didn't need our help, we stayed out of it. We never went out of our way to do things for her that she could learn to do by herself."

It was a decision made for the parents' benefit more than for Lori, because Lori was already fast on her way to learning to do things for herself. At three years of age she taught herself how to roller-skate. She graduated from the tricycle to a bicycle, even though at the time she didn't own a two-wheeler. While a neighbor tried to teach her son to ride a bicycle, Lori eagerly watched. The boy was having a great deal of difficulty and finally gave up for the day. He left the bike in the driveway, and Lori couldn't resist. She picked up the bike, hopped on, and rode away. Interestingly, the bike didn't have training wheels.

"We had to go out and buy her a bicycle of her own then," laughs her mother.

So Lori spent her early years like any other youngster. She went from crawling, to walking, to a tricycle, to roller skates, to a bicycle. It seemed that whenever she wasn't in school, at the dinner table, or in bed, Lori could be found racing around the block with her friends. Since there were no organized activities for girls that age, she had to be content with her bike and her roller skates. However, one evening her dad took her to one of his softball games. She was hooked. She begged to go to every game and sat in the stands studying every move made on the field. It was to have a profound effect on her later.

During her elementary school days Lori continued her active ways. When she was eight years old she started swimming lessons (an activity she didn't care for at first), played softball at recess, and participated in physical education which included track and field events and soccer. When she was ten years old, she participated in the President's Council on Physical Fitness and Sports Fitness Awards Program. Her years of activity made Lori ready.

The program required students to do a certain number of push-ups, sit-ups, pull-ups, and other exercises, along with a 50-yard dash and 600-yard run. Lori easily made the standards in all the calisthenics, but missed the required time in the 600-yard run by one second. As far as she was concerned, that was that. She was disappointed, but felt good that she had given it her best shot.

Her teacher and principal had other ideas, though. They called Lori's parents and asked permission to write the President's Council requesting special compensation due to the fact that Lori was handicapped.

Her mother told me: "We were against it initially. We felt it would be unfair to the rest of the kids who missed out because they couldn't meet the required number of sit-ups or something. But the teachers were adamant and told me Lori was the only student who had passed all the other requirements. They felt since she met all the requirements and missed the running by only one second, special consideration should be made. I finally told them to do whatever they thought was right. And lo and behold, she got the award."

When Lori was nine, she immediately got involved in a swim program connected with Phillips Petroleum Company in Bartlesville. She took the appropriate lessons and mastered all the strokes taught. The stroke she had the most difficulty with was the butterfly. After all, you have to undulate your body, and the legs kicking together are crucial.

At eleven she became involved in the organized competition aspects of swimming. And she thrived on it. Naturally, she had to remove her artificial limb for swimming, but this didn't bother her a bit.

"At first, I had trouble with the kick. As you know, the kick is important to a swimmer, but I just didn't have the necessary equipment."

A perceptive coach soon discovered that Lori had exceptionally strong arms, and taught her a way of swimming that utilized the arms more than the legs.

"It's sort of a modified kick. I just move my legs a little, so they don't slow me down, but I get my speed from my arms."

"Of course, I did have one advantage, I think—that's on the flip turns. After all, I only had to flip one leg. Many people told me I had a better flip than anyone else on the team."

The Splash Club sponsored by Phillips is organized according to AAU age group standards. The kids are encouraged to compete regularly to try to improve their times. They are classified by age, along with ability groupings of A, B, C, etc. Lori reluctantly recalls her attempts to reach the highest level, the Class A swimmer.

"It seems like I always reached the A rating just after I moved up into the next age group. I would almost make the A and then I'd have a birthday. I remember one time when I had just turned thirteen, I made the A rating for twelve-year-olds. My coach was going crazy, congratulating me and all. She forgot that I had just turned thirteen and I sort of wished I was still twelve. But that's what happened every time."

The swimming was a frustrating experience for Lori. Week after week she would train. Most of the time she would spend from one and a half to two and a half hours in the pool, doing calisthenics, etc. And this was done six days a week. In the summer they had double sessions.

But apparently this wasn't enough for Lori. She wanted to take up weight training to improve the strength of her arms—her real asset in swimming—but her coach frowned upon it.

During the summer, like many of the other swimmers, she took up running and even more calisthenics, figuring it would improve her stamina. Over a two-month period of time she built up to running three to three and a half miles daily. The running was done in the following manner. One mile of running, followed by calisthenics, another mile of running, followed by calisthenics, one mile of running, followed by more calisthenics. Around and around Lori logged the miles in the gym. Twenty laps to the mile. The running was difficult for Lori. Each time her right foot hit the floor the stump of her leg would be irritated because of perspiration and stress. But Lori didn't say anything to her coach. She just gritted her teeth and went through it. By golly, she was going to be a Class A swimmer. Stress on her bad leg was practically unbearable, but she didn't want any special kind of treatment. That's Lori. Then one day the man who had made her prosthetic device suggested the running might not be good for her. "In fact, he suggested that I stop. I tried running again for some time but learned the wisdom of my doctor's advice: 'Do whatever you want. If it hurts you then stop.'"

Another frustration was never being able to finish first in the competition. It was something she always wanted to do, but couldn't.

"I finished first in my heat several times, and that was kind of nice, but I really wanted to win it just once, overall."

Hold on a minute, I thought. Here's a girl with a physical handicap talking about winning an event that obviously requires two strong legs. What makes someone like that tick? I asked her.

"There isn't anything I can't do because of this," she answered defiantly, nodding toward her artificial limb. "I can't see that I have a handicap. There are some things I can't do as well as others, but there are some things I can do better."

One of those things she can do better is softball. Where I live, organized softball for girls is just starting to pick up steam. In Oklahoma, it's a way of life. During the summer when Lori's American Legion team won the state championship, they played fifty-eight games. By comparison, in that same period of time, major league baseball teams play about the same number of games. And the girls have a separate high school season in the fall. There are lots of teams, lots of players, and lots of competition. Lori loves it.

"If I couldn't go out and play softball, I'd be really upset. I just really love the game."

While Lori seemed to possess a natural ability for the game, she got a great deal of help from her father. He began working with her at an early age and noticed she moved well from side to side. He also noticed she threw the ball with authority.

"I figured those two characteristics were all that was needed for a third baseman, so that's where we started her. She's got a real good arm. I think that comes from all the swimming she used to do. A lot of the girls couldn't throw the distance from third to first, but Lori handled it easily."

At the plate, she has had to make some adjustments due to her leg, but they weren't all her idea. She was doing pretty well in Little League. She amassed a .476 batting average, helping lead her team to a league championship. But when she went to a fast pitch league, her coach thought she should change her technique a little.

"He thought I could get more power off my bad leg, but the stance proved to be too awkward. I could hardly stand up that way, let alone swing the bat. But then I was back in the school league, and that coach let me bat any way I wanted to, so I went back to my old way and started getting hits."

Does that sound handicapped to you? You'd better say no, unless you want Lori to take aim in your direction.

"I don't consider myself handicapped. Other people might have had doubts before, but once they saw me play, they didn't," she maintains. "Once they saw that I could beat some other kids out, they didn't think of me as handicapped." For example, she can run the base paths with the best of them. "She beats quite a few of the team members and is only three seconds slower than the best," her dad told me proudly.

Like many people who have had a physical problem, Lori has turned it into an asset. She learned early in her softball career that sliding into base in a conventional leg hook slide was a bit hazardous. If her bad leg got caught on the base, it might fall off. To compensae, she ha perected the soewht dangerous, but spectacular, head-first slide, à la Pete Rose.

"My dad and coach both told me to take it easy and be a little more careful, but the head-first slide really doesn't hurt that much. It doesn't hurt my arms, but hurts my sides more than anything."

Other than a few scrapes and bruises, Lori hasn't had any more injuries than her teammates. When she does get hurt, it's usually the result of her competitive nature. She likes to win and pulls out all the stops to do so.

Once, while trying to beat out a ground ball, she pushed a little too hard. She felt something pop in her leg and was sent sprawling to the turf. The pain was intense and the coach suggested they take her to the hospital. Lori was afraid she might have a broken bone and would have to miss the rest of the season. She was relieved to learn that she only pulled a muscle. She was forced to sit out one game, but was back in uniform and on the field for the following one.

Lori has had another adjustment to make. Most of the girls that are on her softball team have been playing four or five years. Not so with Lori. Swimming had occupied most of her time between the ages of ten and fifteen—when the other girls were honing their softball skills. Lori only played a year of Little League softball prior to playing in high school, so she should have been at a disadvantage. Furthermore, in Little League, ball bunting wasn't allowed and this rule aided Lori. But when she moved to high school ball and American Legion fast pitch ball, it was a different story. But she made the team and started.

There has been a long line of people waiting to tell Lori Markle she can't do things. Doctors. Teachers. Friends. Relatives. But the one that takes the cake is the coach from an opposing softball team. Her coach, Larry Fisher, described the incident.

"As we were preparing for our quarterfinal game in a tournament, Lori and Robyn Brookshire, our co-captains, went to home plate for the coin toss. Since the temperature was in the nineties, many of our girls took off their long pants and were in shorts. This exposed Lori's leg and raised an opposing team's eyebrow. Just before we were to bat, I became aware of some talk of a possible protest due to Lori's artificial leg. The protest was to have taken place when Lori came to bat as our D.H. In a roundabout way, I felt one of the officials out on what would happen if a person with an artificial leg or arm played, and they protested. He informed me they would uphold the protest due to the fact A.S.A. rules prohibit persons with artificial limbs from playing and described them as hazardous and could be used as a weapon.

"I had to make a decision as to whether to take a chance with Lori in the lineup or to substitute for her before she came to bat. I knew that either way I went, Lori would be deeply hurt by both, but I felt I knew what Lori would want. She wouldn't want the team to be defeated by a protest because she is a team person and would do whatever was best for the team. I made the change, and when I explained to her you could see the hurt in her eyes.

"Upon explanation to our team, you could see the disbelief and anger on everybody's face. 'Let's win it for Woody,' were the first words I heard. We played an inspired game full of intensity. We played with intensity for the duration of the tournament, which we did win. Lori was a true inspiration to us that day. We all found that we just couldn't believe that someone would be so low as to try something like a protest for a win. But for some it is win at all cost, and it doesn't matter who it hurts."

"That one really burned me up!" she recalls as she told me about it, and her parents verified the incident. "They were a team that tried everything to win," said Mrs. Markle. "But the next day we checked with the state high school athletic office, and they assured us that it would be corrected. They sent us a letter saying that Lori was allowed to play in any game the rest of the season."

Lori played in most games the rest of the season, helping them reach the state championships where they finished second. Not bad for a young woman who was born without part of her right leg and only has one toe on her left foot. And she never once had to use her artificial limb as a weapon!

Don't let her positive attitude kid you. She makes it all sound so easy—so natural. Competing in interscholastic athletics is tough. You have to be good. And although Lori will deny it, she has had to struggle to compete with girls who physically had an advantage. There have been moments when the struggle seemed impossible. The times when she reached the end of the pool with her arms and lungs aching, looking up at the clock, and falling disappointed back into the water to hide tears of disappointment. The times when she reached first, a step after the firstbaseman received the throw, knowing full well she could have turned it into a hit if she didn't have to compensate for her artificial limb. But Lori has refused to quit—refused to take an easier route. Instead, she persevered without ever complaining.

It payed off, for everyone who comes in contact with Lori recognizes her as a winner. Her friends call her "Woody." And since the incident in the tournament they call her "Woody the Weapon." Everyone who meets this fine young athlete is touched by her drive, positive attitude, and joy for living. Perhaps the words of her high school softball coach sum it up best. He called Lori to the dais to make a special presentation at the annual sports banquet. With Lori's proud parents watching, Coach Fischer put his arm around Lori and gave an eloquent tribute that brought tears to everyone's eyes:

I can't think of anyone who has been more of an inspiration to the entire game of softball than Lori Markle. I don't like to call it a handicap, because for Lori, it wasn't a handicap. She never complained a lick. If everybody would go around and not gripe at anything like Lori, this whole world would be a lot better place. She never wanted any favoritism but just always did her job on and off the field. She's just one super girl, and I love her.

Elizabeth
Andersson

Elizabeth Andersson

I'm going to have to pull a fast one on you. I can't use the name of the person featured in this chapter. I think you'll understand. This time the challenge involves fighting back from divorce. Divorce is nothing new. Statistics tell me that about 40 percent of you who are married and read this book have been divorced and are extremely familiar with its effects on a person. Depression. Anger. Fear. Loneliness. Frustration. All side effects—all unpleasant. So bear with me. As they used to say on a television series, I will be changing the names in this chapter to protect the people involved.

When Tom and Elizabeth Andersson met, he was a senior in college while she was a freshman. It was, as they say, love at first sight. Tom was a star fullback on the football team in the midst of a successful season. He was ruggedly built, handsome, and when he smiled at Elizabeth she knew he was Mr. Right.

What began as a blind date arranged by one of Elizabeth's friends developed into a warm and loving relationship. As the football season drew to a close, they were seeing each other regularly. By December they had announced their engagement, and in June, just after Tom received his degree, they were married.

If their courtship and wedding seemed perfect, their first few years as Mr. and Mrs. were even better. Tom landed a successful job with a firm in Wisconsin. They moved into an attractive home and began to raise a lovely family. Elizabeth enjoyed her role as homemaker and developed a real talent in the kitchen. Tom's infrequent trips to the scales were proof of that. Within a short time he jumped from around 180 to 210 pounds. But he still looked and felt good and Elizabeth enjoyed the friendly ribbing about "being such a good cook that Tom's going to just have to go on a diet."

While they never entertained a great deal, they developed a few close friends and enjoyed getting together occasionally. Tom's job was never so demanding that he couldn't take time to be with his family and friends. His three children were charming and beautiful—enough to make any father burst with pride. In short, you couldn't ask for a better family situation. And both were very happy.

Then, something happened. It really wasn't anything of great significance. In fact, it really looks pretty small in retrospect. Yet it happens to everyone, though men seem to be more susceptible to the negative effects. After ten years of marriage Tom turned thirty.

Now I know that doesn't seem like such a big thing (in fact, it probably did a lot of good, because Tom began to reevaluate a lot of things in his life). Yet looking back, Elizabeth Andersson realizes that this was the beginning of the end of their marriage.

"As soon as he hit the big three-oh, things started to change."

The changes were really quite positive. At first. Like most men at that point in their lives, Tom suddenly realized he wasn't a kid any more. While that can be a bit sobering, it usually produces nothing more serious than some occasional healthy introspection regarding career, family, and personal goals. Nothing wrong with that.

The other change was a physical one. In looking at himself, Tom awoke to the fact that he ate too much, smoked too much, and exercised too little. So he stopped smoking, kept an eye on what he ate, and started running. And unlike most thirty-year-olds in such shape, he stuck with it.

Now as far as I'm concerned, Tom did all the right things. I spend a great deal of my time trying to show fitness leaders and physical educators how to get guys to do what Tom was doing. And he did it all on his own. That's great!

Yet Elizabeth doesn't think so. In fact, she claims it was his running that contributed to the decline of their marriage. And even though I don't like to knock something I've been doing for twenty-seven years, I'm well aware of the fact that a person can become negatively addicted to running. I've seen more cases of negative addiction than I care to admit, which proves, I guess, that there really *is* such a thing as "too much of a good thing." Such was the case with Tom.

At first, the running was harmless. Three or four times a week Tom would either get up early and run or run during his noon hour. He was surprised how quickly he shed his weight, and quitting the nicotine really wasn't all that difficult. He looked and felt better than he had since his football-playing days. His whole family supported him in his efforts to get back into shape.

The problem started when he began entering local fun runs. A fun run is just that. It's an opportunity to run with a group of people and see how you do against them. It is not really meant to be competitive, but an indication of how you're doing. But for the first time since he was in college, Tom discovered an area in which he could compete. And to most former football players, competition is everything. The old killer instinct returned, starved by a ten-year layoff.

"His running was never a problem until he started entering competition," said Elizabeth. "Before, he was running for all the right reasons. You know—to lose weight and feel better. We all thought it was a great idea, but once he got into races, he really took his running seriously."

That's quite an understatement. Almost overnight, Tom turned into a different person. He increased his mileage to the point where he was running two times a day, seven days a week. And every weekend it was the same: find a good ten-thousand-meter road race, ten-mile competition, marathon, whatever. Just find a race and get to it. And win!

That's right. Run to win. It became an obsession to him, and probably justifiably. For Tom was good. He was not just your ordinary Saturday afternoon runner. For his age he was one of the best. And when you're good it's hard to keep things in perspective. Among his accomplishments is a two-hour-and-thirty-minute (2:30) marathon which figures out at 26.2 miles to a five-minute-and-forty-five-second (5:40+) per mile pace. That's not just good, it's fantastic at any age. And this was when he was pushing forty. In addition, he won the master's division of a major Midwest marathon a few years ago. No doubt about it. Tom Andersson was an exceptional runner. One driven by a strong desire to win. Perhaps too strong.

"Running was his life. If he missed a day, he would go crazy," said Elizabeth.

Naturally, his time away from the family was being noticed. She began to resent the fact that Tom had no time for his children. They began to argue, something they really hadn't done much since they were first married. And the arguments usually started with a question from Elizabeth. It went like this:

"Why is it that everything that's organized for family entertainment is organized around running?"

And it was true. The only thing the family did together at this time was attend races. They seldom went to movies. They seldom entertained friends. Every weekend they attended a race together. That could be quite positive. In fact, Elizabeth recognizes that a lot of good came from it. Travel together. Meet new people. See new places. Cheer for dad. Enjoy the "afterglow" of success. But every weekend? It got to be a real source of friction between Tom and Elizabeth.

"Our children hardly knew their father, and there were some very difficult problems with the oldest. Their father was rejecting them at this time and our oldest rebelled by getting into trouble at school. I think of them as running orphans."

Elizabeth recognized the importance of running to her husband and did what she could to support his habit of running farther and faster. She even tried running herself, but she could never go far enough or fast enough to please her husband.

"I tried running," she told me. "Oh, how I tried, but I had problems getting into it. I started running several times, and ran regularly once for almost a year in 1975. But it wasn't a positive experience. I was plagued with injuries, suffered from anemia, and had a hysterectomy during that year. It seemed like every time I started running my husband would just taunt me by saying, 'If you'd only get beyond a mile or two you'd feel better.' He believed in long, slow distance. But for him long, slow distance was twenty miles at an eight-minute pace. He was very negative about anyone who, like myself, wanted a nine- or ten-minute pace for only two or three miles."

Her on-again, off-again approach was disastrous. In addition to causing a variety of aches and pains, it did little to enhance her self-image. It also did little to combat another problem—extra weight. While her husband was looking younger and healthier, Elizabeth ballooned. She would get home from work, have a few glasses of wine, and snack on a lot of cheese and crackers. And then eat supper. Before she knew it, she tipped the scales at 185 pounds. In a sense, she was retreating into her own little world, realizing she could never enter her husband's world of competitive racing.

Then she discovered that her husband was planning on running off literally as well as figuratively with a twenty-ish woman who also happened to be a runner. Though the news crushed her, she loved her husband and wanted desperately to save their marriage. They agreed to attend counseling sessions to see what could be done to repair their relationship.

Naturally, Tom's negative addiction to running was discussed. Their counselor pointed out that as long as he gave competition such a priority status, it would be difficult to maintain any loving relationship with people. Tom recognizes that this was a problem, but didn't feel he could walk away from his races.

The counseling also brought something else out. Privately, Elizabeth was told that her husband didn't marry a 185-pound woman seventeen years ago, but a slim, vivacious gal with a healthy self-concept. The words stung, but she knew they were true. It didn't take her long to add that to the fact that her husband's paramour was young, slim, and healthy. She decided the counseling wasn't going to do everything and that she would have to fight to win her husband back. She resolved to start running.

"I thought maybe it would please Tom, maybe it would help me become the type of wife he wanted. Besides, I resented the fact that the 'other lady' had all that time with Tom. I was running to compete with her."

She had visions of literally running back into Tom's life. In addition to running, she tried a lot of crazy things to lose weight. She dieted to lose a few pounds. She fasted to lose a few more. She even tried forced vomiting to drop a few more pounds. Those attempts, along with the running, dropped thirty pounds from her frame and she went from a size 20 to a 12.

While she was running for all the wrong reasons, at least it seemed to help. Trying to win her husband, she ran often. She hated the mileage, yet she wanted to prove to her husband that she still had it—that she could be the woman he wanted. Instead of going home to several glasses of wine and the cheese and crackers, she ran. Whenever she felt hungry, she ran. Whenever she felt depressed, she ran.

True, her running was done out of spite, yet it helped her survive the ordeal of watching her marriage die. I find that ironic. Tom started running for all the right reasons and eventually let it get the best of him. Elizabeth started running for all the wrong reasons, but gradually let it offer relief from her depression. The key, I believe, is attitude.

"I began to actually enjoy the running once I realized I wasn't going to die. Where before Tom was always pushing me to go farther and faster, now I was running for myself. I didn't overdo it. I didn't run hard. I just went at a pace that felt comfortable and quit when I got tired."

Elizabeth started running in August 1978 and ran through the fall. While on the run, she was able to think clearly. She used the time to evaluate her present situation. She was able to accept the fact that her marriage was probably through. While it was a fact she hated to admit, she was able to approach it objectively.

"I decided maybe I'd better go back to school and figure out a way to make a living. I just didn't know how long my husband was going to be around."

So she quit her job in preparation for enrollment at a local university. Her timing couldn't have been worse. The same week she quit her job, her husband walked out on her. Though she had known all along it might happen, the actual event was an enormous shock.

"For about two weeks I went through the whole grief process. There were a lot of tears. I would cry for no reason at all. I didn't sleep. I didn't eat. I felt weak and shaky. I was just a little dishrag, wandering around trying to make it through university registration. There were times when I wondered if I'd ever recover my emotional stability, but my doctor just said the more normal things I would do, the faster I would begin feeling better."

One of the things that helped was the running. Her best relief each day came when she pulled on her sweatsuit and laced up her running shoes. The extra physical activity helped keep her mind off her troubles. And once she got her student identification card, she was able to run on the indoor track at the university.

"It was really an upper for me to be able to run inside and be free of all those clothes I had to wear outside to stay warm."

Speaking of uppers, I asked Elizabeth if she was given any medication by her doctor. Actually, it's fairly common. People experiencing severe emotional stress may be given medication to help them sleep or relax. While I'm somewhat against that practice, I realize for some it seems to be the only answer. She was adamant with her answer.

"I did the whole thing cold turkey. I think I was lucky to have a doctor who didn't put me on medication. He just told me to be patient and keep active. The running definitely was my medication."

Elizabeth still hadn't solved the problem of providing financial support for herself and her family. She was in that limbo between desertion and divorce, with very little money for child support, food, or shelter. She called on an old friend who happened to be a psychiatrist in charge of a depression project at the university hospital. He had told her before about his studies involving running as therapy for depression. This time, her timing was perfect.

"He knew about my impending divorce and must have sensed I was looking for a job. Anyway, he asked me if I'd like to go to work. I asked, 'When?' and he said, 'Now.' And that was that."

The job was incredible. One that I, along with any other runner of average ability would love to have. Her official title was "Running Therapist." Her assignment: run with people.

The doctor explained that the psychiatric staff would do the basic workup on the patient. He would then recommend the therapy and assign the patient to a therapist. The therapist would be given the case history of the patient, but would not try to diagnose, treat, or advise. Just run and be a good listener and help the clients "tune in" to their bodies.

"I couldn't believe I would actually be paid to run," she laughed.

Remember, Elizabeth was still experiencing a great deal of depression herself. I asked her about that.

"Oh sure, Dr. Jones knew that. In fact, I think that's one of the reasons why I got the job. In a sense, I could empathize with the patient. I may not have been a psychiatrist, but I knew a little bit about depression. We weren't dealing with people who were psychotic. Just people struggling with day-to-day anxieties. People who needed some way to cope. I think part of the reason I felt like an effective therapist was because I used it effectively to cope with my own problems."

One of those problems was her future. After the dust had settled and the initial shock of being left subsided, she still had to deal with lawyers, judges, court dates, etc. It had a depressing effect on her, but again running came to the rescue.

"I started to get very anxious as divorce court drew closer and closer. On the morning of my pretrial I ran with two clients, but by noon I was still very anxious. I did not feel very secure about my financial future, and I didn't know what would happen with my three children. Having a judge make those crucial decisions made me very uncomfortable. So I went home and ran three miles in twenty-three minutes—a fast pace for me. Then I walked to get my breath back, then I ran again. By the time I finished I was laughing and feeling very good. After that I went to the courthouse and sat outside the judge's chambers for two and a half hours and waited to find out what would happen to the rest of my life. Nothing was determined, other than the fact that I had to go on trial later, so I did a lot of running between the pretrial and the divorce court action."

One way in which her running has helped her cope with her depression is by improving her self-image.

"I've become a stronger woman because of my running. I can't imagine how I would have dealt with the depression if I hadn't been running. When I come in from a run and look at myself in the mirror and my cheeks are pink and I look healthy, it's really nice. I like what I see in the mirror now. I'm no longer the pudgy one with the skinny husband. People tell me now that I look ten years younger than I did five years ago. That's a perfect antidepressant."

In addition to the psychological effects of running, Elizabeth believes that the running has helped her overcome some physical conditions. Actually, who's to say they are purely physical? As she told me about her health problems during the early years of her marriage, I noted that they were all stress-related conditions. Chronic sinus infections, headaches, and fatigue.

"I used to be in bed for a month every year with these, but since I started running, I haven't had a cold. And that's been over a year and a half."

She still has occasional sinus problems, but they don't bother her nearly as much. She has also always been plagued with arthritis, but her knee is the worst spot and she had to take as many as twelve to sixteen aspirins a day for years just to get through the discomfort. But even that is behaving better since she's started running. She insists that it's the added exercise that's doing it.

The thing I like about Elizabeth's running is her attitude about it. She has a real laid-back approach to it.

"My world does not revolve around my running. It could have been swimming or cycling. Or any type of activity. I just know that it helps. With Tom, running was competitive and compulsive. I run for fun and for my own sanity."

What's Elizabeth doing now? She's literally a different woman. For once she was satisfied to let the events of life come and go; she now has a fine grip on her destiny. She ran for and was elected to city council. She's active in public housing for senior citizens. She takes classes at the university. And she runs.

Her running is still a help to her, but now she finds more joy in knowing it helps others. Each time she watches one of her clients turn the corner and regain control, she inwardly feels a profound sense of accomplishment. "But I can't take credit for their successes because I know from experience how important their self-motivation is."

She related one interesting case about a young man in his mid-thirties. He was very anxious about dying from a heart attack. He was just sure the big one was waiting for him. The psychiatrist and exercise specialist put him on a treadmill and tested his heart's ability to withstand vigorous exercise. In fact, they took him to his maximum level. He did beautifully. No sign of heart disease. Yet he was sure he would drop dead at the slightest exertion. They decided to start him on a running program. His "dose" was to be twice a week. On their first run together, he took off like a shot and got quite a few yards ahead of Elizabeth. Of course, he was not in good shape and within a matter of a few blocks he had to slow down to catch his breath. When she caught up with him she implored him to slow down. She asked him why he was going so fast. He answered, "I hate running so much I just want to get it over with." Elizabeth was glad to discover she finally had an honest patient at least. But she set about to change his attitudes about running. In just a short two months he had a totally different attitude about his running and the possibility of having a heart attack. Moreover, he dropped twenty pounds, and he got up to doing three and a half miles a day. And he's still doing that distance.

Naturally, that makes Elizabeth feel great, but sometimes her job can almost get away from her. Like the day she ran twenty-four miles. Unfortunately, she isn't paid by the mile.

"I really hadn't intended to go that far. But it was a Wednesday and it was just beautiful, with a temperature in the low sixties. I ran with four or five clients during the day, and that's fifteen miles right there. Then I dropped my car off at the edge of town to have it fixed, and when it was ready I decided to run out to pick up my car. That felt real good, too, so after going home I ran six or seven miles with my running club. And I felt as fresh after running all those miles as I did in the morning. So I know if you do it easily enough you're not going to hurt yourself. I've never really trained for long distances and I don't have a running goal. I run just for the pleasure of it."

She has even carried her therapy off duty. Occasionally she will drop in to a neighbor's kitchen and tell her to go run while she watches the kids.

"It tickles me to see them come back after running for twenty minutes and smiling. They were on the verge of tears when they went out the back door because the kids wouldn't shut up for five minutes, and when they come back they're fine."

Rather than talk about distance with the people she runs with, Elizabeth recommends that they just go out and run for a half hour to forty minutes. People are not intimidated at all by that, it seems. But when they get back she says, "Well, you probably ran and walked anywhere from two to two and a half miles." The usual reaction is, "I did? Wow! I never went that far in my life!"

Elizabeth still faces problems with depression in her own life, but she feels she's making progress. She is the first to point out that running was not the cure-all.

"I really don't think there's such a thing as a panacea. The important thing about running is what you do with it, and I think if you approach it with the right attitude, then it is going to treat some of the symptoms that have been annoying you. Such things as fatness, lethargic attitudes, and body tone. Running is great, but I think the fact that I have so many other reinforcing things in my life now helps a great deal. I still feel sad occasionally. I still cry when Willie Nelson sings 'Phases and Stages.' I'm not completely well yet but I'm getting there. When you're married to somebody for nineteen and a half years it takes a pretty long time to get over the shock of realizing it's all over."

I've a feeling there are a lot of Elizabeth Anderssons around. I'm afraid there are also a lot of Tom Anderssons, too. We live in a stress-filled world with heartbreak readily available. Elizabeth's still fighting it. She'll probably fight it for a long time. Yet something she told me makes me think she's going to meet that challenge.

"It was very nice to reach a level of inner peace where I was able to begin to find out who I was as a woman. Running helped me find that out. I run to be comfortable. I run to feel better. I don't think you can separate physical and emotional fitness."

Bob Gilley

Robert F. Gilley

When I first spoke with Bob Gilley, he had just lost one of the biggest sales of his successful insurance career. Just minutes before I called, the big one got away. I expressed my condolences as best as I could, then learned a good deal about Bob when he answered.

"Charlie, that's pretty small stuff compared to what really counts in life."

What really counts to Bob Gilley is good health, a loving wife, and a handsome family. He means it, too. For just a few years ago, when everything seemed to be going for him, Bob's doctor told him he had cancer, and that recovery was doubtful. But I'm getting ahead of myself. It all started in a tree in a small college town in the mountains of North Carolina.

Bob was nine years old at the time,

and like most kids that age, he enjoyed tree climbing as well as hundreds of other activities. He and his friends had a big favorite oak in a neighborhood backyard, and often it was the scene of numerous races. Everyone wanted to be the first to the top, and such things as civility and manners were tossed aside in the quest for supremacy. Which brings us to an event that would shape Bob Gilley's future immeasurably.

"We were all climbing for all we were worth. I was in second place but rapidly gaining on a girl who had a headstart. Anyway, just as I was getting close, she decided to step on my hands to slow me down. I don't really think she was trying to be malicious, but you have to realize what was at stake. Anyway, I lost my grip on the limb and went falling out of the tree. When I hit, I landed on a stump and snapped my thigh bone about an inch below the hip socket. It totally shattered the bone, which is one of the biggest in the body."

Few kids escape their formative years without a broken bone of some kind. Indeed, orthopedic physicians would probably go out of business if youngsters stayed out of trees, off skateboards, or away from activity altogether. But few suffer an injury as severe as Bob's thigh fracture. To compound the problem, the break never healed properly, seriously affecting the youngster's future athletic endeavors.

"It was really traumatic. At the time it happened, I was the fastest kid on the block, the one no one could beat. I had good hand–eye coordination and excelled in any sport. But from then on, it was a complete reversal. Instead of always being chosen first when we chose teams for sports, I was now being chosen last. It was always, 'Who wants Bobby?' That's pretty hard for a kid nine years old."

Not only was it hard for him when he was nine, but there was little improvement when he was ten. The thigh bone, only partially healed, refused to do the things it once had done so effortlessly. Then, shortly after Bob turned eleven, he broke it again.

Typically, he broke it by going all out.

"I was sliding into second, trying to stretch a single into a double in a grade school baseball game."

So young Bob returned to a period of recovery, replete with humiliation and frustration. His bad leg prohibited him from doing the things that gain the respect of fellow adolescents. Although he still tried—never once giving in to the temptation to quit—he just wasn't able to compete.

Bob broke the leg a third time at the same spot in a relatively minor incident.

"I was playing in a table tennis tournament and made it to the finals. I lunged for a shot and slipped and fell on the concrete floor."

It was apparent something had to be done other than set the bone and hope for the best. The bone was breaking without any major provocation. Bob was sent to nearby Charlotte for major surgery at Memorial Hospital. Using surgical methods that were still in the experimental stages, a team of physicians removed some bone from his left leg and transplanted it into his injured thigh. The new bone was held in place with a stainless steel pin. To give the transplanted bone a chance to take hold and grow, the patient must be kept practically motionless. So Bob, just thirteen years old, was placed in a full body cast. He would subsequently be kept in one type of cast or another for the next year.

"First, it was the body cast. After that, they kept putting me in smaller casts. Finally, after a year in casts, they cut the last one off for good. I was shocked. My leg had atrophied and withered to the point where it was useless. It was completely stiff. I literally had to learn how to walk all over again."

There's a favorite story that is passed around the Gilley family regarding this period of Bob's life. Bob had a little red stool that served as his walker. He would push that stool just out of arm's reach, and try to walk to it. More often than not, he would end up falling.

"I had bruises all over from falling so much. I must have fallen over a hundred times. But I kept getting up and trying. It just occurred to me that the only alternative was to spend my life in a wheelchair or on crutches. I just couldn't accept that as a possibility."

After the body cast was removed, young Bob had to learn how to walk not once, but four separate times; he kept breaking his bad leg. After each break, a cast was applied to his full leg for a couple of months. When the cast was removed, Bob was shocked. His leg was without much form and definition. It was like a foreign object to him. Walking was impossible. Each time he would learn to maintain his balance and then practice walking every day. After the third break the doctors told him something that scared him.

"They told me that if I broke it again, it would probably never heal to the point where I could walk without some type of aid. I didn't particularly like the idea of a life on crutches, so I quickly got involved with physical therapy."

Even though physical therapy in those days was relatively primitive, Bob would visit the facilities daily. His regimen consisted primarily of swimming and a whirlpool treatment for flexibility.

"I tried one other approach that now seems kind of humorous but that I think really worked. That was a Charles Atlas course. Anyway, it really helped me build up strength, not just in my bad leg, but all over."

Bob did exceptionally well with his physical therapy and the Charles Atlas course. He slowly regained strength and was able to walk without aid, though he limped noticeably. However, one day, about two years after his surgery, he received what appeared to be the crowning blow.

"I was in high school and was helping set up bleachers one day for an assembly. I picked up the end of a seat bench and my right knee buckled on me. To this day, my knee sits off-center. I figured that was just about it for me as far as sports were concerned."

To a high school sophomore who was just thinking about making a comeback and returning to the varsity baseball team, this was a crushing setback. The injury didn't seem serious—in fact, he was able to walk the next day—but it showed young Bob just how weak his leg was. If it couldn't handle a simple task like setting up chairs, how would it ever handle the rigors of competitive athletics? The injury, however, did have a lifelong effect on Bob.

"I had always really loved sports and really wanted to be a baseball pitcher. But when I went out for the tryouts the coach told me, 'You've got to be kidding. That leg is just too weak to pivot and run and push off.' He was polite about it, but he was trying to tell me to forget it."

It didn't work . . . or perhaps it did. It depends on how you look at it. It didn't discourage Bob in the least. Instead, it galvanized his decision to make that team regardless of the price he would have to pay. Bob Gilley went to work.

Every day after school, Bob would go out and run on his own. He couldn't go far and he couldn't go fast, but he didn't miss a day. At first, his weak, injured leg slowed him down with a characteristic limp. He knew he had to correct that somehow. He reasoned that the limp was caused by weak muscles that hadn't returned to their once sound condition. So he started lifting weights. Again, every day, in addition to his running, Bob would visit the school's weightroom and lift weights for an hour. Soon the limp was disappearing, and he was able to run through drills that simulated the types of activities he would be expected to perform on the baseball diamond.

Once tryouts began, Bob continued his own private training, but had to do it after practice. That meant he would attend practice for two hours after school, then stay after for an hour or so to complete his workout. It required rigid mental and physical discipline, something he didn't always possess.

"There were many times when I would walk in the door after my workout, toss my glove down and declare, 'That's it!' I mean, I really just felt like quitting. You know, when you see all the other guys doing things so much better than you, and you realize without this crazy leg problem you could beat them at anything, it gets pretty discouraging. But whenever I felt like that, my mom would always tell me that I could do whatever anybody else could do. She encouraged me to never give up. But, she always let me decide."

Finally the day arrived when the final team selection was to be announced—always a tense moment in high school athletics, as any boy or girl will tell you. If you are quite sure you made the team, you want to rush down to the coaches' office and find the list. If you are one of the doubtful ones, you almost want to run and hide. Bob was one of the doubtful ones, and he wasn't sure he wanted to go down to the locker room. He was afraid he would find his name missing from that all-important list.

When he got to the locker room and looked over the list, he held his breath. His eyes passed over each name, and his doubts grew. He got through the first nine names, and had started on the second nine, when the excuses started forming in his mind. "If only I didn't have this bad leg. I'll just work harder next year. I know I should have worked more on my batting."

Then he saw it. Never mind that it was the last name on the list. It was his. Bob Gilley. A member of the varsity baseball team! He couldn't believe it. He ran to find his coach, bumping into him in the gymnasium.

"Gee, thanks, Coach! I just saw the roster."

"Thanks, nothing, Gilley. *You* made the team, not me. And you made it 'cause you deserved it. Now get dressed for practice. I don't want anybody late, you hear?"

It was music to Bob's ears. He didn't have to be told he was just a scrub pitcher that probably wouldn't see much action. That didn't matter to him. At least he was on the team. Give him a chance, and he'll show everybody what Bob Gilley can do!

Well, Bob didn't go on to become his team's star pitcher that year. In fact, he played very little. But he never gave up—never quit going the extra mile. He continued to finish each practice with his training regimen, only this time he did it with a great deal more enthusiasm. He decided that since he was able to make the team, he needed another goal. He decided to shoot for success by his senior year. He would use his junior year to catch up with the rest of the team.

"Sure, I was glad I made the team, but I really wanted to see what I could do. Being last man in the lineup just wasn't my idea of success. So I kept working, and it payed off."

I'll say it payed off. By the time Bob was a junior, his coach was using him as a regular pitcher. More and more batters went down swinging at Bob's pitches. Then it all came together his senior year. First, he was elected by his teammates as team captain. Second, Bob became the team's number one pitcher, which means he was used against the best opponents on their schedule. Finally, behind Bob's leadership, his team captured the championship with an undefeated 9–0 record. I'd call that success.

"I can't describe how good it felt. Every time I struck out a batter or retired the side one, two, three for the inning, I would think back on the days when I couldn't even walk. It felt great."

Bob has an amazing attitude regarding his leg problems as a youngser. I expected a trac of bitterness, but Bob looks back on it as being one of the best things that ever happened to him. Naturally, I was puzzled and wanted to find out why.

"Well," he answered, "for one thing, my handicap opened up a whole new world for me: music."

This was a surprise to me. When Harry Welch, Assistant Executive Director of the Charlotte YMCA phoned me about Bob, he spoke of his athletic pursuits. He never said a word about music. I soon discovered that in the greater Charlotte area, Bob Gilley is known more for his music than his athletics. He is one of the leading baritones in Charlotte. He has two degrees in music. He is the soloist for one of the largest churches in Charlotte. He also has soloed with the Charlotte Symphony Orchestra and the North Carolina Symphony among many. And all of this from a tree climbing accident?

"The way I look at it, I would have never gotten involved in music if it hadn't been for that accident. You see, when I was a freshman in high school, I was learning to walk all over again. Naturally, I was on crutches, and sports were only a dream. I needed some outlet, a means of expressing myself. In fact, I was just visiting my high school music teacher the other day, and she told me she remembered when I came into her music room after school one day. She asked me what I did, probably referring to whether I sang or played an instrument, and I told her, 'One thing I can't do anymore is pitch a baseball, but I will someday. In the meantime, I need to do something else.' Anyway, she told me she could always use singers, and that started me off in aesthetic fields like art and music which I'm sure I never would have gotten into if I were just a jock."

While Bob credits that tree climbing accident for his musical accomplishments, he also believes it had an even more pronounced effect on his life, because Bob's story doesn't end on the pitcher's mound. Nor does it stop on center stage with the symphony. In fact, that's where it should probably begin. For when Bob was just enjoying great success as a businessman, musician, husband, and father he received what currently must be the most feared announcement faced by anyone these days: he was told he had cancer and that he most likely would not live much longer.

"I think the accident with my leg gave me a lot of discipline. It gave me the ability to set my jaw and say, 'By God, I'll do it!' I used that technique with the cancer. Actually, I think the cancer was a simple thing compared with the five or six years of frustration with my leg. I've often thought what might have happened if I had had a trouble-free childhood—if everything had been smooth sailing. Would I have been able to cope with the cancer so well?"

Just prior to his thirty-ninth birthday, Bob was in his doctor's examining room for his annual physical examination. Being an insurance salesman, he is very conscious about health and the value of regular checkups. As the doctor performed the routine examination procedures, the two engaged in small talk. Then, the questions came. The doctor had just discovered a small lump in Bob's right groin. When he asked how long it had been there, Bob was surprised. He had never noticed it before.

"Then he really came at me with the questions. They sounded just like those seven warning signs mentioned by the American Cancer Society. I'm very aware of good health, so I said, 'Hey, I've seen those questions before, and they sound pretty serious.' He told me he thought it was, and sent me into the hospital for exploratory surgery."

When he awoke from what was to have been the relatively minor operation, he discovered there was nothing minor about it.

"They hadn't done just a biopsy. Instead, they opened me up from top to bottom and side to side. What they found was a tumor the size of a small orange. It was malignant, but the worst was yet to come. They told me the type of cancer was very tenacious—a slow growing carcinoma that is difficult to kill. They gave me little hope, but started me right away on chemotherapy."

He didn't have to tell me about chemotherapy. Basically, it's simple. It is an attempt to kill the cancer before the cancer kills the patient. To kill the cancer, highly toxic chemicals are administered. The key is to achieve the proper level. You want it poisonous enough to kill the malignancy, yet not so poisonous as to cause death to the patient. Even under the best conditions with the proper levels, the patient must undergo tremendous suffering.

"I had twenty-two measurable side effects. The most trying were the nausea, diarrhea, weight loss, headaches, and loss of strength. The loss of strength bothered me, because I felt I needed my strength to fight this thing."

That's a key to understanding Bob Gilley. He had already decided to fight. He was surrounded by patients plagued with the same tragic disease. He watched several do nothing but lie around and eventually die. He vowed that wouldn't happen to him.

"I saw too many people in that large cancer hospital just give up and die, so I decided to do something to build up my strength. On my own, I started visiting physical therapy. The staff told me I was wasting my time, but I went anyway. Every day, no matter how sick I was, I walked down to therapy and lifted weights. Sometimes I would lift a couple of times, go throw up, and return to the lifting. I just reasoned that if I missed a day, I would be weaker the next day."

His self-styled therapy not only baffled, but bothered the staff of physicians assigned to him.

"First they said I was wasting my time. When that didn't stop me, they said I was wasting my money. That didn't work either since I knew it wasn't costing any extra to use the facilities. Then they told me I was upsetting hospital routine. I really got mad about that one. I told them it was my time, my money, and that I wasn't taking anyone's place in the regular hospital. I really think they wanted me to just stay in my room and follow the routines. That's what all the other cancer patients were doing, but I noticed many were also dying."

Don't get him wrong, though. Bob is not anti-doctor. In fact, he credits his own personal physician for offering encouragement.

"My own doctor was great. He told me the therapy was the right thing to be doing. And the nurses were fabulous. They cheered me on all the time. They kept seeing the progress from my daily visits to therapy."

Bob added another dimension to his attempt at recovery. He noticed the depressing effect the cancer ward had on him, so he made every effort to stay out of it as much as possible.

"One thing I did was check out every day and go for a walk. No matter how sick I was, I would tell the head nurse I felt fine.

Then I'd go out for lunch or a long walk. One of my favorite activities was to go across the street to the service station. I'd just sit down on a tire and shoot the bull with the guys. It was more important for me to escape the reality of the cancer hospital and create a more normal reality of my own. So I'd just go over and sit with the good ol' boys and drink a Pepsi."

After three weeks in the hospital, Bob was responding well enough to chemotherapy to be sent home. That didn't mean the treatment was over. It simply meant he could go home for three weeks, then return for a week of treatment, then return home again, a schedule that continued for almost a year.

You would think such a drastic interruption in his life would affect his business. Not so. As unbelievable as it sounds, he led his insurance company in sales that year. Not locally. Not statewide. But nationally!

"I even find that hard to believe, but I really had a lot of support from my partners. I have two business partners and we own the business together. They told me to take the year off and we would still share the profits equally. That shows you how great those guys are. But I felt it was important for me to be doing something so I went to the office every day. I had a cot in there, and when I got weak or sick I would just lie down for a while. I did the research and telephone work, while my partners were out in the field. It worked out quite well for all of us."

I don't want to paint Bob's recovery as all bright and cheery. Indeed, one of the biggest difficulties was the emotional strain. The Big C strikes fear in the heart of anyone associated with it. Bob discovered he wasn't immune to such fear.

"Emotionally, it's a terrible experience. There's always that fear element nagging away in the back of your mind. I would wake up in the middle of the night and feel pains and wonder just how long I had. Sometimes I would begin bleeding and it wouldn't stop. I would think, 'Hey, man, this is it.' It's something you never escape."

There were other times when the depression seemed to be too much to take. It would turn to anger, then resentment.

"Sometimes I would get to thinking I was doomed. After all, I've had more operations than my two children, wife, parents, and four siblings combined. I have been hospitalized more than all of them combined. When the cancer came, I just about gave in. I would think, enough is enough. Sometimes I would just drop out. Sometimes I would say it's not worth it and quit. That would last for maybe a day, then I would snap out of it and get back to work."

Bob tried to resume an active life following his cancer treatment, but even that proved to be a hardship. He would go down to the YMCA on his lunch hour and see the joggers, handball players, and basketball players doing their thing and react with anger. His emaciated body was just not able to compete on their level, and that bothered him. Just like the days of trying to make his high school baseball team, maybe that was good for him. Seeing others do things that he knew he should be able to do brought out the old competitive spirit in Bob.

"The guys at the Y were very compassionate and supportive, but they were doing something I wanted to be able to do. It made me angry, so I started working harder every day. Now it was not only a bad leg I was working against, but a body weakened by chemotherapy. But I just kept working and taking one day at a time. Pretty soon, I began to improve."

Bob gives a lot of credit for his comeback to a positive mental outlook. He received a lot of support in this area from one of his physicians, Dr. Carl Simonton, a pioneer in the area of holistic health. His program, which Bob adopted after chemotherapy, is really quite simple: proper nutrition, exercise, relaxation, and biofeedback technique.

In addition to the direct aid of Dr. Simonton, Bob was following the writings of Norman Cousins, former editor of the *Saturday Review*. Cousins literally laughed himself to health, after discovering he had a supposedly "fatal" illness. Actually, a combination of heavy vitamin doses and a program of positive thinking has been attributed to Cousins's remission of the disease.

"I believe it," says Bob. "I believe that negative feelings produce negative results, and positive thoughts can cause positive things."

Crazy? Unbelievable? Fantastic? Maybe. But then, maybe not. I talked with Bob about this at length. I'm well aware, and so is he, of the fact that most people view anything other than prescription medicine as hocus-pocus. To a certain extent, we may never know for sure what makes people get well. Bob agrees.

"You know, Charlie. It's all so complex, and I don't think anyone truly understands what makes us sick or makes us well. I don't think any one thing made me get better. I think it has to do with good physicians, early detection, nutrition, exercise, and attitude. I wouldn't want to say which is most important."

Now, Gilley is known as the proverbial "comeback kid." He plays racquetball four times a week, and he plays with the best. "I give it all I've got, and I win more than I lose and that's satisfying after where I've been.

"I find the further I'm behind, the better I play. My adrenalin starts flowing, and I know I'm going to win. I think a lot of it goes back to my upbringing as a child. My parents always told me I could do anything anyone else did. For me, there is simply no other way."

Since his bout with cancer, Bob founded and serves as chairman of Dayspring, Inc. Dayspring provides emotional support through counseling for cancer patients. As if that isn't enough, Bob also served as president of the Drug Education Center in Charlotte during 1978–79. Add that to being president of the Charlotte Association of Life Underwriters, president of the Charlotte Chapter of the American Society of Chartered Life Underwriters, and you get a small peek at the busy life he leads. Oh yes. He has sold over a million dollars of insurance a year since 1976.

Bob Gilley's favorite childhood story was "The Little Engine That Could." I'm sure you are familiar with it. Every other train had the ability to make it up the mountain, but just didn't want to. The little train really lacked the equipment, but simply believed it was possible to haul that payload up the mountain. Sound familiar?

There is no way Gilley could have learned to walk four different times. It was an impossibility for him to think of making the baseball team. Cancer should have been his demise. Maybe so. But it's been five years since he walked out of the hospital. His schedule with community work, church, and musical events is packed. His business is thriving. His family is proud of him. His racquetball opponents respect him.

I'm not sure, but I would almost bet that each night, as Bob drifts off to sleep, his wife hears a soft, tired voice repeating, "I think I can. I think I can. I know I can!"

Virginia Murling

Virginia Murling

If you saw her running alongside the road, you'd probably laugh. Most do. It's hard not to. First thing you would notice would be the jiggling. Everything seems to be jiggling, but in a different direction. Her rear jiggles. Her stomach jiggles. Her thighs jiggle. Her breasts jiggle. As you approach, you will probably stop laughing. Because you will notice her eyes. You can't help it, because she makes it a point to look directly into your own. They seem to say, "Go ahead and laugh, buddy, until you join me here alongside the road in sweatshirt and tennis shoes."

Once you've passed her, you'll probably feel a little funny about laughing. Most of us do when we realize we are laughing at someone else's expense. In fact, you will proba-bly feel a little embarrassed. When you get home, you will probably do something you haven't done in a long time. You'll dig out a pair of sneakers from the closet, pull on a sweatshirt and shorts, and go run. A half-mile later, laughing will be the farthest thing from your mind.

That's what seeing Virginia Murling tends to do to strangers. We Americans have gotten used to seeing streamlined bodies plodding along our nation's highways. Indeed, you can hardly drive to the corner store without dodging a nylon-and-mesh-clad fitness freak of sixty who looks thirty. It has gotten so commonplace that we no longer make promises that we will start "getting in shape" when we get home. So you can imagine the shock of seeing a 240-pound woman, dressed in a pink warm-up suit, plodding along rather ungracefully. It's downright ludicrous. Until you realize that the bouncing behemoth you saw was on her fifth mile of an eight-mile run. Like I say, you don't laugh very long.

I was a little apprehensive about meeting Ginny. I found it pretty easy to talk to people about their arthritis, heart problems, or diabetes, but how do you talk to someone who is bigger than she wants to be? What would be the best word to use? Obese? Overweight? Heavy? Fat?

I'd been prepared a bit by Dee Howell, a friend of mine who was once Ginny's instructor at the YMCA in Rome, New York. Dee was instrumental in getting Ginny started on a fitness program. She told me not to worry because Ginny was unusually open about her problem. She couldn't have been more correct, for I found Ginny a delight to talk with.

Ginny's story really isn't much different from the stories of many middle-aged housewives. I hope that doesn't sound too chauvinistic. When it comes to being overweight, there are no barriers due to sex. There are as many fat men as there are fat women. But each group seems to have different reasons for being too heavy. Ginny's pounds came from having children, cooking big meals for the family and then eating them herself, and staying home most of the time. Those three things can pose a problem for the housewife who is also trying to stay slim. Most housewives see the results in ten or twenty pounds of extra weight. Ginny saw it in one hundred to two hundred extra pounds.

Though her adult life is fairly typical, Ginny's younger years

were not. While she doesn't view it as being particularly disadvan-
taged, by most standards her childhood was rough. Her mother
died when she was nine years old, depriving Ginny of the stability
of home and family. Since Ginny was born when her father was
already well into his fifties, he found it difficult to keep Ginny, her
sister, and brother together. He did the best he could, but by the
time Ginny was twelve she was beginning to become a problem.
Nothing serious, but enough so that the county thought she'd be
better off in an orphanage.

"I was just wild, that's what it was. I was twelve and looked
sixteen. I just kept getting wilder and wilder, and the county didn't
go for that so I was put in an orphanage."

The orphanage was successful in directing her boundless
supply of energy in the right direction.

"I was very active those years. I played softball all the time. I
was always doing something active. I was never obese at the time,
probably because of all the activity."

After graduating from high school, Ginny returned to her
father to help take care of him. He was getting up in years and
needed someone to cook and take care of household chores, and
Ginny felt responsible. She got a job with the telephone company,
got married, and settled in her hometown to be near her father. As
a young working wife Ginny never had a serious weight problem.
She was fairly active, worked hard, and was able to stay right
around 130 pounds. Then she became pregnant.

It was a happy time for Ginny and her husband, but it was also
a time of added stress. First, Ginny's husband was anxious to
move upstate to Rome, New York, and establish a new business.
Ginny wasn't too fond of that idea for she knew about the hard
winters in that area. Also, she couldn't think of leaving her father
alone. Second, Ginny began to gain weight, more than she knew
was normal for an expectant mother.

"I weighed a hundred and thirty-six pounds when I got
pregnant, and gained fifty-six pounds almost overnight. The
doctor just went into orbit. And I didn't do anything about it."

Unfortunately, that established a pattern that Ginny still
struggles against. She practically ate herself into oblivion. She was
no longer working, so the temptation to snack went unchecked.
She knew she was putting on weight, but she just didn't care.

"From that point on, I didn't do anything as far as physical activity was concerned. I'd sit, watch television, and eat. I ate constantly. I was up to three hundred pounds in no time."

After the baby was born, Ginny continued her sedentary existence. She didn't drive, so she never left the house. Occasionally she would put her son in a stroller and take him for a walk, but even that was too much exertion. She just sat around and watched television. And ate.

"I really don't know why I ate. I guess I just liked food. I would eat and eat and eat. There would be days on end where I would never go out of the house, and it would be an effort for me to go from the kitchen to the cellar to do the laundry. So most of my time was spent sitting and eating."

We might think that type of lifestyle is lazy. I know, until I met Ginny, I viewed people who were overweight as simply needing to get busy and get losing. But do you realize what it's like carrying another person on your frame? I asked Ginny about it.

"Everything you do is difficult. Just getting out of a chair is tough when you weigh three hundred pounds. I found myself avoiding simple tasks, just because it took so much out of me trying to perform them. The only thing I could handle was sitting in an easy chair or a sofa. I know it sounds crazy, but that's just about all I did."

If you don't buy this line of reasoning, try this little experiment. Go to a supermarket or hardware store and buy an eighty-pound bag of water softener salts. Hoist it up on your shoulders and walk around for five minutes. The fact is, one reason the obese have difficulty beginning an exercise program to lose weight is that even the slightest activity is too taxing. They are simply carrying around more weight than their muscles can handle.

The next seven years were much the same for Ginny. She weighed well over three hundred pounds and it was all she could do to watch over her small family at the time. She wouldn't leave the house to visit friends because it would mean too much work. She wouldn't go dancing with her husband because she'd tried that and had barely been able to make it through one dance. She had few hobbies or outside interests, because those too would require more effort than she had energy for. So for those seven years she continued to sit around and eat.

Eventually, she and her husband decided they would like another child. When she got pregnant she weighed 310 pounds. Her physician put her on a strict 1,000-calorie-a-day diet enabling her to lose 56 pounds while pregnant. She got down to about 200 pounds due mainly to the close adherence to the diet. The diet convinced her that her problem was simply with eating. When she would quit eating she would lose weight. At this time she seemed to have some control over the situation. She hadn't weighed 200 pounds in years and it felt good to be somewhat "thin" again. But by the time the baby was six months old, Ginny and Dick made the move upstate to Rome, New York. The timing couldn't have been worse as far as Ginny was concerned.

"The first day it snowed. It didn't stop until five feet had fallen. I would just look out the window and get depressed. And naturally, I didn't go out. I don't think I went out in the snow the entire winter. I just stayed home and ate. I was really frustrated and upset. Everything went wrong. The well went dry, the window shades didn't match, I was depressed. My daughter was sick all the time, and my only relief was to eat. In no time I had gotten back up to over three hundred pounds."

So Ginny returned to the pattern that had plagued her for years. For the next seven years life was pretty much the same as it had been the previous seven years. This time, however, there were added difficulties. Her husband opened an auto upholstery business in his garage. Like most business enterprises, the business took a lot of his time and returned little profit. Her second child was sick most of the time, requiring constant attention—attention that was exhausting. Her weight continued to soar as she gained back most of the weight she had lost to prepare for her second pregnancy. The business was a constant struggle. Ginny's world seemed to be closing in on her.

Through all of this, however, Ginny was never really concerned with her weight. She had resigned herself to the apparent fact that she was simply going to be fat all of her life. She knew she was fat; she knew she was different. She just didn't let it bother her.

"If I really thought about being fat, it bothered me. But I would just tune it out of my mind. Occasionally I would get upset with myself thinking that once I was thin and now I was really in bad shape. But I would just get those periods when I would eat and eat and eat, and I just didn't care what I looked like. I honestly didn't think that it would be possible for me to do anything about the way I looked."

So when a friend invited her to a meeting, she was a little reluctant to attend. After all, it was her usual custom to make excuses for staying home. She didn't particularly enjoy getting out of the house. It always meant having to deal with the stares and the comments. But she relented and said she would go.

The friend called the meeting TOPS, which Ginny later learned meant Take Off Pounds Sensibly. Although she was a little skeptical of the title, she enjoyed the company and the support of the other women. She met other women who were obese, but were gradually shedding pounds and inches. She learned about nutrition as well as the importance of exercise. Occasionally a guest speaker would visit and explain some facet of nutrition and health. The group would sing together and play games and in general have a very good time. As she continued to attend she was able to take some weight off. For the first time, she became aware of the fact that it was possible to do something about her weight.

Ginny did very well with TOPS. Although she was never able to do the recommended exercises, she made good use of the nutritional information, and trimmed herself down to 220 pounds. That was her lowest weight since before her first child. She was quite popular with the group, and if you know Ginny you would know why. She's a real cutup and likes to have fun. Soon she was elected leader of the group. Her weight continued to come down, and for the first time in several years things looked bright for Ginny. Then came a big surprise in the form of an announcement from her physician. She was pregnant again.

"It was quite a shock, and I must admit I was terribly upset. I didn't tell anyone except my husband. I kept going to TOPS and kept losing weight. Believe it or not no one found out until I was already seven months pregnant. And from then until I had the baby, I only gained seven pounds."

After the birth of her third child, a girl, Ginny started gaining weight again. And when Ginny puts on weight, she doesn't fool around. In no time she was up to a new high—345 pounds! Even she has difficulty believing it.

When she tipped the scales at 345, Ginny decided to go back to TOPS and see if she could get rid of some of those pounds. True to form, Ginny dropped a hundred pounds in a relatively short time. As Dee Howell is fond of saying, she lost a person!

It was during this period that Ginny met Dee. Dee had been invited to speak at TOPS, and Ginny remembers being a bit perplexed about it.

"I knew who Dee was, because I had been taking my girls to the gymnastics class at the Y where Dee was an instructor. So I wondered what in the world a gymnastics teacher could say to a bunch of fat ladies. All I could imagine was her trying to turn us into a bunch of ballerinas. My girlfriends knew I could get a little mouthy so they told me to behave that night."

In addition to behaving, Ginny paid attention to what Dee was saying, and it seemed to make sense to her. She was telling the group that calories could be controlled by either diet or activity. She told the ladies that walking for half an hour would have the same result as not eating a piece of pie. By doing both they would receive the double benefit. It sounded good. Ginny was curious, however, to find out what type of activity she could do. After all, walking from the refrigerator to the sofa was about all the activity she could handle.

At the meeting, Dee began a group activity session. She asked all the ladies to reach beneath them and grab their chair seats. It turned into one of the funniest sessions of all time.

"I couldn't believe it. I reached, but my seat had disappeared. I tried as hard as I could, but I couldn't find that seat. It was funny, but it was also a bit shocking. I realized that I was so fat I couldn't complete a simple task like that."

The little experience with the seat sent the entire group into hysterics. Usually the group is very supportive, but this time they couldn't help themselves. Women were falling out of their chairs and laughing so hard. Even Ginny thought it was funny, and looks back at that experience as pivotal.

"Everyone was laughing and so was I. But for some reason, something clicked that night. I decided to try this exercise thing."

Dee recalls that night and her reaction to Ginny. "I was simply overwhelmed at her size. She just seemed huge to me. I really wanted to ask her to start coming to my class at the Y, but I was afraid for her. I just didn't know if someone her size would be able to do much of anything. Yet I really wanted to do something for her."

It took a while before Ginny got up enough nerve to go to the Y. Every day when she would drop her girls off for their classes, Dee would meet her and ask her when she was going to start coming to her class. Each time the answer was the same. Then one day she decided that she should learn how to swim. So she enrolled for swimming lessons at the Y. That in itself took a lot of courage. It had been twenty years since she had put on a bathing suit, and that was when she weighed about two hundred pounds less than she did now. However, she followed through with her plans and took swimming lessons. But she still wouldn't go near the gym.

Then one day she found herself in the gym. She can't really explain how she got there. When she walked in the gym she met a friend. She approached Ginny and asked her to run around the gym with her. Ginny has no difficulty recalling that day.

"When one of my girlfriends suggested we jog a little I thought 'Big deal.' So we started. The gym was divided in half by a large door so we were only going to be running around half of the gymnasium. I almost died. I thought we would never get around that gym. I immediately decided people who run must be crazy. I mean, it was awful. My lungs were on fire. My throat was burning. My legs were rubbery. I just collapsed when we finished. And that was just one lap!"

I know it's easy to say that one time around the gym was difficult. Hard. But for Ginny to experience it is something else. Picture this: You're a casual observer at a fitness class. It's eighty-five degrees in the shade. The unfortunate are at work, while the sane are sipping lemonade on their front porches. But Ginny is in an exercise class. The normal clamor of the class has a new noise—Pflop–wheeze–pflop–wheeze–pflop–wheeze–pflop–wheeze–pflop–wheeze. Around the corner of the gym comes a large, gray blob. Upon closer scrutiny, you see that the blob is really a rather portly middle-aged lady topped with blond, frizzy hair. Beneath two stout legs ride blue nylon shoes. If they could talk they would probably be screaming. Instead, they dutifully carry a puffing Ginny Murling on her run around the gym. She is sweating, and she looks flushed. She has run one-half a lap. She has another half to go. A distance you take for granted. Ginny can't. Taking from 220 to 250 pounds around a gym floor on a frame designed to hold 150 pounds maximum is a real challenge.

When Ginny told me about how she felt when she was running, I was curious. My experience in getting people to begin exercising suggests that a bad first experience is a turn-off. If the first session is too rough, they will never return. I couldn't believe that Ginny went back the next day. I asked her about that.

"For me, the key was the support I received. Especially from Dee, but also from the other girls. They were all going to this program called 'Drop In.' Everybody encouraged each other and there was no competition to see who was best. Even though I could hardly move I went back the next day."

So Ginny returned the next day and this time ran two laps. Again the pain returned, only this time it was more intense.

"I still don't believe that I went through with it. When I got done that day, everything ached worse than it had the day before. I really thought I was going to drop dead. But after a few minutes of recovery, I felt pretty good about myself. After almost twenty years of doing absolutely nothing physically, just to know I could run two laps around the gym was really something."

Ginny stuck with it with relentless determination. While many are encouraged by progress, Ginny saw little. One of the exercises the group did together was sit-ups. The first time Ginny tried one, she couldn't do it. She wasn't too alarmed. After all, this activity thing takes some time. The next day she tried, and still she couldn't get off the ground. She got a little concerned, and thought maybe it would take a week or two. So she kept at it. Every day she would show up, get in the circle, and while the others were doing their sit-ups she would try to get up just once. Still to no avail. Two weeks later, after trying every day, that simple bent-leg sit-up was still impossible. Now it was a question of stubbornness. If it took her the rest of her lifetime, she was going to do that sit-up. A month later, she tried and the results were the same. Two months, ditto.

"Finally, after six months of trying to get my upper body up off the gym floor, I did it. I think the whole town cheered. It was really great. But now I can do sixty."

Initially, the exercising brought little change in Ginny's weight. No matter how hard she worked she stayed around 220 pounds. The change came in appearance. When she started at the Y, she wore a size 22½ dress. The exercising shifted everything around so soon she was wearing a size 18, though she still weighed 220 pounds. That had a tremendous effect on her as far as motivation was concerned.

"It had been years since I had been able to wear an eighteen, and I felt if the exercise did it it was worth it."

Such motivation was important to Ginny. The first four months of her active life were tortuous. Remember, we're not talking about a young housewife trying to drop ten or twelve pounds. Ginny was in her mid-forties, one hundred pounds overweight, fighting against twenty years of sitting and eating. Those are tough odds to work against.

"Those first four months were agony. When I got home I would simply die. I would just collapse on the sofa and stare. Every muscle, every bone in my body ached. The only part of me that didn't hurt was my mouth. But the neat thing was that I was feeling pretty good inside. I could see the results in the mirror, and I liked the sense of accomplishment. I liked knowing that I was doing more than just sitting around and eating."

Once she overcame the initial pain, Ginny was hooked. It was four months before she decided she felt better. That was when the aches and pains started to disappear. She was running inside at the time, but someone suggested she try running outdoors as some of the other girls had been doing. So she went outside to run for the first time.

"It was fantastic! For the first time since I was a little girl, I was seeing things again. It was March and it was snowing when I went outside, but that didn't bother me a bit. In fact, it was kind of fun. I never dreamt that I would ever enjoy snow. But I went very slowly and I told the other girls to go ahead. I went up around the circle that they had followed and came back and they told me it was one and an eighth miles. I was really pleased. I thought it was just great and I did that for a few weeks."

When she first started running outside, Ginny would run only a mile or so. That was primarily because she had a lot of people telling her to be careful. Dee was quite concerned about Ginny overdoing it, and kept in touch with a medical doctor who was a consultant to the Y. When Ginny first started running her resting heart rate was ninety-eight. After about a half-mile it would shoot up to over two hundred. Naturally this caused some concern, so Ginny was advised to go slowly and not to worry about the miles. So she ran her mile in about twenty minutes and enjoyed her surroundings.

One day, the group of girls she was running with got a little bit ahead of her. Ginny watched where they headed and followed. It became an adventure to her. She was farther out than she usually went, but she still felt pretty good. She finally lost sight of her partners, but kept running after them. The route circled back and ended at the Y. The girls had already showered when she met them in the locker room. Naturally she wanted to know how far she had run. When they told her she had gone three miles she couldn't believe it.

"I just felt great. It really wasn't that hard. And I couldn't wait for the next day to see how far I could go."

Thus began a personal contest. Her goal was to run in the Bonne Bell Women's 10,000 Meter Race in Central Park (New York City) later that summer. The 6.2 miles represented a major challenge to Ginny. At the present time, Ginny had only gone three. The race had already begun as far as she was concerned.

The very next day she increased her mileage to three and a half miles. Following Dee's instructions she stayed there for a few days. When she felt comfortable at that distance, she jumped up to four miles. Her pace was now in the neighborhood of fifteen minutes a mile, so she was running steadily for sixty minutes. That's quite a lengthy run for anyone. At the end of the four-mile run she would be tired, but she knew she had to be able to run six if she was going to finish the race. And there was no way Ginny Murling would start a race without finishing it. So she kept running, increasing her mileage whenever she could.

Ginny was still over two hundred pounds, and her training was wearisome. The runs were now stretching to two hours since she was trying to cover eight miles a day. This placed tremendous stress on her feet, legs, and lungs. When I talked with her about it, however, she told me it was nothing. Evidently she thinks I'm stupid. It was anything but easy. Running eight miles is not easy for anyone. Easier, perhaps, but still a pretty amazing feat for most of us. And those distance whizzes should remember that Ginny has to carry an extra person each mile that she runs. When Ginny Murling's foot hits the ground her body knows it. And if she's not careful, I'm sure she pays for it with all kinds of aches and pains.

Finally, the day of the race arrived. Dee had taken a group of women from the Y to New York. Most road runners are concerned about getting a good start. Ginny was just concerned about starting and finishing. When the dust settled at the starting line, there was Ginny plodding along at her thirteen-minute pace. She was quickly left behind, but it didn't bother her a bit. At two miles she started to labor. At three miles she wondered if maybe she had gone out too fast. At four miles she noticed that some were starting to finish. With a mile to go she wasn't sure she would be able to finish. But eighty-four minutes after the gun signaled the start of the Bonne Bell 10,000 Meter Race, Ginny Murling finished the first road race she had ever entered. The same Ginny Murling who used to sit in an easy chair and look out the window between bites, had just finished running a 6.2-mile road race.

"It was a tremendous experience. Just to know that I could do that after not being able to do so many things before. Always before I would sit around and do nothing. There would be days and there would be weeks before I would even go out of the house. So I just felt great. I just had a ball."

Naturally, Ginny gets her share of harassment while running along the roads. It's commonplace for any road runner to receive some type of comments or criticism from motorists passing by. Being two hundred pounds just adds to the problem.

"Sure, I get some harassment. I've been called just about anything on the road. But I've got a good sense of humor."

Once, around Easter, Ginny displayed her humor. She donned pink leotards, pinned a large cotton ball to her derriere, and fastened long, white rabbit ears in her hair. Then she wore that outfit in the gym.

"I got a lot of strange looks that day," she laughed. Sometimes she just outsmarts the name-callers.

"I remember a six-mile road race I was in. There was a thin, poor little girl behind me with huge breasts. Naturally they were flopping all over the place. Some guys were riding bikes along beside her just bothering the devil out of her—you know, using really obscene language and all. And I thought, 'I'm next.' So when they pulled up beside me I told them not to go too far ahead of me because I was in bad shape and I might not be able to make it to the finish. It must have struck a compassionate nerve, because they rode with me the rest of the way and never once said anything to me."

Since she has started running, Ginny's life has changed remarkably. Dee says she's simply a totally different person. Ginny agrees.

"One thing I do now that I never dared do before was dance. Before, my husband and I would never go out for a night of dancing, because I simply wouldn't be able to keep up the pace. Now we go out quite often. Last Saturday night they played three real fast tunes in a row from the fifties, and we stayed right out there on the dance floor. I was really puffing and sweating by the time we were done, but I loved it. I know I wouldn't have been able to do that before I started to run. Also, I wouldn't be able to keep up the pace I've been keeping lately. With the three kids I have to do a lot of carting back and forth here and there. Before, I wouldn't even drive."

Currently, Ginny's life is being lived at a tremendously fast pace. In addition to carting her children here and there, every other month she volunteers as a driver for the Meals on Wheels program in her community. Yet if you want to find Ginny, the best place is at the local YMCA. She's there most mornings. She walks, swims, jogs, and does just about anything else she wants to.

There is something else about Ginny. She would never mention it herself, but one of Ginny Murling's greatest assets and special qualities is her ability to help, inspire, and motivate others. Bonnie Hyde, her fitness leader, says: "Anyone who comes to the Y, regardless of their age, sex, or physical condition, is helped by Ginny's willing, friendly, and common sense advice."

The effects are more than social and psychological. I mentioned that when Ginny started the program, her resting pulse was around ninety-eight. Now it's down to seventy. At one time it was even as low as fifty-nine. In addition, her blood pressure is normal, 120/70. In short, Ginny Murling looks better and feels better than she did twenty years ago. She credits this to her running.

So where's Ginny now? Modeling regularly for *Vogue?* Prancing around the Riviera in a string bikini, the fantasy of every man who sees her? Setting records in the marathon? Well, not really. Ginny Murling is still struggling—still meeting the challenge. As hard as she tries, she is unable to get much below two hundred pounds. She still loves to eat, and probably does too much of that. Every time she bends over to put on her running shoes, she's reminded that she still has a long way to go.

But you know what? Ginny Murling has met the challenge as far as I'm concerned. Of all the types of people I meet, the obese are the most difficult to get to exercise. They just won't get off their duffs. Ginny might only be able to do sixty sit-ups. She still might look a bit large. And true, it does take her twelve minutes to run a mile. But she's out there every day, rain or shine, working, running, improving. I think she'll make it!

William Haughton

William R. Haughton

Lieutenant William Haughton was pleased with the job his men from Charlie Company, First Engineer Battalion, First Marine Division had done clearing the Punch Bowl of mines. The army of the Republic of Korea had mined this desolate valley so heavily that you could hardly drop your handkerchief without setting off a shrapnel-loaded blast. But the brass had decided to take control of the Punch Bowl, and Haughton's men were doing just that.

The North Koreans were adept at hiding mines. Clearing one of their minefields required patience, a steady hand, a good dose of courage, and plenty of luck. Most of the mines were buried several inches below the surface, requiring each man to gingerly poke around with his bayonet until it hit something solid. You just hoped you didn't hit the fuse, because, if you did, you left a terrible mess for the corpsmen to work with. Up to now, the men from Charlie Company had done a remarkable job and their leader, Lieutenant Haughton, decided to give them a break. Bending over and poking around the ground in the hot Korean sun is hard, tedious work, and the men welcomed this brief rest.

True to his nature, however, Lieutenant Haughton refused to slow down. While his men sat down on the rocky terrain to rest, Haughton headed up the hill to find a suitable route for a road.

Suddenly, a loud explosion split the stillness of the Korean countryside, and without having to look, the men from Charlie Company knew what had happened. In that brief instant of chaos, the rugged lieutenant was thrown several feet into the air amid the rocks and debris hurled by the force of the explosion. Tiny, razor-sharp pieces of metal and dirt were propelled in every direction, seeking a target. The scene of dust and gravel turned gruesome as bits of skin, blood, and bone flew in every direction. Almost as quickly as it happened, it was still again for a moment. Then Lieutenant Haughton's men sprang into action to try and rescue what was left of their commanding officer.

"Watch your step!" gasped Haughton as he saw one of his men approach. But it was too late. Private First Class Harry Stassinos, a former quarter-mile champion from Wyoming, was the first up the hill to Haughton's rescue. In his hurry, he failed to keep an eye on the ground beneath his feet and another deafening explosion rocked the air.

The young private writhed in pain and panicked as he saw the dry earth around him turn a sickening red from the blood rushing from his wounds. Searing holes pocked his face, chest, and arms, while exposed bones from a shattered leg screamed their agony. He could not contain himself, but wept and cried out in fear.

"Take it easy, buddy," came a calm yet strong voice.

Stassinos looked toward the voice and couldn't believe what he saw. There lay Lieutenant Haughton in a puddle of mud wet from his own blood. One leg was blown off just below the knee, the jagged edge of raw bone jutting grotesquely into the sand. His other leg was barely hanging by the frayed threads of his trouser leg. His face was caked with dirt and blood. Yet he spoke calmly to try and cheer up the young private.

"The corpsmen will be here soon, and we'll be on our way to a nice vacation."

The private could hardly believe that Haughton was alive, let alone offering encouragement. But just as Haughton predicted, the corpsmen finally made it to the two fallen Marines and soon they were airlifted to a hospital just behind enemy lines.

Doctors worked on both men most of the night. Haughton required eight pints of blood. His shattered left leg was cleaned as well as possible and "trimmed." In civilian parlance, that means his lower leg was amputated about 6 inches below the knee. The right leg was a mess! As the medical team was preparing to trim that one as well, Dr. Graham Pierce walked into the operating room. When a chaplain had asked Haughton if there was anyone he wanted to contact, the lieutenant asked for Pierce, who had grown up with him in Dallas and who was stationed somewhere along the front. Luckily, someone followed up on the request, for it was Pierce who insisted they try to save the right leg. They placed the leg in a cast, but had to leave the wound open.

The next day, Haughton and Stassinos were flown to a United Nations hospital in Seoul. They spent an eventful night there. Just after dark, air raid sirens began to scream and the loudspeakers announced that enemy planes were approaching. Everyone that was able to move ran for cover. Haughton had no choice but to lay still and pray. The bombs could be heard dropping just outside his window, yet none hit the hospital.

The next morning, the lieutenant was flown to the U.S. Naval Hospital in Yokosaka, Japan. He was kept there for two weeks so that he could gain enough strength for the long, arduous flight back to the States. The trip home, strapped on a stretcher with many other wounded men, was strenuous, but he arrived in mid-October, 1951, at the U.S. Naval Hospital "Oak Knoll" in Oakland, California. This was the Navy "amputee" center.

As it turned out, the battle had just begun! Recovery was no easy process and demanded every ounce of grit and determination that Haughton had. Fortunately, he had plenty of both.

The first step to recovery was to get the right leg to heal. There was almost two and a half inches of bone in the lower leg that had to be removed. Moreover, there was almost thirty inches of skin and flesh that had been blown away. Since there wasn't enough flesh around the damaged bone, there wasn't enough blood supply to cause the wound to heal. Operations using bone graft techniques were tried, but none seemed to work. Although the flesh gradually began to grow around the bone, allowing surgical skin grafting to take place, the bone still refused to heal.

At one point, a Navy physician approached his bed and tried tactfully to tell him that the leg would have to go. Haughton thought for a moment. It was becoming tougher and tougher to keep his positive mental attitude intact. Maybe the doctor was right. Yet the physician was neglecting one important factor. In spite of the setbacks and pain, Bill Haughton was not a quitter. He simply could not give up.

"I'm afraid we have done everything medically possible to save the leg," he began. "It just doesn't look like we can do any more. The muscles and ligaments are in pretty bad shape and I personally feel you will never be able to use it again. However, since you won't let us amputate, I'm going to put the leg in a walking cast and let you walk around on it."

That was all Lieutenant Haughton needed to hear. Hearing the words, "never able to use it again," resounded in his ears as the ultimate challenge. "I made up my mind I was going to make that doctor eat those words," he laughs. The doctors supplied the walking cast; now it was up to Haughton to supply the will. His doctors would soon discover that he had an unlimited supply. As soon as the plaster was dry, Haughton walked. He could manage only a few steps before the excruciating pain blinded him to the point of passing out. But he walked. Each day he walked a little farther, dragging the clumsy cast behind him. Ignoring the advice of the medical staff to slow down and be patient, Haughton walked. Some days, the pain was so bad that walking seemed out of the question. He wanted to stay in bed those days but the words "never be able to use it again" would echo in his mind. So he walked. And walked and walked. The days dragged into weeks, and the weeks into months, and Lieutenant Haughton walked. Finally, after fourteen months, the bones in the leg showed signs of mending and the skin grafts seemed to be experiencing circulation. The doctors examined the leg again and told Haughton he had won the first battle in a series that once seemed hopeless. They told him the leg had healed, and that the main reason was probably his own positive attitude. In fact, the doctor who first gave Haughton permission to walk later used him as an example to prove the power of the patient's attitude in the healing process.

"I used to see him in Chicago every other year because we both had conventions that met there at the same time," Haughton recalls. "And it was always the same thing. We would go out to lunch together and he would put my leg up on the table and pull the pant leg back and tell them [his doctor friends] the same thing he told me. 'Doctors can't heal.' And he told them he was convinced the patient's attitude was the biggest single thing to healing."

So Haughton overcame the problem with the "good" leg, but there was still another difficulty to face. How was a man to exist with only one leg? Especially a man who was used to an active life? Again attitude seemed to be the answer, for Haughton never pictured himself as being handicapped.

"I think the key to everything in life is attitude," says Haughton. "It has been ingrained in me that you face your difficulties with a positive attitude. You have to."

Haughton had, perhaps, a special reason for being able to face the future with only one leg. His grandfather fought in the Civil War, or as he puts it, "the war of northern aggression." During a battle he caught a lead ball in his leg. He was sixteen years old at the time, and the wound seemed to heal properly. Years later, after his family was born, he developed osteomyelitis and his leg had to be amputated. The loss of the leg barely changed his lifestyle. A primitive, artificial leg was attached to the stump, and soon he returned to farming. Haughton recalled seeing his grandfather doing everything a man with two legs could do, and in many cases, he did it better.

"My picture of having one leg instead of two was that of a healthy and successful man," said Haughton. "So from the start I had a positive feeling about it."

Haughton could hardly wait to be fitted for an artificial leg, and when he got it, he started right in learning how to use it. It was awkward, but it gave him the mobility he had been deprived of for so long.

Soon, Haughton was on a plane headed back to the States. He was officially an outpatient at the military hospital in San Diego, but he regularly hitched rides back to Dallas where he began to form a small business. By 1955, the hospital declared him fit and able to resume a normal life, even though he had been doing that ever since he strapped his artificial leg on for the first time.

To celebrate his new status, Haughton headed for New York to see the World Series. On his way home, another car crashed into his, resulting in a fracture to the knee on his good leg. He was taken by ambulance to that one place he hoped never to see again: the hospital.

Once again doctors were faced with the challenge of trying to heal Haughton's body, only this time, the leg they were working with was already scarred and discolored from the original injury. There was little to do but encase the twisted and broken limb in a plaster cast, and hope for the best. But Haughton knew that hope accomplished little. He started by looking for something to do to stay active.

"I had always done everything—played all sports. Golf seemed to be the likeliest thing to take up, so I grabbed my nine iron and started to work on my short game."

It wasn't exactly that easy, though, as Haughton soon found out. What had once seemed a simple pastime became a task that would be called impossible except that Haughton had removed that term from his working vocabulary. He put a washtub at one end of his yard, hobbled back to the other, and tried to hit the balls into the tub. On his first shot he fell down. So he got up and tried again, and again fell down. He kept at it until he learned how to compensate for the weight of the cast. By leaning slightly forward and shifting his weight more on his artificial leg than his broken one, he was able to hit the ball without falling down. Next, he worked on accuracy, for it wasn't enough to hit the ball. Anyone could do that. The trick was to put the ball into the washtub. It wasn't long before he mastered that. While he was pleased with this little victory, he was more excited about a discovery he had made about his broken limb.

"The more I used it, the better it got."

He continued to use it until two months later the cast was removed and Haughton was back in action. And action for Haughton has never meant simply going to work every day. He had always been active in various team and individual sports, but at this point, baseball, football, or tennis seemed out of the question. The weightlifting in Japan was fine, but now he needed something more. Something that would keep his whole body in shape. He just couldn't sit still.

He checked around and found a health spa nearby. In those days, a "spa" was little more than a small pool and an exercise room tucked away in some building. This place was no different, yet it was all Haughton needed. Each day at 6:00 A.M. Haughton showed up at the spa to begin his program of exercise. To begin, he lifted weights, did a few calisthenics, pulled through a few sit-ups, then swam a few laps. And though he did this as most men in Dallas were rolling over for another few minutes of sleep, it still wasn't enough for Haughton. So he started running, or at least, he tried to start running. Everything seemed to stand in his way. For one thing, the spa had no running facilities: no Tartan surface indoor track with pacing lights and oversized stopwatches. For another thing, Haughton really shouldn't have been able to run. The artificial leg was awkward and exerted severe pressure on his thigh whenever he tried to run. The "good" leg wasn't much better. He could move the foot from side to side, but he had no control over lifting it up and down. Consequently, the foot flopped uncontrollably when he tried to run.

He surveyed the situation and decided a narrow, dimly lit hallway about thirty feet long would be his "track." The legs? They would just have to do their best to keep up with Bill Haughton.

So he started running. He was quite a sight, with an artificial leg that creaked along and a "good" leg with a foot that flopped. But he ran. Back and forth. He ran. For five years.

"Then I heard about Cooper's clinic," he recalls, referring to Dr. Kenneth Cooper's new Aerobics Activity Center in Dallas. "I was there the day it opened. We did our calisthenics out on the lawn because they were still working on the gymnasium. I've been going there ever since, and that has been the greatest asset of all."

It was at the Aerobics Activity Center that Haughton really began to approach his fitness program seriously. He began to run more seriously so that a few trips up and down an old hallway turned into three-quarters of a mile on the track. He discovered the treadmill testing program, which offered him a chance to objectively measure and evaluate his progress. He was also introduced to a group of other men who were serious about taking care of themselves. It all provided an incentive to continue in his program and to constantly shoot for improvement.

Still, it wasn't easy. Anyone who tries to do something about his or her physical condition faces a number of hardships. Weather, business, family, and a whole catalogue of excuses stand in the way of most Americans' quest for a healthy life. But for Haughton, such excuses seem minor. He has never been able to run even one complete mile without being forced to stop by cramps. So far, his maximum distance has been three-quarters of a mile, but his goal is three.

Even though he hasn't achieved the distance that he would like, there are many who believe that the work Haughton puts in on his running program is equivalent to much more. Treadmill tests on both able-bodied and disabled people have suggested that an amputee uses four to six times more energy. That would translate his three-quarters of a mile into three to five miles.

The treadmill has provided Haughton not only with exercise, but also with humorous satisfaction. The first time he stepped on the treadmill, he lasted twelve minutes. Four years after that he went nineteen, and two years later he was up to twenty-one minutes. His latest attempt is one he loves to talk about. He reached his personal record of twenty-one minutes and felt fine. So he kept going. At twenty-four minutes, he was a little winded, but showed no signs of stopping. At twenty-six minutes, his doctors must have looked worried because Haughton winked and said, "Relax." At twenty-eight minutes, the incline was tough, but Haughton was tougher. Finally, at thirty minutes, Cooper pulled him off.

"I guess they thought I would pull a muscle or something," he says with a gleam in his eye. "They told me that was more than even Roger Staubach of the Cowboys does!" he added.

Haughton approaches all his activity with the same rugged stubbornness. Numerous friends and acquaintances have told him to be careful or slow down or, worse, quit, because a man with one leg isn't supposed to be able to do certain things. Obviously, Haughton doesn't buy that line of reasoning.

"Really, I don't think there's anything I can't do," he insists.

Like skiing. Many people consider downhill skiing a skill-oriented sport that is for the able-bodied only. Even Haughton feels that way about it, but then, he also considers himself able-bodied. So he and his wife cannot let a season pass without a few trips to the mountains of Colorado. They are both excellent skiers and the trips add a vibrant quality to their active life together.

One trip, in 1972, almost did him in, however. He and his wife were on one of their yearly jaunts to Colorado to "gun the Monarch Pass," as he refers to his skiing expedition. He gunned a little harder than he should have, hit a mogul, and went head-first into the slope. Once again, pain ripped through his body and he sickeningly recalled the awful moments spent in hospitals at home and abroad. He also wondered if the damage this time might be more than his damaged legs could take. The ski on his artificial leg didn't release as it was supposed to and the consequent torque of the ski hideously twisted the knee joint, breaking the bone in six places.

Even in the pain and shock of the accident, Haughton displayed a stoic sense of humor. To occupy himself while waiting for the ski patrol to show up, Haughton had his wife set his artificial leg in an upright position—with the ski still attached!—off to the side in the snow. He chuckled to himself as he looked at the ski boot with what appeared to be part of a leg jutting into the crisp mountain air. Then he resumed his position sprawled in the snow and waited anxiously for the fun. Soon the men from the ski patrol approached, surveyed the scene, and, in Haughton's words, "almost lost their cool." When they regained their composure they asked the downed skier what had happened.

"I guess I broke my leg off," was his casual reply.

It took a while for the patrol to calm themselves. After all, it wasn't every day they came upon such a sight, and their manuals didn't tell them how to handle such a situation. Haughton couldn't stand it any longer and broke up in laughter. The patrol saw little humor in the situation and almost refused to help.

When they finally got Haughton down the mountain and into a local hospital, the seriousness of the situation became evident. The X-rays showed the fractures to be of such magnitude that setting them would be almost impossible. The doctor came into Haughton's room and tactfully tried to break the news. He told

Haughton that the joint was broken in six places. He told him that surgery was impossible. He told him that setting the bone would be impossible. Then he told him something that did little for his reputation as a medical expert. He told Haughton that the leg wasn't much good anyway so why not amputate above the knee?

The words were barely out of the doctor's mouth when Haughton was in the lobby waiting for an ambulance to take him to another hospital.

"He sounded like that Navy doctor back in Japan who wanted to do that to my other leg, so I said 'no way' and got up and left that guy."

With the bone still not set, Haughton flew back to Dallas where his own doctor tried desperately to set the bone and save the leg. What followed was a series of painful attempts to set the bone. First, the doctor tried to set it by hand manipulation. It was a slow process. First, the leg was X-rayed. As soon as the film was available, the doctor read them and then tried to move the bones back into position. Then another X-ray. The results showed that the bones were not set properly, so it was back to the doctor and try to set them again. After doing that a few times, it appeared the bones were set. A cast was put on, but four days later it had moved out of position. After several other attempts, it was decided to use a pin to secure the bone. The pin was inserted and the bone healed. The next year, Haughton returned to Colorado and skied, and he has been skiing ever since.

In all that Haughton has done, his wife Betty has stood by his side. In fact, much of their time spent together is involved in the pursuit of an active life. Not only do they ski together, but they also play tennis together, golf together, and run together. Once, while running several blocks from their home, the foot on his artificial leg broke off, temporarily halting his morning run. His wife had to run on home, get the car, and return to pick up Haughton, who was sitting on the curb, holding his leg in his lap and waving at passing motorists. Obviously he enjoys her companionship in their activities together, but he recalls it wasn't always this way.

"Without my wife I'd still be in a wheelchair," beams Haughton.

The early days of his recovery were, at times, intolerable. The pain, the frustration, the embarrassment. The days when it seemed like he was going backward rather than forward. The days when "never be able to use it again" seemed to be a reality. During those days, Haughton needed more than his usual strong supply of courage. He found it in his family. To this day, his wife and four lovely daughters provide an inspiration to continue.

"Whenever anyone, and there have been many, told me something was impossible, they were there, spurring me on."

In turn, Haughton has become a source of inspiration for others who have lost a limb. He recalls the days in the hospital in Japan when an officer came by to cheer him up and told him it wasn't so bad to lose a leg. Haughton thought it was easy for him to say that because the man had two good healthy legs.

"Then a WWII veteran came into the room and danced around a little. He didn't say much at all. Just danced. When he was done, he pulled his pant leg up and showed me he had lost his leg in the Pacific. Now *that* cheered me up and gave me some hope."

So Haughton has done just that.

"I have gone to see every amputee that I have heard about or read about just to show them what can be done. I remember once I visited a boy in the hospital who had lost his leg. He had the nurses tie pillows where his leg would have been because he didn't want to be able to look down and see what was not there. He just didn't want to face the fact that he was 'crippled.' So I talked with him a little while, then ran in place for him. The next year, he played on the football team. Just by seeing me dance and run, he no longer looked at himself as crippled."

Conquering his handicap was not the end of Haughton's struggles. In 1969, he suffered another serious medical setback. Bothered by an irritable lump on his tongue, he checked into the hospital for tests. The diagnosis revealed he had cancer of the tongue. This time, surgery cleared up the problem, but Haughton believes it was more than that. On his wall in his office hangs a quote from the German philosopher Goethe. It refers to the sovereignty of nature and reflects Haughton's own views about the healing process.

"It's like the Navy doctor told me when he told me to start walking. 'Doctors think they can heal wounds, but they can't.

Nature does the healing.' If we'd just let nature run its course, the miracle happens."

So now, Haughton assists nature by running his own course. He believes strongly in keeping himself healthy and fit, and pursues a program of fitness at the Aerobics Activity Center with religious fervor. Every day that he is in town, Haughton visits the Center at 6:00 A.M. That means he must get up at 5:00 A.M. When he arrives, he joins a small group of dedicated regulars and spends the first twenty minutes stretching. That is followed by ten minutes of sit-ups, with a total of two hundred in sets of twenty-five. That's when he feels he's ready to run, so he heads for the track and puts in his half to three-quarters of a mile. After the run, he works out on the weight machine for thirty minutes. He then takes a break in the steamroom where he shaves, followed by a fifteen-minute swim. Then it's shower, dress, breakfast, and off to the office. A two-hour ordeal accomplished, but the sequence never varies. Even on the bad days.

"Everybody will have some bad days. If you let that be defeating, it will be. If you say you are whipped, you are. It's what you make it."

Deanna McKenzie

In November of 1966 Deanna McKenzie was lying in a UCLA hospital ward bed wondering, "Why me? Why do I have MS? I've been a good mother, wife, and Christian. Life's not fair. Sure, I had an uncle who had MS and died when I was little, but this is me. I don't want to die. There are lots of things I want to do. What's going to happen to my husband and children? I don't want my life cut short. This is the worst thing that could have ever happened to me."

The woman next to Deanna must have read her thoughts. She asked Deanna if she wanted to talk. Deanna was ready and willing. Over the next couple of days their relationship matured and blossomed. They shared some pretty intimate thoughts on life, disease, and the future. Deanna found out that her new-found friend had a brain tumor. She was in significant pain and partially crippled. She was undergoing tests to determine the extent and nature of her tumor. And then she was going to have surgery.

Deanna opened up to her new friend. She said that her multiple sclerosis started three years before. It began when she was pregnant for the second time. Three months into her pregnancy she noticed that her hands went numb. One morning she had a hard time talking to her next door neighbor. Her mouth and jaw seemed stiff and immobile. That same week she observed, as she walked down the aisles in a food store, that she tended to brush against the aisles. The same thing happened as she walked through doorways. She was concerned. She checked with her doctor. He felt the changes were probably due to her pregnancy. She shouldn't worry.

As time progressed her right leg started to drag. Her speech slurred significantly. So much so that she sounded as if she were drunk. She also developed a urination problem, but, fortunately, medication seemed to manage that quite well.

But the numbness persisted, especially that of her hands. Things got so bad that there were times she would pick up a hot pan and not realize that it was scalding hot. She noticed that her body often went numb from the waist down. Her obstetrician was concerned and monitored her closely, but he maintained that the changes were probably due to her pregnancy.

When her baby girl was born Deanna was happy. She was also cautiously optimistic. She hoped she would return to her old ways physically—no more numbness, leg dragging, and slurring of speech. But one week after her daughter was born her vision faltered. Worried, she contacted her obstetrician. He suggested that she see an optometrist. After a series of thorough tests the eye specialist could not find anything wrong. But he recommended that she see a neurologist.

The neurologist placed Deanna in the hospital and put her through a sequence of exhaustive neurological tests. Afterward, his diagnosis was not definitive. He would only confirm that Deanna had a demyelinating disease. He did not call it multiple sclerosis but nevertheless recommended that she visit an ophthalmologist. There Deanna underwent some more tests which measured her balance and walking abilities.

When Deanna came home from the hospital she was depressed and upset with the diagnosis. So was her family. It was the only time she ever saw her husband cry. "I had never really seen him that sad. He'd never been around sick people before. It was quite hard on him and my family. My parents, of course, were very sympathetic. Perhaps too much so. I think they felt sorry for me.

"I also developed a lot of self-pity, a sort of 'woe-is-me' approach. I thought about taking something to get out of everybody's life. I remembered that my uncle died a difficult death being unable to eat properly because of immobility of mouth and throat muscles. I didn't want my family to suffer through that kind of ordeal. Of course, this depression and introspection made my condition worse." Her eyesight became more blurred and her arms and legs would numb for days at a time.

A few years after Deanna was released from the hospital a nurse friend told her about an experimental program at UCLA under the direction of Dr. N. S. Namerow. She was told that if her doctor would recommend her she could get into the project. Deanna requested permission from her physician and got it. Soon she received a letter from the executive director welcoming her to the research project. In the letter the doctor alluded to the fact that she might have multiple sclerosis. It was the first time that anyone had told her there was the possibility of her having MS.

The research project, therefore, was the reason Deanna was now in the UCLA hospital ward bed. While there, she received a series of experimental serum shots to help her. And she met with many, many doctors who were trying to understand more about her condition and the progress of her disease.

The women spent ten days together in the UCLA hospital sharing life's experiences. On the tenth day, Deanna's pastor came to visit her. He told Deanna that he felt it was appropriate for both the women to pray for healing. They agreed it would be a good idea. The pastor laid his hands on them and asked that they be healed. He then departed. Ten minutes later Deanna was transferred to another ward. The woman with the tumor remained behind.

The very next dy her friend cae to visit her. "I wa shocke," said Deanna. "When I left her she was in significant pain and crippled, and now she was walking."

The friend told Deanna she felt she was cured. Her pain was gone and she could walk normally. Deanna was fascinated with the woman's experience. As they talked the woman explained that she was going to have a series of X-rays that morning. Since she had shared her feelings of being cured with the staff, they wanted her X-rayed. Deanna decided to go to the X-ray with her friend and find out what really happened. Deanna said, "When they took the X-rays of her skull the radiologist was amazed. He reported that he could not find a trace of the tumor. The doctors called it a spontaneous remission. I called it a miracle," Deanna told me.

This incident was a turning point in the development of Deanna's disease process and her attitude toward it. "I became actively involved in my own progress. My friend's healing revived my spirits more than anything else. I decided to pull myself up by my bootstraps. I figured if I was going to fight this disease I had to have a positive mental attitude. An attitude which could lick this disease. I recalled that my multiple sclerosis seemed to get worse when I was feeling under a good bit of pressure and stress. I was pregnant. My sister and a friend came to live with us for a time, I had a three-year-old at home, and my parents came to visit. Maybe that started the MS ball rolling. I don't know. But I felt positive thinking was now in order. It was the only way I thought I could survive.

"I also figured I should do something with my life. Selling real estate fascinated me. I had a friend who enjoyed it and I wanted to give it a try. My husband wasn't that excited about my doing this, however. He wanted to know if he wasn't making enough money. He was afraid my working would be disrupting to the family."

But Deanna felt she needed to do more with her life, and real estate seemed like a good way to go. But in a short time she discovered that real estate agents keep odd and difficult hours. Her schedule would have kept her away a great deal of the time, especially on Saturday and Sunday. She felt the tug of two loyalties—job and family. She did not want her job to ruin her family life. So she decided to direct her attention and energies elsewhere. She thought teaching would be more compatible with her family life.

Her son and daughter attended a cooperative nursery school. Gradually she had felt herself getting more and more involved—

and more and more interested. Deanna describes her involvement best. "After the real estate episode I was seeking new directions in my life. Education seemed a natural. I took a course of study at UCLA on nursery education. In time, I got my certificate. Later I became the director of the cooperative nursery school."

The decision to take nursery education courses was fortuitous. Deanna's courses in early childhood stimulated an interest in nutrition. She saw an important relationship between the type of food eaten and properly developing children. Furthermore, she had a child in her classroom who was diagnosed as hyperactive. The child's doctor recommended a change in his diet. The improved nutrition had a remarkable effect on him. He was no longer screaming, jumping in and out of his chair, and generally disrupting the class. The shift in eating habits had a calming effect on him.

But it wasn't only the child who was affected. Deanna was affected as well. "The childhood courses at UCLA and the radical change in the student impressed me. I started to study nutrition and multiple sclerosis seriously. I thought maybe I could do something to affect the outcome of my disease. The mental attitude was of paramount importance, but it seemed as though I should be doing other things as well. After all, when you're being treated for MS you don't take medicine like you do when you have some traditional disease. It was frustrating not to be 'doing anything' for the disease. So I thought better nutrition would be helpful. I supplemented my diet with vitamin B complex, vitamin C, and some E. I also became very conscious about the amount of sugar and white flour that I ate. I cut back on my salt. I wanted to make sure that I had everything going for me in terms of nutrition. I was not going to take any chances."

Then in late 1977 Deanna's husband was transferred to the Midwest. It was the first time she hadn't been employed in some time. She had plenty of time on her hands. She started exercising at home. When the weather broke in April she started to do some walking. She thought it would be good for her. She felt it would help complete the circle of her rehabilitation.

When Deanna first tried walking, it was difficult. Walking by yourself can be a drag, especially if you're not used to it. And if you have a significant disease such as Deanna did, that compounds the problem. So she walked with a friend. Deanna had a significant limp or foot drag, and the muscles of her leg had deteriorated significantly. The muscles of MS patients lose their strength and tire quickly because they are not as well supplied by the nerves as they should be. So the muscles atrophy and fatigue rapidly. That was the case with Deanna.

The first time they walked a mile—at least it seemed like a mile—Deanna got very tired. Halfway through the walk she had to sit down from exhaustion. It wasn't that she was out of breath, but her legs were trembling; they were like rubber. Deanna says it best: "We walked maybe half the distance, a half-mile at most. Then I sat down. I wondered what I should do. Going home was the only alternative.

"We walked very slowly at first. We also did a lot of talking. The talking seemed to take my mind off the walking and the weakness of my legs. When I got home my legs felt like putty. They wanted to jump constantly. My legs were that much out of shape. At times I wanted to quit."

But Deanna didn't quit. The challenge to improve herself physically was there. Each week Deanna gradually increased her distance. As she did she noticed she seemed to be getting stronger. Her leg muscles were starting to firm up. But the best thing of all was her state of mind after the walk. "I really felt good. Tired. But mentally I was proud and felt on top of the world. It gave me a great positive attitude."

In the fall of 1978, a friend told Deanna about a fitness class being held at a local community college. Intrigued, Deanna signed up. After all, it seemed as though this might be a good motivator for her—something that might keep her going through the cold winter.

It was at this class that she got turned on to fitness and started to see some significant physical changes. For example, when the class started, the instructor had them do a variety of exercises. Included were such things as walking forward, backward, and sideways. Walking forward was no problem. But walking backward was another story. "I could hardly do it," said Deanna. But over the weeks more physical improvements were made. "Stepping sideways was very difficult for me. These kinds of exercises took real effort. But I noticed more and more progress. I felt my body was getting stronger. It seemed as though the increased exercise was improving my multiple sclerosis condition. I felt as though I could keep up with most of the class. I wasn't embarrassed at all. I really wasn't that far behind the rest of the group."

The class ended in December. Deanna was so excited with her progress that she signed up for the class again in January. Of course, while she was taking these courses she walked with her partner—three miles a day. During January, however, Deanna decided to pick up her pace and start jogging. "I did it because it was so darn cold. I did it to keep warm. When walking I had to bundle up too much to keep myself from freezing. So I figured by going faster I would keep warmer. I knew the running would help me. Furthermore, I thought if I ran I wouldn't be in the cold as long."

Deanna and her friends began a pattern of walking, jogging, walking, jogging. In a matter of weeks they were covering two to three miles in this manner. That seems like quick progress, but the nine months of walking and exercising had paid off. It had strengthened her legs to the point that she could tolerate the increased activity of running.

Deanna had no pain while doing this, just leg fatigue. But she kept at it because of the good feelings she had.

"The exercise, the running, and the walking helped me mentally. It allowed me to maintain a solid positive mental attitude. Of course, it made me a lot stronger. My legs were less fatigued. So now I had seemed to bring it all together. For my multiple sclerosis I felt that the most important things were and are a positive mental attitude, good nutrition, and proper exercise," Deanna said.

As Deanna told me this I asked her if she was familiar with some of the work Dr. Arthur L. Kaslow from California was doing. She said no but would be interested in knowing his approach. I briefly explained to her what I had read in a Detroit newspaper article, written by Betty Blair. Dr. Kaslow is the director of the Kaslow Medical Health Care Center in Santa Barbara, California. He has excellent medical credentials and a traditional medical background. He does not feel, however, that traditional medical techniques are working with multiple sclerosis patients. He feels that better nutrition, proper exercise, and the ability to handle stress are the keys for the MS patient.

Interestingly, the American Medical Association has been critical of his work, but Jacob Blass, director of patient services for the Southern California Chapter of the National Multiple Sclerosis Society, said he's impressed with Dr. Kaslow's approach to disease.

Blass noted, "I certainly haven't had any negative feedback from multiple sclerosis patients treated by Dr. Kaslow, and at least two have told me about their successful treatment and appear outwardly free of symptoms. But whenever a patient is interested in the nutritional approach I recommend him. He's the only doctor I know about who is developing overall programs to treat multiple sclerosis."

After listening Deanna said, "I'm only a lay person but I think Dr. Kaslow is right on target. It takes a lot of things to fight this disease but I would say these three are essential."

As we talked, I asked her about the current status of her disease (she has had MS for sixteen years). She told me she thought she was doing very well. Ever since her experience in the hospital as a research patient she feels her condition has improved. "Every once in a while I slur my speech, but it's not as bad as before. I definitely have more control over my legs. And the numbness from my waist down has gone away. I still have a slight numbness in my hands, though. But even that has subsided. I no longer have trouble bumping into doorways or against the aisles. And my leg no longer drags."

She did mention, however, that her eyesight has declined. Deanna explained, "MS can attack the optic nerve. The nerve endings deteriorate, which disrupts the process of transmitting signals to the brain. This is quite common in MS patients. My right eye has deteriorated to the point where I can just barely read normal print. But my left eye is still pretty good. Fortunately, my health has not deteriorated. I feel pretty good about that."

I asked her what Dr. Namerow thinks about her wellness regimen. Deanna told me that she sees her doctor every three months. It's part of the research procedure. Even when she lived in the Midwest she flew back for consultations. She and her family have again moved back to California. Each time she visits the doctor he is more and more impressed with her progress. "He and his staff take notes on every bit of food that I take, all my exercise, and my comments about positive mental attitude. They are very thorough. At one time they had me keep all my urine for a month. I had to store it in gallon bottles. The last time I visited he could not believe how well I am. Even though the symptoms come and go with MS, my symptoms have been largely in remission."

Dr. Namerow now thinks that people with multiple sclerosis may be allergic to themselves. So the new phase of the research project is to try experimental drugs on the patients. He's dividing the patients into two groups. One group will receive the experimental drug and the others a placebo. But Dr. Namerow is so pleased with Deanna's progress that he doesn't want to muddy the water. So she'll not be receiving either a placebo or the experimental medication.

All the doctors are impressed with the strength of her leg muscles and her coordination. Her ability to perform neurological tests such as standing on her toes and walking a straight line have the doctors shaking their heads in disbelief.

Deanna continues, "I'm so normal now the symptoms of my disease are very slight, very subtle. My last meeting with the doctor was in December [1979]. He cannot believe how strong my legs are. He pushed his thumb into my thighs and was taken aback by the strength of the muscles. Because of my progress I would not have to see him for another six months. That's the first time he's told me that in thirteen years."

Dr. Namerow is fascinated with Deanna's approach. He is especially interested in the positive mental attitude she has. And he wants her to meet with several MS patients to tell them her story and her approach to living well.

I asked her why. Deanna responded, "Most MS patients are severely depressed. They're also bitter. That attitude is the worst thing for the disease. I know that when I'm down, as I told you before, the disease seems to flair up. He knows that my positive way of thinking helps me. And hopefully it will help other patients."

I then asked her what she would say or do to help these patients out of their doldrums.

Deanna responded, "I would tell them that this is what worked for me. I don't know whether it will work for you, but it certainly is worth a try. First and foremost you've got to reduce the stress. I tell them that it can be devastating. To help overcome this stress I'd have them write down goals for the future. Things they would like to do ten years from now, one year from now, and one month or one week from today. Next I'd tell them to clean up their attitude. Be enthusiastic about life. Get excited about things they do. I know that the worst thing for me is depression. It's then that my symptoms really get activated. To avoid depression you must do things. Go to school. Get a job. Get involved in your church or some social project. Get busy so you don't have time to be sick. That's how I feel. I'm too busy in my marriage, family work, and other responsibilities to get sick.

"Second, I tell them to start to do something about their disease. Do not sit idly by and be a passive patient. Two things that I know you can do are to exercise and improve your nutrition. I'd recommend a vitamin B complex supplement, vitamin C to help them handle stress. I'd also recommend some vitamin E. They should also cut down their sugar, white flour, and salt. Finally I tell them to exercise. Do whatever they can. Walking is probably the easiest and best. Do it with a friend, and they'll keep you at it. It will help your spirit, mind, and body."

Randy Nelson

Randy Nelson

There's something about a wheel-chair that makes me cringe just a little. Every time I see one, a wave of pity sweeps over me. I, like most people, think a wheelchair represents a lack of freedom. Indeed, don't we all refer to it as "being confined" to a wheelchair? My whole orientation to people in wheelchairs is changing rapidly, and one of the major reasons is Randy Nelson.

I heard about Randy from Pat De-Boer, a friend of mine from Grand Rapids, Michigan. She knew about the book I was working on and called one day.

"Charlie, you've got to see a guy up here who plays for the Grand Rapids Pacers."

"The Grand Rapids *what?*" I asked incredulously. In Michigan we have the Tigers, Lions, the Pistons, and the

Red Wings. Recently, they have done very little to jog the memory, but the Pacers? I had never heard of them.

"The Pacers. They're a group of men who play wheelchair basketball."

Right away I cringed. Sure, it was a nice try. But really. Basketball is a tough, demanding sport. It was invented for people with two good, strong, and preferably long legs. I just couldn't see the purpose of trying to play such a competitive sport while being pushed around in a wheelchair. To placate Pat, I told her I would check into it.

I'd almost forgotten about the whole idea when I saw a poster in a local merchant's window. It announced the benefit basketball game at the nearby college, featuring wheelchair basketball. Well, I thought, I'll go see what this is all about. What I saw was impressive. While it was an exciting game featuring a professional wheelchair team against local personalities, the abilities of the "pros" was amazing. As a game it wasn't much; the poor able-bodied players didn't stand a chance and the score was terribly lopsided. What stood out in my mind, however, was the skill and mastery of the professional team. I decided to follow up that suggestion and arranged to meet with Randy.

I met with Randy and a friend of his, Tom Kelderhouse, who is the mainstay of the Pacers when it comes to fund raising and organizing wheelchair athletes in the Grand Rapids Area. In fact, Tom could have been the subject of a story for this book. He enjoys competition in wheelchair archery, table tennis, and field events. In the 1968 Paralympics in Tel Aviv, Israel, Tom won gold and silver medals in archery. Unlike most professional athletic teams, the Pacers is not on a massive budget with the players earning six-figure salaries. It takes men like Tom, as well as all of the team members, to obtain the financial support for travel and equipment expenses.

The Pacers play a rough twenty-four-game schedule which takes them throughout the Midwest. They play such cities as Cleveland, Toledo, Columbus, Chicago, Milwaukee, Lafayette (Indiana), and Quint Cities (Iowa). Since the players hold regular jobs they can play only on the weekends. The team will travel to the opposing city for a "doubleheader": one game is played Saturday evening and the second at noon on Sunday.

When I got to the appointed location, I was a little perplexed. While Tom was sitting in his wheelchair, Randy was not. In fact, there was no other wheelchair in sight. He must have noticed my look of bewilderment because they both laughed.

"Somebody's got to push me or I'd never score a point," joked Tom, nodding at Randy.

I laughed but I was still confused. Mercifully, they let me in on their joke.

"I only use my wheelchair for basketball or running," said Randy. "I have some impaired motor ability due to polio, but I *can* get around without the chair."

Before I could ask my next question, Tom answered it for me.

"Randy's able to play in the league because of our player classification system. Players are given either a I, II, or III classification, according to the nature of their disability.

"Because my disability is relatively minor, I'm given three points," added Randy. "We have to adjust our lineup to make sure we never have more than twelve points on the floor at one time. That keeps it fair and gives every level of disabled person a chance to play."

Player Classification

Class I: Complete spinal paraplegia at T-9 or above or comparable disability where there is a total loss of muscular function originating at T-9 or above.

Class II: Complete spinal paraplegia at T-10 or below or comparable disability where there is significant loss of muscular function of hips and thighs.

Class III: All other disabilities.

Team Balance

Each classification will be given a numerical value or factor as follows:

          Class I: 1 value point
          Class II: 2 value points
          Class III: 3 value points

At no time in a game shall a team have players participating with

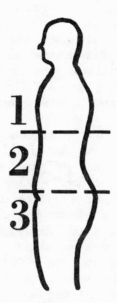

a total value points greater than twelve (12) or have more than three (3) Class III's on the floor at the same time.

If T-9 and T-10 and some of those other terms from the illustration throw you, don't feel bad. It sent me to my old college anatomy textbook to refresh my memory. Actually, the terms are quite familiar to the disabled. The player given a classification of I is quite seriously disabled. While he has control over his arms, he is unable to move his upper body at all. For example, if he bent over at the waist, he would not be able to sit back up on his own. A player classified as II would have control over his trunk and upper body muscles, but would not be able to use his legs. A III is given to those players who, like Randy, may be able to stand, and perhaps walk, but only with great difficulty. Which brings us back to Randy.

In 1952, Jonas Salk and a team of scientists were putting the finishing touches on a vaccine that would literally eliminate polio. It was September, the time of year when the dreaded disease often struck in epidemic proportions. In that same year, more American children died of polio than any other communicable disease. The virus made its way from their intestines to their central nervous systems, where it destroyed cells upon which life depended. The unfortunate became paralyzed and died. Those who escaped death faced a life of varying degrees of paralysis and immobility. Randy was one of the lucky ones.

"I don't remember much about it because I was only five at the time. I recall being very sick one afternoon in September. I complained of a headache and a stiff neck. My mom checked my temperature and it was quite high."

Throughout the early part of the fifties, such symptoms were ominous. The time of year, the temperature and headache, and Randy's age were danger signals. Randy's mother took him to their family doctor who promptly admitted him to the hospital. Shortly after he was admitted, the results from the lab were announced: Randy, age five, was a victim of polio.

"I was in the hospital for a long time—about five months. I remember being a little scared at night and I wondered why I hurt so much all over. The paralysis began to set in within a couple of days, but generally I did pretty well. I think being so young helped me adjust."

The hospital routine consisted of complete bed rest with daily physical therapy sessions. The therapy in vogue at that particular time was moist heat.

"I vividly remember the hot packs because they were so painful. They kept saying, 'The hotter they are, the better you'll get,' but I really hated it." When he got out of the hospital, Randy joined the ranks of thousands of youngsters across the continent who had to wear braces in order to stand. He also needed crutches in order to walk.

"It didn't really bother me that much. Sure, there were moments when I got a little frustrated, but generally speaking, I adapted pretty well."

His bout with polio affected his posture and gait of walking. Randy tilts his body to the left. Furthermore, as he walks he limps badly, favoring his left leg. He had good mobility, but the destruction of the disease on the central nervous system never allowed him to have the carriage and gait that most of us are blessed with and take for granted.

The really rough times came during his adolescence.

"During my teenage years, I really had a hard time of it. Occasionally I would question, 'Why me?' I don't think it was bitterness, really. It just hurt to see what others could do, knowing I would never have a chance. Knowing I would never be able to run as fast as my friends. Knowing I would never be able to play football. Knowing I would never be able to play basketball. I must say, however, I had tremendous support during those years from the school, my parents, and the community."

Randy attributes a great deal of his success in adjustment to the fact that he grew up in a small down in rural northern Michigan, Sutton's Bay. Like most small towns, everybody knew everybody else. Wherever Randy went, people would wave, shout a greeting, or lend a helping hand. The fact that they understood and were in his corner meant a lot to Randy. And even though he was afflicted with a disease that should have kept him on the sidelines, his friends encouraged him to join in their activities as much as he could.

"I could stand at the plate and hit a baseball, and then a friend would run the base pads for me. Also, I could shoot baskets, and even would get involved in half-court pickup games. I had as good or better shots than a lot of my friends, but I just couldn't rebound or lead a fast break or things like that. Yet I was always invited to join in."

Sandlot competition with his friends provided an outlet desperately needed by young Randy, but as he entered high school organized competition occupied more and more of his friends' time. He noticed, for the first time, he was being left out and the only reason was his disability. He had the desire, the knowledge, and the discipline; he just lacked the ability to compete in interscholastic athletics.

"It really hit me hard. All of a sudden I realized I was different. It really hurt, but I kept close to sports by being a manager or statistician for the various teams. I did anything that kept me involved with athletics."

After high school, Randy entered Central Michigan University where he majored in social science. While in college he increased his activity level a bit by taking up swimming. He enjoyed the university pool and felt good after a swim. The buoyancy of the water seemed to minimize his disability, and it allowed him to stay in shape. Still, Randy is competitive and needed more than just a few laps by himself in a pool. He wouldn't find the answer until well out of college.

Randy got his degree in 1968 and spent the next two years as a substitute teacher in northern Michigan. In the fall of 1970 he accepted an invitation from some friends to spend homecoming weekend at Michigan State University. What a weekend it was! In addition to the parties, the dances, and, of course, the game, Randy found a special attraction that weekend. Her name was Chris, and though it was a relationship that began quite casually, it gradually blossomed.

In 1972, Randy and Chris were married, then moved to Grand Rapids, where they both landed full-time teaching jobs. Everything was going great for the Nelsons. They had a comfortable apartment. They enjoyed teaching. Randy especially liked working with his high school students. And married life was very agreeable to both. But Randy still felt a need to do something competitive. He thought a city of that size should have something to offer.

"I called the recreation department and asked them if they had any program for people with physical handicaps. They told me about a basketball program at a local gym, so I decided to check it out."

On the appointed night, Randy drove over to the school gymnasium, parked his car, and walked in.

"I couldn't believe what I saw. I had no idea until I got there it was going to be a bunch of guys playing basketball in wheelchairs. As soon as I realized what was going on, I wanted to leave. I was totally against it. I thought, 'Hey! I don't need one of those!' I really had to fight the stigma of the wheelchair. I had never had to use one. I remember once in high school I had to have some corrective surgery. After the operation I had to wear a back brace and it made walking very difficult, even with crutches. So my dad went out and got a wheelchair for me. It was only going to be a temporary thing, but I would have no part of it. I just plain fought it. You know, 'I'll be damned if I'm going to use that chair!' But my dad told me I had to. Still, I think I won that one. I was in it for a day and that was it. I mean, I had always taken pride in being able to get around without one, and here these guys were wanting me to get in a chair and join them. I'm still surprised that I stayed."

But stay he did, perhaps more out of politeness than anything else. He hopped in a chair, feeling as long as he was there he could at least give it a try. Within minutes, he realized he had some ability.

"I made more shots than I missed and realized I might be able to be good at it. That provided positive reinforcement to offset the stigma of the chair. Before the practice was over, I was beginning to enjoy it."

That lasted until the next morning. When he woke up, he didn't know if he was going to make it.

"I could hardly move the next day. My arms ached so badly I could hardly lift them. My hands were a mass of blisters and I really felt miserable. I realized very quickly what terrible shape I was in. In fact, when I got to school, I couldn't write on the chalkboard. I just couldn't get my arms up and hold them there."

Given his attitude about wheelchairs, and the soreness of his entire body, it's a wonder that Randy went back. But he did go back and became a regular member of the team. The Pacers were just getting organized under Tom's leadership. Randy enjoyed the companionship of the other players, but he enjoyed the challenge of competition even more.

"Gradually I began to accept the chair. It really didn't take that long at all. I realized I could do things playing basketball with that chair that I could never do without it. Once I worked through that, I couldn't wait to get to the practices."

The next summer, Tom loaned Randy a chair as Randy began a personal campaign to improve his wheelchair basketball skills. Every spare moment was spent practicing. He worked on dribbling. He worked on shooting. He worked on maneuvering his chair. He wanted to excel. That's just his way of doing things.

"My wife tells me I'm too competitive, even in cards. I guess I figure I've missed a lot. This is something that came to me after twenty-five years of being unable to compete in something physical. Maybe I'm trying to make up for lost time."

By the time the season rolled around, Randy was ready. However, the Pacers were not. Remember—they were a brand-new team. They discovered you don't just build a team overnight. The first two years were plagued with setbacks.

First, it was difficult to get players. Just getting someone to give it a try was tough enough, but if they were lucky enough to get a new body out on the floor, he usually didn't return. Like Randy, the new ones thought it would be quite easy. Once they discovered how much work was involved, they decided to pursue something that required a little less sweat.

Another problem in those days was equipment. Tom innocently thought all he had to do was go out and get wheelchairs for the team. He soon found out that wheelchairs are a lot like shoes. Just as I can't wear my everyday shoes to run in, Tom learned you can't use a regular wheelchair for playing basketball. They just aren't built for that. For one thing, the foot pedals on normal chairs may be at varying heights on different chairs. The result on the basketball floor is a lot of cracked shins every time novice players get near one another.

It wasn't until they started playing other teams that the Pacers learned just how inexperienced they were.

"We were pretty horrible," recalls Tom. "We only played three or four games that year and it's a good thing. We played the Detroit Sparks who were the national champions that year. They beat us ninety to twelve. It was very frustrating, and some of the guys felt like quitting. But one good thing did come out of that game. We noticed the chairs were quite a bit different than ours, so we got a copy of the plans of their chairs. They had built their own, and we figured we could do the same."

The chair building seemed to be the factor that began to knit the team together. Things really started to click for them as their work began. It started when the people at Tom's company offered to pay for the materials for the first ten chairs if the guys would build their own. Tom grabbed the offer and went out and bought the materials. The wheels alone cost $500, to say nothing of the upholstery, the tubing, and the other materials. Soon, everyone was getting in on the act. Somebody volunteered to sew the upholstery. Another said he could do the cutting and the grinding of the metal parts. Another group offered to do the welding. It took all summer, but when they finished, they had twelve custom-made basketball chairs.

The next year was an improvement, though they still had a losing season—and they were losing more than just games. They were still losing players. Randy explained why.

"Those first few years were tough. Each year we'd win a few more games, but it wasn't overnight success. We'd win a couple of games and pick up a few new people. They would come out thinking it was going to be a lot of fun and we'd have a workout. After one or two nights, they'd quit coming. The main reason was they couldn't stand the physical pressure. First of all, it's like anything else that's physical—you have to dedicate yourself to it totally. You have to *want* to do it. Second, it requires a lot of work, and that sometimes means pain. You've got to be able to put up with some pain. Most people would take it for a little while, especially if they're winning. But we weren't winning a whole lot then, so the dedicated ones really stood out."

I was dumbfounded. Here's a guy in a wheelchair talking like Vince Lombardi. I began to discover that these weren't your typical Sunday afternoon jocks who got a charge out of shooting baskets for half an hour or so. They were athletes in every respect. As we talked more, I began to sense the dedication that I thought was reserved only for the able-bodied. Randy must have been reading my thoughts, for what he said next really illustrates what many of us feel.

"You know, there's a stigma attached to the wheelchair. We all have it. People think that those in wheelchairs are somehow different from people who aren't. I know I had to work through that. What happened with me was that I realized you can still feel the thrill of accomplishing something physical whether you're in a chair or not. The excitement of being involved in a close game is the same. Once a guy experiences that, he's hooked."

Randy should know. He's been in some awfully tough games. They push and shove and get angry, just like they do in the NBA. In fact, Randy confided that he's had a guy take a swing at him once.

"But that doesn't happen often," he laughed. "It's just that anything that you have in a basketball game involving able-bodied players you'll have in one of our basketball games."

Recently, Randy was selected to coach the team, and it couldn't have been a better choice. In order to make sure they are competitive, Randy drills his team unmercifully. To get them through a tough thirty-game schedule, he knows he has to have them in shape. And remember, whatever he has them do he does himself, too.

A typical workout for the Pacers is much like a workout for any able-bodied team. They begin with some warm-up drills, then shoot lay-ups for a while. Remember, all this from a chair. Following this, they work on speed and endurance. First, Randy puts them through that dreaded, but necessary drill: wind sprints. Down the floor as fast as you can go. Screech to a halt. Pivot. Back up the floor, all out. Pivot. Back down the floor. Again. And again. And again. And if you're not going fast enough, you get yelled at.

When that's over, they usually head for the free throw line, to practice free throws while they are still winded, simulating a real game situation. After some fast break drills, a little work on their offense and defense, and some rebounding drills, they usually finish up with about forty-five minutes of scrimmage.

By the time the practice is over, the guys are pretty much wiped out. The only difference between them and an able-bodied team is where it hurts. Both sweat. Both can't seem to get enough air into their lungs. Both have cotton mouth. While legs are rubbery for the able-bodied; arms, shoulders, and hands ache for the wheelers. Oh yes . . . the end of the practice is a welcomed moment for both.

It pays off though. The Pacers advanced from a motley group of rookies to an experienced, highly-skilled unit that posted a record of twenty-two wins against only seven loses in their 1979 season. In a tournament, they beat the seventh-ranked team in the nation. Last year they finished second in their conference. The team that beat them was ranked second in the nation. This year, they will play at half time at one of the Detroit Piston basketball games. They're big-time and they love it.

"Every year the crowds get bigger and bigger. They cheer for you and get rowdy and make lots of noise. It makes you feel great."

Randy is more than just the coach. He is probably the best player on the team. For the past five years he was selected to the All Conference Basketball Team. He was also voted the Most Valuable Player for the past two years at the Lake Michigan Basketball Conference.

Recently, Randy decided he needed something to keep him in shape in the off-season. While he was trying to decide what to do, Tom received a phone call from the sponsor from a local road race. He asked him if they had any entries for the wheelchair division. Without really thinking, Tom said, "Sure!" And took the news back to Randy who had done some work in wheelchair track and field.

"All in all," said Tom, "we had thirteen people in that first run. It was a two-mile fitness race, and it was really fun. We decided to do a little running to keep in shape for basketball."

As was the case in basketball, once they became familiar with the sport, they were hooked. Part of becoming familiar with running is learning about modifying their chairs. After all, going downhill in a chair can be tricky. You can reach speeds of twenty to thirty miles per hour. Or more. That could be downright dangerous in a normal chair. So they did a little research and began modifying their chairs. In fact, both Tom and Randy have three chairs—one for regular activity, one for basketball, and one for running.

Once the equipment problem was solved, the real work began. The first hurdle was to get enough space. As a runner, I seldom worry about where I'm going to run. Because of the running boom that has swept this nation, most motorists are used to seeing middle-aged guys like me plodding along the roadside. But what about the wheelchair runner?

To gain confidence as well as ability, Randy started running at a local track. However, he soon got tired of running around in circles. One day he selected a route along roads that were infrequently traveled and gave road running a try. To his surprise, it wasn't all that bad.

"I'll have to admit, at first it was kind of scary having those big cars and trucks going by. But once you get used to it, it's no problem."

Actually, wheelchair runners are bothered more by potholes than motorists. Consider Randy's aggressiveness when he's on the road. Like most dedicated runners, he doesn't like to have to stop in the middle of a run and wait for traffic to thin out. On one occasion, he even hit a car, though just grazing it and not once stopping. In wheelchair parlance, I guess you could say he never missed a stroke.

Another problem, somewhat related, is the weather. Since the wheelchair runner depends on good traction for mobility, slippery roads pose a particular hazard.

"There's a company that makes special treadmills you can use with your wheelchair in the house," said Tom. "It's supposed to simulate running. But personally, I like running because it lets me get outdoors. I just couldn't see spending an hour in my basement working with that thing."

Along with the snow and ice, the winter months bring darkness rather early. When Randy gets out of work at five, it's usually dark. Running in the dark is never safe even for able-bodied runners, but the wheelchair is at an even more serious disadvantage.

"We need to see the surface we're running on," said Randy.

Consequently, the two will often visit lighted parking lots for their running. They have one where they have marked out a course that's about a mile in length. They make the circuit ten or twelve times to get their mileage in for the day.

In addition to some of the hardships of running in a wheelchair, Randy has had his share of light moments. Perhaps he has had more. Consider one of his first road runs with Tom.

It was Sunday morning, Easter to be exact. One of the nice things about Sunday morning runs is that the runner has the entire road to himself. Tom and Randy were enjoying the freedom of being able to wheel right out in the middle of the road. They turned out onto a flashy five-lane highway where the center lane is reserved for left turns. It seemed like an ideal lane for wheelchair runners, so they both moved into it. It was toward the end of the run when a car came up alongside them, and the driver rolled down the window. From inside came the smiling voice of a pleasant little old lady.

"God bless you and happy Easter." That made Tom and Randy's day.

Actually, support like that is not out of the ordinary. Randy has found that most people are very positive about seeing him on one of his runs.

His introduction to running has made him more mobile as well. For example, when visiting his parents and/or in-laws near Sutton's Bay, he will often take a run from one house to the next—some seven miles away. "At one time I thought the only way I could get there was by car, but all that has changed. I just tell my wife if she doesn't hear from me in two hours she'd better start looking. I may be in a ditch or have lost a wheel.

"The young kids especially seem to get into it. I know when I was teaching, my students thought it was really neat that their teacher played basketball in a wheelchair. During lunch hours I would go down to the gym and get into a pickup game with them. Naturally, they all wanted to give it a try too, so I let them get in the chair and give it a try. I think the exposure is important. I think it's important to be out on the streets, even if it might mean some embarrassment. What I'm concerned about most is to be able to show people that a disability is not necessarily disabling. That a handicap is only as big as you make it."

Listening to him talk, I couldn't help but wonder if I would go to all the trouble to run as they do. It's easy for me to slip on a pair of shorts, lace up my shoes, and be off. Preparing to run with a wheelchair is almost as much work as the run itself.

First, there's the hassle of always having to carry an extra chair around, for normal chairs just won't do. Then there's the matter of the hands. Ten or fifteen miles can turn a pair of rugged hands into hamburger, unless special care is taken to protect them. That means first taping the hands, then pulling on a pair of gloves, then taping again. That takes time. So does strapping the legs into position so they don't interfere. By the time Randy would be ready, I would be two miles into my run, and thinking about my shower on returning.

Still, he wants no special treatment. I asked him about the controversy over allowing wheelchairs into major road races like the New York City Marathon. I cited the argument that goes like this: Because spectators, motorists, and other runners aren't used to wheelchair competitors, the chairs should be banned for their own protection.

"Nonsense!" says Randy. "If they do that, they ought to ban a lot of so-called 'able-bodied' runners from running. I ran in a race in Grand Haven where there were a lot of people running who weren't in shape. It was ninety degrees in the shade, and they were dropping like flies. I saw some people vomiting blood. It's an individual choice. I know the risks, and personally I think they're minimal for people in wheelchairs."

Randy has adjusted well to the special problems wheelchair runners face, but in addition, he has to face the same problems of any able-bodied runner: pain, fatigue, exhaustion.

"Sure it's tough," said Randy. "You're always worried about hitting a bump and tipping over. Your hands get sore. Blisters develop. Going uphill, you feel like just letting your arms relax, but if you do you'll start rolling backward. And you're always wondering if some motorist might run into you. But it's worth it."

His wife Chris thinks so, too. You could just feel the pride in her voice as she spoke about her husband's accomplishments.

"You know, I'm used to seeing people in wheelchairs. But when I saw those guys come over that final hill at Grand Haven, I couldn't help it. I just cried. But they were tears of joy. I was so proud of him."

By now, I think I understand the wheelchair athlete well enough to second-guess the answer to my next question. But I had to ask it anyway, just to confirm my belief. Why, when all the odds seem to be against them, do they do it?

Randy was very direct, but I knew I deserved it.

"Charlie, ask yourself why *you* run. And your answers will be the same as mine. People think we're different because we have a physical difference. The same thing that might motivate you is the same thing that might motivate me. We're both human, Charlie."

I still cringe when I see a wheelchair, but for a different reason. I keep thinking of the runner, thrusting his arms down in a pistonlike manner, much like the push of a locomotive. I see the hands taped, ragged, perhaps a bit bloody. I feel the relief of finishing a long run that leaves the body tired but the spirit soaring. I cringe in the same way I do when Darrel Dawkins leaves the earth to deliver a slam dunk. Or when Walter Payton slithers for extra yardage. Or when Renoldo Nehamian skims the hurdles for another world record. I cringe with respect.

Chris Stutzmann

There are thousands of success stories about people who have been rehabilitated after a heart attack with exercise. Steve McKanic, whom you met earlier, is one of my favorite stories. And while it is common today for physicians to encourage, even command, their patients to exercise, it wasn't until the mid 1970s that this concept caught on.

In the 1950s and '60s there were few stalwart physicians who strongly advocated vigorous aerobic exercise for cardiac patients. Terence Kavanagh, M.D., Medical Director of the Toronto Rehabilitation Centre in Canada, was one of these early advocates. In 1967, he pioneered research in the use of endurance exercise for the treatment of post-coronary-attack patients. Operating out of a small public hospital, he carefully documented changes occurring in patients subjected to regular cardiovascular exercise.

But the event which set Kavanagh's work apart from his contemporaries was the 1973 Boston Marathon. In April of that year Kavanagh took a group of eight documented heart attack patients to run in that World Series of running, a race which is 26.2 miles in length and tests the mettle of normal, fit individuals. One man was told by Dr. Kavanagh he could run only half the race because of insufficient mileage, but the other seven were cleared. Kavanagh's team slipped unnoticed at the back of the pack of several thousand runners who gathered for this Patriots Day race. As the men ran, Kavanagh ran alongside of them and checked them periodically. All seven finished, setting medical history by being the first documented post-coronary patients ever to complete the grueling 26.2-mile run.

In terms of medical research, the men who ran in the race played only a small role in the battle against degenerative heart disease. But their determination, desire, and successful completion captured the attention of doctors and laymen alike. Their run in a top marathon probably did more to change the attitude toward post-coronary rehabilitation than any other research study.

Of course, Kavanagh's work did not begin or end with the Boston Marathon. Since 1967 more than twenty-five hundred patients have been under his care which advocates exercise. Now, more than seven hundred people each year undergo his exercise therapy at the Centre. Soon more will be accommodated with an expanded facility.

With that kind of track record I thought it was appropriate to visit Dr. Kavanagh, his staff, and his patients. Jo Kennedy, his able assistant who has worked with him since he started the program, made provision for me to observe Dr. Kavanagh's program in operation and to talk with six of his patients. I sat down and discussed at length with Peter Myerson, Chris Stutzmann, Dave Wood, Bill Belitski, Bill McCort, and Ken Smith their feelings toward Dr. Kavanagh and their heart attacks. I found some fascinating things.

Interestingly, Kavanagh not only runs marathons and other races with his patients, but also exercises with them almost daily. He lectures to them in group sessions. He and his staff closely prescribe the proper intensity, duration, and frequency of exercise for all patients. They are under constant supervision.

Dr. Kavanagh does not mince words with his patients. If someone tells him that running is boring, the doctor asks him if he dislikes himself so much that he can't spend a half-hour all alone. If a patient refuses his advice and tries to go too fast too soon, or run in an unauthorized race, Kavanagh tells him to follow his advice or seek another physician.

Dr. Kavanagh challenges his patients to exercise, to take good care of their bodies, and to get the most of what they have left.

To a man, the six patients I interviewed felt that they were alive today because of Dr. Kavanagh. They felt lucky to have met him and to be residing in Toronto. They said if Kavanagh challenged them to race up to the top of Mt. Everest their only question would be "when." Kavanagh is their guru. And while I would like to tell you their six success stories—and hundreds of others—I think Chris Stutzmann's story tells it best.

"I hate to run," Chris Stutzmann kept insisting all through my conversation with him. "I log a lot of miles and spend a good bit of time on the track as a member of Kavanagh's Long Distance Club, a club which is often referred to as the world's sickest track club."

All this got me thinking. How and why does Chris do it? How and why has he run fifteen marathons? And, how and why does he run between thirty and sixty miles a week?

"My trick is, right away in the morning, weather permitting, I go run. Get it over with. The longer I postpone it, the harder it gets for me. If I leave it for the evening, I might find a reason not to run. In fact, if someone gives me a good excuse not to run I take it."

There. That explains how he pulls it off. He sneaks out first thing and does his running before his body has much opportunity to argue. But to find out why Chris does it we have to go back to 1968 when he was forty-one years old. At that time he owned four coin laundries in Toronto. He sold laundry equipment, worked fifteen to sixteen hours a day, and was on call 365 days a year. The stress was killing him.

But it wasn't only his work that was killing him. Chris smoked heavily—twenty-five to thirty cigarettes a day. And he wasn't sedentary, he was downright lazy. "If I had to go around the corner for a pack of cigarettes," he said, "I'd take the car. I got so sedentary it was ridiculous."

But Chris managed to quit smoking six months before he had his heart attack. I asked him why. "First, I was coughing every morning when I got up. I was sick and tired of that. Then the Minister of Revenue said that the Ontario government was going to tax cigarettes heavily. And whoever didn't like it could stop smoking. In other words, he was saying, 'You idiots can't stop, so you'll pay the increase.' So I got mad and I said *I'll show you*. I smoked every last cigarette I had in the house and then I stopped." But the damage was done.

The night before Chris had his heart attack he was opening a brand-new coin laundry. Part of that job involved dumping salts into a large commercial water softener. Chris lifted about twenty of the hundred-pound bags from the floor to his shoulder and high above his head to empty them into the water softener. For ten years prior to that he had done nothing strenuous whatsoever. He feels this unexpected extra activity may have contributed to his heart attack.

The actual attack came about three o'clock the following morning. "I woke up with pain in my chest," he said. "I thought it was indigestion, so I got some Bromo Seltzer and went back to bed. But I couldn't sleep. I felt pain in my left arm, and my wife called the doctor right away. I was mad at her for calling the doctor for what I thought was just a bad case of indigestion, but she insisted.

"The doctor came into the house, checked me out, and then sent me to the hospital. He said he came thinking he could spare me a trip to the hospital, but after checking me he said he was afraid I'd have to go anyway."

After two days in the hospital they came to Chris with the bad news that he had had a heart attack. Being only forty-one years old with a wife and two children, ages twelve and seventeen, and to have to be there while the doctor told him there wasn't much hope was more than Chris could take. "I got really scared," he told me, "because in those days they didn't train you for anything, so you would more or less be a cripple for the rest of your life. The doctor said I should watch going down to the basement; I might not be able to come back up. And, of course, all you have to look forward to is another heart attack. I was so scared . . . as a matter of fact, I'm still scared. That is why I'm still running."

Twelve years ago when Chris had his heart attack there weren't many doctors around who were keen on fitness for heart attack patients. In fact, Chris spent five weeks in the hospital after his attack. He was told "no more work." His future looked bleak. Fortunately, his cardiologist was one of the more progressive ones at that time, because he gave Chris a list to follow. He told Chris, "For two months I want you to do absolutely nothing. Then after two months start walking. Fifty yards a day for one week and then the next week increase it to one hundred yards and so forth."

But that wasn't enough for Chris. "I wanted more, but I was depressed, scared, and confused. I felt I needed something because I was a real basket case. But I didn't know what. I was scared to do anything for fear of having another heart attack. I ran right over to the doctor every time I felt a little bit of something which I would have probably never noticed before. My doctor must have gone crazy seeing me every week or every second week. For every little pain here or there I would say, 'Do you think this could be the heart?' But he was very patient and understanding and he said, 'No, Chris, your heart is okay, but I would rather see you come once too often than not come and have something happen.' But I was afraid to do anything. It was a sad story. Today my wife tells me that she saw me deteriorate badly. The only positive thing that happened in those years is that I lost weight."

In 1970 Chris's family physician sent him to the Toronto Fitness Institute, a private fitness club. He was there for a month or so, but it was too expensive, and he was forced to quit.

"Then in 1971, I read about Dr. Terence Kavanagh's program at the Toronto Rehabilitation Centre. I saw a picture of the Governor General running with Dr. Kavanagh and a group of heart attack patients for about five or six miles. So I went to my doctor and said, 'Listen, what is this? Can I join this program?' He told me he could send me there if I wanted to. I said, 'Of course I want to—how much is it going to cost me?' He told me there would be no direct cost to me, that the program would be paid for by a grant from the Ontario Ministry of Health, and all Ontario residents are covered for it by their Ontario Hospital Insurance Plan (OHIP).

So arrangements were made for Chris to enroll in Kavanagh's program. After all the preliminary information was taken, Chris was scheduled to take an exercise stress test—a test which measures a person's heart and body's ability to withstand vigorous exercise.

The test proved to be an experience in itself. "I got in and I was supposed to have a test at ten o'clock in the morning. Since my heart attack I was conscious of my weight, and I was never hungry in the mornings anyway, so I always skipped breakfast." It seems there were some technical delays and it wasn't until two o'clock that Chris had his test. He still had not eaten! It was a fairly strenuous test. After all, running on a treadmill for several minutes at faster and faster speeds and on a higher and higher incline is no simple task. When it was finished the attending doctor said, "This is one of the best tests we've ever had," to which Chris replied, "The best test my foot, I think I'm going to faint."

That is all Chris can remember. When he woke up he was lying on the floor. They were preparing to give him oxygen. Everyone was fearful he had had a heart attack. Fortunately he was still on the EKG machine and everything appeared to be okay, but the staff couldn't figure out why he had collapsed. At this point, Jo Kennedy rushed in. She asked Chris when he had eaten last. He told her. She quickly called for orange juice. She was convinced his problem was a lack of blood sugar depleted by fasting and exercise. The orange juice seemed to revive him. However, just to be sure, they sent him to the hospital in an ambulance. While there, it happened that Chris's cardiologist checked his room. Chris told him what had happened and the cardiologist checked him out. He, too, concluded that the problem had to do with a lack of sugar and nothing concerning his heart. So he released Chris that same afternoon.

That was Chris's first experience with Dr. Kavanagh's Rehabilitation Centre, a dubious one at best, but it didn't scare him off. For he went back to the first exercise session.

At that session Kavanagh met with a group of fifty or so new people, Chris included. Dr. Kavanagh told the group that they were embarking on unexplored territory. He said, "There's a lot we know and an awful lot we don't. Up to this point we have found exercise to be quite helpful, but you must follow our guidelines and advice. It's up to you to either accept the program or opt out. But you must follow our guidelines."

Chris was glad to be in the program. "I was constantly under Dr. Kavanagh's and his staff's supervision. On my own I was afraid to walk. I wanted to but I was afraid of another heart attack. But with Kavanagh I was under the direct care of a physician.

"At first we began by walking, then walking and jogging, and then jogging. The program was very specific. They told me to walk or jog a certain distance at such and such a pace. I was to walk three miles at a twelve-minute pace. Everything was done with great care. I was relieved. Happy to be involved.

"I think we all knew at this time that Dr. Kavanagh was putting his career right on the line with us. This was specifically true when he took the first eight men to the Boston Marathon in 1973. Ken Smith, one of the eight runners, says it best for everybody at the Centre. 'We told Dr. Kavanagh that if any of us failed in this marathon, if we had any kind of heart problem, then he would have to go so far away to practice medicine that it would have cost us about ten dollars to send him a postcard.'" But they didn't fail, and Kavanagh is still on the leading edge of science when it comes to cardiac rehabilitation.

The objective of Kavanagh's program is to bring any heart patient up to an hour of exercise, five days a week. This is as far as they are required to go. If individuals want to do more, they can join the long-distance group, a club which has more freedom than the immediate post-coronary group.

Chris had not always lived a sedentary life before his heart attack. He moved to Canada in 1954 from Ljubljana, Yugoslavia. He was born in Pancevo City, Yugoslavia, a city of about thirty thousand, ten miles from Belgrade. In Ljubljana he worked as a truck driver and gradually worked through apprenticeships and schooling to become a mechanic and tool and diemaker. He stayed in shape during his twenties by playing soccer. He was quite good—in the second level of the national league. But when he reached thirty he stopped playing and adopted a totally sedentary lifestyle.

When he moved to Canada, Chris started out as a tool and diemaker and also sold life insurance. But he soon got out of that business: "Life insurance was hard on my nerves. It's a nerve-wracking business for me. I had an ambition to make a certain amount of money and then retire by the age of fifty-five or at least by sixty. So I placed a lot of demands on myself."

In 1957 Chris started his own general insurance agency and took some accounting, business, and law-related courses at the University of Toronto. But the insurance business was too much; he worked five years as an accountant and then began his own coin laundry and dry cleaning business. Today he sells laundry equipment but is out of the coin laundry business.

By the time he had his heart attack in 1968, Chris had become sedentary, ate copious amounts of food, and weighed 235 pounds. Today he is down to 170. He lost the 65 pounds in one year.

Chris's heredity may also have contributed to his heart problem. His mother suffered from a bad heart for almost fifty years, and his brother died at age fifty-two of a heart attack. Also, most of the people from the part of Yugoslavia that Chris comes from eat high cholesterol foods like bacon, ham, and pork.

Chris has not licked his eating habits, but doesn't plan to—and with good reason. "After the war I was a prisoner-of-war in Yugoslavia and we were starved. I swore to myself if I ever had the chance, I would never be on a diet again. I really lived up to that in Canada. I ate until I had food coming out of my ears." Yet although he ate high cholesterol foods, his cholesterol level was only 140 when he had his attack. Since normal is 150-250, he and Dr. Kavanagh believe that other factors caused his heart attack.

Dr. Kavanagh's rehabilitation program was the best thing that could have happened to Chris. Kavanagh and his team made Chris start slowly. First he was to walk two miles; he kept a diary and checked his pulse. Every so often his prescription was increased until he was allowed to do three miles at twelve minutes per mile. He was held at that pace for two years, which upset him, because most of the other people who entered the program at the same time were advancing much faster than he was. So Chris arranged to discuss it with Dr. Kavanagh.

"Listen, Dr. K," he said, "how come for two years now I have not been allowed to increase my exercise? Is something wrong with me? If there is, tell me. I want to know. Don't beat around the bush."

Dr. Kavanagh took out all of Chris's diaries and said, "Well, it's very simple. You are supposed to do three miles, at twelve-minute miles. That's thirty-six minutes. But for the last year you've never gone slower than thirty or thirty-one minutes for three miles. You're doing it faster than you're supposed to."

"Well, isn't that supposed to make me fitter?" Chris wanted to know.

"No," replied the doctor. "We will tell you when to go faster and further. If you don't, you will probably push yourself too much and perhaps precipitate some serious problem. You must listen to our plan and not surge ahead of schedule. Once you show us you can follow our advice we will let you advance."

Chris took that advice to heart, and within two months or so, and with Kavanagh's consent, he was running each mile in eleven minutes. A few months later he was running ten-minute miles.

"When I reached that point I was asked to join the Long Distance Club, of which there were six or seven members. I was told that, if interested, I should come out to the track Sunday morning. They would check us out, and the doctor would tell us if we could participate or not. Chris was excited. After all, the Long Distance Club members were the guys who had run in the 1973 Boston Marathon. "For me they were heroes," Chris told me.

"So on Sunday I reported to the track. The medical team cleared me and said, 'Let's go for six miles.' [The Long Distance Club runs a six-mile loop or multiples thereof near the Centre.] I thought, oh, my, that's the end of the world. I've never gone more than three. Different things flashed through my mind: Can I do it? Will I be able to make it back? Will I have chest pain? Will I have another heart attack? But I decided to go along.

"It was amazing. I ran the six and I didn't find it any harder than the three. I had no pain. Nothing. That was it. I was hooked.

"I soon learned to trust the medical team. I figured they knew what they were doing. Besides, Dr. Kavanagh ran with us at the time, and that gave me great confidence.

"I told my wife. From now on I will run five days a week, of which two are in the club. You can have the other time, but these two days are mine, with the club."

This decision and jump in mileage occurred in the spring of 1974. Considering how much Chris disliked running, it's surprising he stuck with it so long. The reason, he thinks, is because of his wife. "I'm lucky. I have full cooperation from my wife, Anna. As a matter of fact, I think she pushed me into this. She realized more than I did what kind of a nervous wreck I was and how scared I was and that I was becoming a cripple. When she realized what this Centre did for me she was a hundred percent behind it. Anna even went to the track with me, to sit there and watch me doing my laps. I hated to do it, but she sometimes ran with me and supported me and kept me going."

I asked Anna how she felt.

"Because of his shape of mind, and health—something had to be done. He was always thinking about his heart and the possibility of another attack. Then I saw the progress he made at the Centre. I knew it was good for him and supported his participation in the program wholeheartedly. It was just what Chris needed."

Chris's association with the other members of the Long Distance Club had a profound effect on him. He soon set his sights on running a marathon—the ultimate fitness test: a test that Chris felt would possibly allay his fears of another heart attack and possibly death, a feat that would surely improve his mental attitude about himself and his disease. So Chris set out in earnest to reach for his impossible dream. And although in the sophisticated 1980s it may sound corny, Chris was going to strive when the heart is too weary and run where the brave dare not go. He now had a challenge and he was not going to fail. He chose the December 1974 Hawaiian Marathon as his goal.

Most of Chris's training runs in preparation for the marathon were six miles in length. Then once a week he would run ten or twelve miles. Slowly, ever so slowly, his mileage on the long day increased. All the while, he had to battle a strong desire to stay in the comfort of his home. Toronto, as we all know, is not the banana belt of the world from November to April. And the icy blasts from the arctic can deter even the best-intentioned runner or fitness enthusiast. But Chris hung in there month after month. Then in June 1974 he ran eighteen miles in practice. Over the summer months he gradually increased his mileage. In September he ran his first twenty-six miles in practice with Dr. Kavanagh at his side.

"When I ran my first twenty-six miles in training I could hardly believe it. I was like a child under a Christmas tree with eyes sparkling, and I went into tears. Because even during my younger days when I played soccer and was in good condition, I knew I could never run twenty-six miles. It got me so high that I felt, if I can do this now, at my age and after a heart attack, I should think I'm healthy.

"All the while he was upping his mileage and preparing for the marathon distance, I knew he could do it if he put his mind to it," Anna said. "Dr. Kavanagh gave him all the confidence that he needed. Chris trusted him and saw his health improving. So he became more and more sure of himself."

Chris ran twenty-six miles two or three times before his first official marathon in Hawaii. He even chose to run in the Skylon Marathon in Buffalo, but he did not run a full marathon. He simply ran twenty miles to get used to the race pace.

Then in December 1974, Chris went to Hawaii. He was ready. As he ran, he paced himself to go slowly. He wasn't about to blow finishing his first official marathon. He didn't push himself. He ran comfortably and well . . . and finished just two seconds under five hours (4:59:58). When he finished he felt well enough that he could have gone another mile or so if necessary. He felt his rehabilitation was complete. "Sir Edmond Hillary when he first scaled Mt. Everest, or the first astronauts when they stepped on the surface of the moon could not have felt better. I had reached the unreachable—my moon! With tears in my eyes, I hugged Dr. Kavanagh, and thanked him for getting me there. My wife put a kukui nut lei around my neck, which I still cherish very much. You can tell my wife had confidence in me and Kavanagh. She had purchased the lei well before the marathon," Chris recalled.

"My wife knew I could run twenty-six miles. But my friends wouldn't believe it. They said, 'Come on, that's impossible for you. After all, you're sick.' But then it came out in the newspapers and they were utterly amazed. They asked, 'How does it feel?' and I said, 'Listen, it's nothing but sheer agony.'"

Chris has put himself through this "sheer agony" many times:

three times in Boston, twice in New York, three times in Toronto, once each in Ottawa, Detroit, Reno, and Dublin, and twice in Honolulu. His best time ever occurred on his second trip to Hawaii where he ran the marathon in four hours and eleven minutes. He's run the New York City Marathon in four hours and thirteen minutes.

To this day Chris still has to fight the desire to stay home and take it easy. Even his training runs are shortened by his mental attitude. Going further distances is a problem for Chris. "During the first two or three miles I think the whole thing is stupid. A bunch of bull. It is all hard labor. But as I go four, five, or six miles I feel a lot better. I solve many business and personal problems. I can honestly say this part of the run is better—almost enjoyable. But somewhere between six and eight miles I usually conclude that I've had enough. I rarely go over eight miles on my own. To go further I must run with the Long Distance Club or in other organized runs.

"Surprisingly, I don't have any aches or pains. My problem is all in my head. If I could find a better way to stay as fit as I am, and feel as good as I do, I would do it. But, of course, there isn't. Running for me is sheer agony. Discipline."

But Chris recognizes the benefits of running: "I skied back home in Yugoslavia when I was young but I hadn't done it for twenty or more years. Now that I am in better condition I take my whole family skiing. It's something the family can do together, so I'm still keeping it up. I have become more active in a lot of things, and my mental attitude has changed so much, you could almost say I'm a completely different person. Exercise has made me feel better. I have a completely different outlook on life. Making money and worrying about the future isn't important to me anymore. I used to be uptight quite a bit, but running calms me down and soothes my nerves."

Another thing that keeps Chris running is a fresh approach to problem solving. "When I'm out there running my mind is completely clear and the air is fresh and a lot of things that clutter up my brain begin to fall into place." He has solved many minor, and even some of his major, business problems while running.

"The running gives me peace of mind. I would have worried

myself to death after my heart attack worrying about this pain and that. The running built up my health and my confidence. So I keep at it."

Chris desires to have the good life, which for him must include a full stomach. He realizes that it doesn't matter how many calories you take in; as long as you burn them up, you won't gain weight or endanger your health. "Let's face it," he observed, "three or four miles a day would be enough for me to maintain good health. But I really enjoy good food and an occasional drink. So this is why I endure the agony of an additional mile or two." Or ten or twenty-six.

Even with all those benefits Chris says, "I'm the joke in the group because of my attitude toward running. I have to push myself really hard to keep up. I don't need much excuse not to run. If my wife would ever say, oh, don't go today, go tomorrow, that would be all right with me. Yet I'm quite regular."

So Chris runs for many reasons, but the fundamental reason is rooted in that frightening experience he had back there in the hospital twelve years ago. When he stared death in the face. "So I run. I run to live. I might be crazy, but I happen to believe that if I didn't run I probably wouldn't be alive any more."

Hulda Crooks

Hulda Crooks

Can you imagine being eighty years old? It's hard for me to comprehend. From prairie sod homes of the frontier to lavish condominiums of a megalopolis. From the horse and buggy to the sleek El Dorado. From the Wright Brothers' first airplane to jet travel, supersonic transports, space travel, and moon walks. I don't know about you, but I think of eighty years old as being old. And when I think of someone fortunate enough to live to be eighty-three, I usually picture white hair, wrinkled face and hands, no teeth, and a rocking chair. After meeting Hulda Crooks, I'm not so sure any more. Oh, she's got wrinkles all right, and exquisitely beautiful white hair, but she doesn't sit on a rocking chair, and she has her own teeth. And a lot more. Like the Senior Olympic's track record for 1,500 meters. A scrapbook of her eighteen trips to the top of Mt. Whitney—by foot. And a warm, engaging personality. In short, Hulda Crooks is a phenomenal woman.

Naturally, one of the first questions I asked Hulda when I met her was what sort of lifelong health program she had been on. I envisioned a youngster taught to eat nutritional foods, exercise regularly, get plenty of sleep, and so on. I was shocked to discover her truly healthy way of life began later in life. While in her early thirties, she thought she might soon die. She was tired all the time. She had suffered an attack of pneumonia and had undergone major surgery, followed by some twenty-five years of poor health. I guess that's as good a place as any to begin the story of this sensitive, dynamic, wonderful human being.

Hulda was born of German parents in western Canada in May of 1896. She grew up on a farm and can still recall the sod home she lived in as a child and the vigorous physical work which was a way of life. She worked in garden and field, milked cows and fed calves, and spent most of her early years outdoors. Unfortunately her diet was unbalanced and too rich.

"I grew up on a diet that consisted largely of meat, potatoes, butter, cream, and eggs. In addition, in my father's country store I had free access to a barrel of candy and a gunny sack of peanuts, both of which we sold by the pound to the country people. I ate these extra snacks between meals in addition to three big meals a day."

This pattern of eating caused her weight to rise, regardless of the daily chores. She was simply eating more calories than she was burning off through physical activity. Before she was sixteen, Hulda weighed 160 pounds—too much for her 5-foot-2-inch frame—but no one seemed concerned about her weight, for a hefty Fräulein on the farm was always an asset. Still, her older brother would tease her and say that by the time she reached twenty she would be as tall on her side as she was on her feet.

Education in rural Canada was even less of a priority than good nutrition. By the time she was eighteen, Hulda had completed only five grades of country schooling and seemed destined to the perfunctory life of an overweight, poorly educated farm lass. Then in 1914 her life took a drastic change. It began with her acceptance of the health and Bible teachings of the Seventh Day Adventists.

She became a lacto-vegetarian, giving up all types of flesh food as well as tea and coffee. The change, however, was more than dietary.

Her new-found faith also inspired her to return to school. It was no longer enough just to plod along taking things as they came. Hulda decided it was time to take charge of her life and get as much out of it as she could. So she attended a Seventh Day Adventist academy in western Canada. Like most young people from the farm, she had to support herself. When she wasn't in class or studying, she worked in the school kitchen. Gone was the exercise of farm life and long hours she used to spend outdoors. It was a Spartan, indoor, sedentary, existence, but it did have one benefit. Since she was away from home and the accompanying rich food, Hulda gradually began to lose weight.

For the next thirteen years, Hulda was in school. But the pressures of having to work to support herself while pursuing her schoolwork undermined her health. In 1923, after completing two years of college, she set out for Loma Linda University in Loma Linda, California, where, at the age of twenty-seven she started to work for a diploma in dietetics.

"I knew I was losing out," she says, "but I thought just a little bit more and I'll be through."

So Hulda hung on for more education, continuing the daily indoor grind of work, study, more work, more study, and little sleep. Finally, in 1927, she received her diploma.

"But I wasn't worth much. I was nervous, anemic, and perpetually tired. Year after year of indoor life, as I worked for my support and education, took their toll. So while I had gained an education, I had lost my health."

Fortunately, not all was lost. In that same year, her fiancé, Dr. Samuel A. Crooks, "took me literally for better or worse." Her beloved Dr. Sam had just finished his medical training and had begun his teaching career as an instructor in anatomy at Loma Linda University.

It would make an interesting story if I told you he discovered a miracle drug that immediately brought Hulda back to good health. While he gradually led her to a complete recovery, his "miracle drug" was really quite simple. Get Hulda outdoors as much as possible. He started subtly. Although fond of tasty food, he gave her little praise for spending long hours in the kitchen cooking, baking, and washing piles of dishes. "Improve your mind" was his constant admonition.

Hulda didn't complain when he suggested they get outdoors and go for walks. It had been years since she had taken the luxury of a leisurely outdoor stroll. So Sam knew what he was doing when he would look up from a book some afternoon and say, "Let's go for a walk." He also knew what he was doing when he started giving Hulda books. He gave Hulda any kind of outdoor book he could get his hands on. Hulda's eyes sparkled as she recounted the first book her husband brought her.

"We were out walking one spring afternoon and we came across a field of yellow daisylike flowers with white tips. 'I wonder what these are?' I exclaimed. Without a word Sam reached into his back overall pocket and pulled out a book. It was written for laymen and had the flowers arranged by color. I turned to the yellow section and there it was—Tidy Tips. The surge of pleasure that swept through me when I found the name of that sunny-looking flower elated every cell of my being. It was better medicine than anything ever ordained on a prescription blank.

"My husband was the key to my recovery. He knew my love of nature and its therapeutic value. He encouraged every interest I had in the outdoors and this helped my mental attitude. You see, poor health makes one introspective. I thought about myself. I worried about me. I remember shortly after we were married that I was afraid I might soon die, because I felt so tired all the time. But I thought, 'Oh well, if I die, I won't be tired anymore.' My husband understood this. He didn't tell me not to worry. Instead, he schemed to get me outdoors to turn my thinking to things other than myself. And it worked."

Gradually, Hulda's strength and energy returned. Her husband's constant encouragement to return to the outdoors she loved was the perfect antidote. Outdoors she had energy. Outdoors she had strength. Where once she could barely walk around the block, she could now walk for miles or work hours in the yard. She gardened, raised love birds, calves, and goats. Dr. Sam would urge her to minimize her indoor work and increase her outdoor interests.

Because of these outdoor activities and nature study Hulda picked up a good deal of new-found strength. During the 1940s she started to explore mountains and began climbing some of those mountains near her home in Loma Linda. Unfortunately, Sam had a heart condition that prevented him from climbing high mountains with her, but he encouraged her to go with friends. He showed a keen interest in anything she learned or saw. One day in the early forties while they were driving in the vicinity of Lone Pine, California, Sam pointed out the car window and said, "See that peak? That's Mt. Whitney. The highest mountain in the continental United States." "It looked awesome," Hulda recalls. "Little did I realize that one day I would climb it."

Then in 1950 just as she was regaining her health and all seemed to be going well, tragedy struck. Her husband died of a heart attack. Hulda was devastated. The man she had loved was more than just a husband. She felt he was largely responsible for her new-found health and her present lifestyle. And now he was gone. For an instant she felt as if her own world had ended. Yet over the years she had developed an antidote for life's problems. She had cultivated the spirit of gratitude for her many blessings. Whenever she felt low, she would just think and reflect on all the good that was about her. And above all, she had reached out for a close fellowship with her Creator as an enrichment of her mental and spiritual faculties. Her positive attitude and firm conviction of being a part of God's plan pulled her through.

"Alone I carried on as best I could. It was hard, but I knew Sam had expected me to keep right on living and doing the things I enjoy. A familiarity with nature and my love for the outdoors helped tranquilize my emotions."

Her friends knew the impact that Dr. Sam's death had on Hulda, and rallied to her support. Knowing the therapeutic value of the outdoors for her, they frequently invited her to go to the mountains with them. On one of her climbs of Mt. San Gorgonio, the highest peak in southern California, and a peak on which Hulda has stood probably more than twenty times, she learned a precious lesson from nature. On a windswept northern slope, pine trees struggle from one level of difficulty to the next, continually adjusting to meet the heavy onslaught of the elements. First they lean; a little higher up the slope they bend, then go prostrate, ever upward toward the crest and the sunshine. At last, though reduced to the size of shrubs, they stand erect at the summit.

"There I saw them one morning as the sun rose in splendor and crowned each worthy head with gold."

To Hulda the struggling pines on the side of the mountain were very much like herself. Throughout her life there had been many setbacks, and there would doubtless be more. Yet the reward would come when one day she would reach the summit and, like the trees, be crowned with gold. The lesson embedded itself deeply in her outlook on life.

Hulda did a lot of climbing in those first few years after Sam's death, and drew comfort from nature's object lessons. Her health continued to improve until she was able to hold a full-time job. She felt best when she walked a lot, so she got rid of her car, which had two immediate benefits. First, it decreased her expenses, and, second, it increased her daily exercise. With today's rising gasoline prices, I personally find that to be a more and more attractive solution to the energy problem, both the oil industry's and our own personal supplies of energy.

Hulda's new full-time job was a fruition of Dr. Sam's advice to "improve your mind." She was hired as a research assistant under Mervin Hardinge, M.D., Ph.D., at the Loma Linda University School of Medicine's Department of Pharmacology. She proved her value as an assistant to Dr. Hardinge, and co-authored a number of papers and articles on nutrition with him. In fact, if you would browse through such prestigious journals as *The American Journal of Clinical Nutrition* or *The Journal of the American Dietetic Association,* you would run across several articles in which her name appears as one of the authors.

Although Hulda had climbed several smaller mountains, something was tugging inside Hulda to try something higher. During these years her association with the university students stoked an interest in climbing Mt. Whitney. Whenever she heard them talk of climbing this great mountain, she wondered if it would be possible for her to do it. She wanted to try but didn't know how to get started. Hulda desperately wanted to ask the students if she could go along, but was afraid she wouldn't be able to keep up and would be a nuisance.

"Then in 1962, when I was sixty-six years old, a couple of friends of mine invited me to climb it with them. They were going to try to climb Mt. Whitney and wanted me to go along with them. I felt free to try because I knew they would go at my pace. Furthermore, I camped in the mountains around Loma Linda for ten days and had just climbed Mt. Grayback so I knew I would be ready."

I'd like to stop here and tell you just a little about climbing a mountain of that size. Though Hulda was quite adept at climbing mountains in the 11,000- to 12,000-foot range, she would be attempting to conquer all 14,495 feet of the highest mountain in the continental United States. Though Mt. San Gorgonio is a respectable climb, the additional 2,000 to 3,000 feet of Mt. Whitney are particularly trying. To use a colloquial phrase, it separates the men from the boys. Or perhaps we should say the young from the old. Beyond 7,500 feet, the air gets thinner with each step and you start to feel it. Above 10,000 feet altitude sickness is not uncommon. And many people who have attempted to climb the majestic peak are forced to turn back because physically they just can't handle it. Now at sixty-six years of age, Hulda Crooks was going to give it her first try.

So in August of 1962 Hulda and her two friends started their climb. They began at Whitney Portal, which is ten miles from the summit and hiked to Mirror Lake, four miles up at an elevation of 10,600 feet. They would camp there until the second morning when they would go the remaining six and a half miles to the top. They reached Mirror Lake late that afternoon, gathered wood, built a fire, set up camp, and ate their supper.

The next day was spent in camp but Hulda was up at three the following morning. She wanted plenty of time to reach the top that day. After a quick breakfast of split pea soup, zwieback, dried fruit, and nuts, the three strapped their sleeping bags and tents on their backpacks and by four o'clock were on the trail, using flashlights until daylight. It wasn't long before Hulda started feeling the effects of her high altitude climb.

"As we got higher and higher up the mountain I became more and more tired. It wasn't altitude sickness, I don't think. I was just plain tired. Then, at the twelve-thousand-five-hundred-foot level with three and a half miles to go I was almost too tired to keep moving. Gradually my pace slowed. I feared that I would just have to admit that a sixty-six-year-old woman was too old for such a climb. I cringed when I thought about others telling me with a laugh, 'We told you so.' I was hungry and tired but I thought that eating my lunch might just bog me down. It seemed I was in a real predicament. I was ready to quit. Then I remembered some grapes I had brought along. I had seldom brought along such an unusual indulgence for the trail, but I ate them and revived almost immediately. I felt that I had renewed energy. My tired body was once again ready to climb, so we started again. In a few hours we reached the top. What joy! Happiness! I had made it! I thought I could see forever. It was a tremendous feeling. I now had climbed 'that peak' Sam had pointed out to me almost thirty years before."

That first climb was tough on Hulda, but it was even tougher on some others. On the way up, she and her party came across a man who was having a lot of difficulty. He was leaning against a rock apparently unable to climb any higher. His hiking partner confided to them that his friend was forty-six and might not be able to make it to the top. Then at the summit, they ran across a couple of young hikers who had climbed at nearly twice their speed. They were miserable with headaches and nausea. They had come up faster than their degree of physical fitness could adjust to with comfort. Yet Hulda and her friends, having climbed at a comfortable pace, enjoyed the beauty of their surroundings in comfort.

That first climb had an addictive effect on Hulda, for the following year she couldn't resist and climbed Mt. Whitney again. Her first two trips up the peak had been preceeded by a training hike up San Gorgonio to prepare her leg muscles, lungs, and heart for the more demanding Whitney climb.

When the third year rolled around, Hulda headed for her mountain. Only this time she failed to get her preliminary warm-up trip and could barely make it to the first camp two and a half miles up the trail. However, after a day's rest, her feisty spirit prevailed and she made it to the top. From that point on, she knew any problems she would run into in mountain climbing would not be so much a matter of age as a matter of exercise and conditioning.

Prior to her fourth Whitney trip, Hulda reached the ripe young age of seventy. While doing research for the Dean of Loma Linda University School of Health, she came across articles on running as a means of improving physical fitness. It was brand new to her, and in true Hulda fashion she decided to give it a go.

"I tried it one morning under the stars in my backyard. I figured no one would see me so early in the morning and think that I was out of my mind. However, my renter happened to look out his bathroom window that same morning while shaving and later told me he nearly cut his face when he saw me running around in the backyard. I ran across the yard from one corner to the gate. After one trip back and forth, I was puffing. So that ended my run for the day. But I kept at it and a few days later I was up to two times across the backyard, then three, then four. After several weeks I could do it six times. I was so proud of myself that I decided to measure my prodigious distance. After all, I thought I was really going places with this running. So I stepped it off. Much to my chagrin it was only a sixth of a mile. I felt like a peacock when he drops his tail feathers."

Undaunted, however, Hulda continued. But she was still unsure about taking to the roads.

"After all, I didn't want people to think I had gone nuts. But after several weeks I finally got up enough courage to take to the road. I would run down the hill, about a block. And when I was short of breath, I would just stop a few moments to catch my breath and then run another block. Fearful of injuring my heart, I took it easy. It took six months before I could run a half-mile nonstop."

Reaching the half-mile landmark was no bed of roses for Hulda. At first, she found that it was difficult to maintain a regular running schedule. It seemed that all sorts of little things served as good excuses and reasons for not running on a particular day. She was either too busy, too tired, or too something. Think of it. At an age when most people are satisfied to quietly live out the rest of their lives according to routines they had established throughout the years, here was Hulda trying to find the time to run a half-mile a day. Even though she wasn't too regular at first, she didn't give up. She grew to enjoy the running and found something lacking in her life the days she didn't run. Within six months of that first nonstop half-mile, Hulda was running a half-mile six times a week. After a few months of that, she decided it just wasn't enough of a challenge. So she upped her distance to a mile, and found she could do it rather easily. In fact, her jump from a half-mile to one mile was so insignificant that she started to run a mile each morning at 5:30.

Running that early in the morning, often before it is fully light, caused some problems for Hulda. When you're young it's easy to adjust for hazards in the pavement. A pothole, some loose gravel, or a crumbling curb are easy to skip over. If perchance you stumble, youthful balance takes over and after a couple of strides you're right back on course. But when you're older, it just doesn't work that way. Consequently, Hulda fell several times.

"It's too easy to fall because we are used to walking on smooth surfaces. Older people don't lift their feet as much as younger ones and a little unexpected bump of a half-inch can throw you. All I have to do is catch my toe a little bit and I'll fall. I've fallen four times in thirteen years. But my bones are strong and I haven't broken a hip. I tell people that I bounce pretty good."

Despite the falls and occasional soreness, Hulda continued her running. So when it came time for her to climb Mt. Whitney for the fourth time she decided to forego her preliminary training climb on San Gorgonio. Instead, she figured her running would hold her in good shape. Her reasoning paid off.

She recalls that her fourth Whitney climb, without a preliminary training climb, was "surprisingly easy. My extra exercise paid off."

It would be unfair and somewhat inaccurate to say that Hulda's running simply made her a more efficient mountain climber. What began as a somewhat capricious attempt to improve her physical condition, thus making it easier for her to climb mountains, gradually took on more significant implications. She noticed that running was having a tremendous benefit on her overall health, physical as well as mental. She enjoyed the sense of accomplishment she felt after she completed a run. She liked the way it seemed to get her day off on the right foot. She was also pleased with the effect it had on her lifelong problem of poor circulation.

"For forty-five years I filled hot water bottles to take to bed on cold nights—one at my feet and one on my stomach. I would always have to get up at midnight to refill them. But two years after I started running I became aware that my feet stayed warm even after the weather turned cold. At first I was bothered. I was afraid that my feet were warm due to some low grade infection. I asked my doctor about it, and after a few questions he assured me that this phenomenal change was perfectly all right. He explained that my more vigorous heartbeat was sending a better flow of warm blood to my extremities."

News like that from a physician has a way of making a seventy-two-year-old woman feel as if she could conquer the world. But tragedy struck Hulda's life again. In 1969 her only son, Wesley, died unexpectedly.

"I put him through medical school after Sam died. He was so brilliant. He left three children whom I had to make sure were raised properly. Now I have three grandchildren and two great-grandchildren."

Typically, Hulda was able to turn this tragic experience in her life into something positive.

"I decided to count the happy moments of each day. My son's death was a thorn in my life, but God gave me grace to live with this thorn. I had to battle with disappointment, depression, anger, and frustration. But I recognized the effect of these things on your mental attitude. Disturbed emotions, when fostered, can undo the benefits of the best regulated program. Anger in all its forms— hostility, frustration, jealousy, hatred, wounded pride—as well as fear in its variations of anxiety, worry, depression, and the like sap your life forces. They affect your circulation, upset your digestion, disturb your sleep, raise your blood pressure, and rob you of the joy of living. So I began looking at whatever good came to me be it seemingly ever so little, and I was grateful for it. I thought about the things that met my needs and gave me joy. I lingered over each 'find' with a thankful heart. This grew into a most rewarding habit."

Since this tragedy over a decade ago Hulda has continued her active ways. If anything, she seems to have picked up the tempo a bit. In 1971 she started long backpack trips of a week or more. The next year she crossed the Sierra Nevada range from Sequoia to Whitney Portal, an 80-mile trip. Two years later, she completed the 212-mile John Muir Trail which she had begun in segments five summers ago. Not ready for the rocking chair at eighty-one, she started working on the Sierra Club's registered list of 268 peaks in Southern California. She now has over 50 peaks to her credit, in altitudes up to 11,500 feet.

Hulda has climbed Whitney eighteen times in the past eighteen years. Most of these climbs have been pretty much the same, but her climb of Mt. Whitney in August of 1979 stands out as her most significant one. At the ripe old age of eighty-three, Hulda Crooks was about to become a celebrity, for during this year's climb the NBC Television Network filmed her Whitney trip all the way to the summit. As far as Hulda was concerned, she would just as well have made the climb without them.

Instead of taking the customary seven hours to reach the peak it took ten. All the picture-taking slowed them down. Besides, most of the members of the camera crew (who were considerably younger) just weren't in good physical condition. The delay took its toll on Hulda. She had hardly eaten anything since 2:30 in the morning, yet she didn't feel like eating. She did have that little extra bunch of grapes again, which she ate, but she didn't think it was enough for ten hours. Looking back, she feels she should have taken more fresh fruit along. She still wasn't nauseous, but the long climb, the pressures of the filming, etc., were beginning to have an effect on Hulda. Add to this a rain squall at the base camp and reports of a summit snowstorm. It was enough to dampen the enthusiasm of most of the fellow hikers and film crew. Still, Hulda retained a confident, positive mental attitude on the way up. While most of the people around her were saying the hike could not continue the following day, Hulda's reaction was to keep climbing. She had seen bad weather before and it hadn't stopped her. Sure enough, the rain stopped and the group was able to reach the summit. It was an exciting time not only for Hulda but for the NBC film crew as well.

The celebration was short-lived, however, for on the way down Hulda became nauseated. In addition, her hip was hurting her quite badly. The film crew seemed to breathe a sigh of relief when Hulda decided to pitch camp at the 12,000-foot level and take the last six miles in the morning. All in all it was a most memorable climb, though Hulda feels she can do without the notoriety next time.

You would think walking, jogging, backpacking, and climbing mountains is enough of a fitness program for a forty-year-old, let alone for someone in her eighties. Not for Hulda. After increasing her daily mileage throughout the years, Hulda decided to give the Senior Olympics a try. She was averaging two miles a day six times a week. In 1977 she placed first in the 1,500 meters. She returned in 1978 to totally dominate the Senior track world. First she won the 800 meters with a time of five minutes and forty-eight seconds (5:48). Then she won the 1,500 meters in 10:59. Finally, she won the 5,000 meters in 39:49, establishing a new record for her age group.

In addition to her track competition, Hulda also participates in quarter (6.2 miles) and half (13.1 miles) marathon runs in the Loma Linda area. Naturally, you don't run in a thirteen-mile road race on two miles a day (her customary running distance). Consequently, prior to a longer race, Hulda increases her training mileage up to six miles several times a week. If you are eighty years old and doing what Hulda does, you're bound to attract some attention. As a result, Hulda is a local celebrity in Southern California. People stop and cheer when they see her coming, and more than one individual has told her she is an inspiration.

Her publicity in Southern California has caught the interest of television networks. While I was visiting with her in her apartment she pulled out a scrapbook and showed me pictures of her appearance on "The Tonight Show Starring Johnny Carson." Sure enough, there she was with America's favorite late night talk show host along with Michael Landon and Dinah Shore, whom he had just interviewed before Hulda came onstage. In January of 1977 Hulda appeared on "To Tell The Truth"; in September of 1978, she was on "Good Morning America"; and in January of 1979 she was invited to appear at Detroit's Fisher Building to be a guest on the famous radio program, "Focus." Instead of taking the elevator up to the twenty-first floor that contained the studios of WJR, Hulda walked all the way up via the stairway. This year, she planned to return to Detroit and walk to the top of the Renaissance Center, a newly constructed seventy-story skyscraper. Those plans were scrapped when the security officer refused permission. Spoilsport!

In fact, people seem to be impressed with Hulda wherever she goes. Can you imagine the response she gets along the mountain trails of California? I've done my share of backpacking and I must admit I haven't seen anyone her age hiking over the mountains. One year when she was coming down Mt. Whitney, a young fellow was coming up and when he met Hulda he just bowed and kissed her hand. Another time she met an older man who had heard about her and had also heard she was on the trail that particular day. When he met her he took off his cap and bowed to her. Pretty heady stuff for an overweight farm girl from western Canada, but Hulda takes it in stride and with great modesty. She is pleased her way of life interests people, and often uses these situations as an opportunity to share her views on health and happiness.

Most often, it is the young people that are most impressed by her lifestyle. They are simply fascinated that someone of her generation is out doing things, seeing things, and enjoying life so much. She has a deep concern for today's young people, consequently she carries a little tract to hand out to them explaining what has given her joy in life. She's given out over sixteen hundred of these on the trail. They are always readily accepted.

Her prescription for other people to live well is simple.

"My advice to anyone is to live simply and to be active," she says. "Eat simple food and do something. Don't just sit in front of the TV. Get a hobby. Find a type of exercise that you like and get enough rest." She also encourages young people to take good care of their health.

"If you take care of yourself when you are young, you'll be able to enjoy life when you're older. Exercise makes you feel good. And when your body feels strong you will also undoubtedly feel emotional well-being. Too often people dwell on a small problem until it gets bigger than it really is. They forget to trust the Lord when problems and trials come. You feel much better about yourself and about life when you look for the good things around you."

Looking for the good things around her has kept Hulda alert and active during the years when many people begin to fail both physically and mentally. She retired at age seventy-eight from her position as research assistant. Some retirement. She still works there, but as a volunteer research assistant. She is able to discuss current research on diet and exercise with obvious familiarity. She can quote studies from a variety of sources much like a Ph.D. fresh out of graduate school. In addition, she still runs, she still hikes, she still climbs mountains, and she shows no signs of letting up.

Hulda's zest for life makes an unforgettable impression on anyone. As I sat in her small apartment I knew that my life had been touched by one of God's special people. Her apartment is arranged in such a way that it allows her to enjoy the great outdoors. Her flower gardens are plentiful and reflect her green thumb. Hulda's pleasures are simple. Her lifestyle, sincere and serene. Her openness, her enthusiasm, and her strong convictions impress you—I will never forget her.

Mike McCarrick

Mike McCarrick

Thirteen-year-old Mike McCarrick of Longmont, Colorado, skis, plays football, tennis, and soccer. He swims, wrestles, and mows the lawn. He serves as an altar boy, cooks, and has won scouting awards. He rides a skateboard, bicycle, and horses. When he grows up he wants to be a truck driver and travel around the country with his dog Cuddles. Someday he hopes to water-ski, ice skate, and walk.

That's right, walk. Mike was born with a crippling birth defect called congenital spinal agenesis—a birth defect of the spine. It is a disease which is first cousin to spina bifida, which means a life of total immobility in a wheelchair.

"When Mike was born, the joints of his legs were wrapped around his waist," Mrs. Barbara McCarrick told me as I was sitting in their living room. "He also had severe club feet. The funny thing was I didn't think his condition was that bad when he was born," his mother continued. "When they first brought Mike in I was so groggy nothing really registered. The doctors told me: 'Mike is paralyzed from the waist down. The motor nerves of his legs did not develop at all. He will have no leg movement. Furthermore, he will have no control over his bladder and bowels.' The doctor was explicit and kind. But the prognosis was not good. But I was too out of it to understand the implications of the discussion."

"When I started to think more clearly," Mrs. McCarrick said, "I still wasn't concerned. I figured with all the advantages of medical science the hospital in Denver would correct his problem. I really didn't face the idea that Mike would be in crutches and braces for years and years to come."

Medical science tried to help Mike. Early in his life he underwent a series of more than eight operations. He had extensive therapy. Mike's parents, Barbara and Dick McCarrick, had to drive him four or five times a week down to the Colorado Medical Center in Denver, a drive that's almost one hour long. There his legs were methodically and carefully exercised by a physical therapist.

The doctors continued to caution the McCarricks about entertaining any high hopes, however. Although Mike's health was okay, the medical consensus was that he would spend the rest of his life in a wheelchair. Muscles will only work if they are stimulated by motor nerves. And Mike's nerves did not develop.

When Mike was a baby his paralysis was no problem. Although there were three other children in the family, two girls and a boy, Mike was like any other child. His mom and dad carried him around. But as the months crept by, things changed. With three other children under five in the house, Mike had to fend for himself.

Although each of his legs was in an entire body cast, with a bar between his feet, Mike learned to scoot along the floor to get to his play things. At first he had to do some fancy maneuvering. His legs were immobile. His lower body was nearly twice as heavy as a normal child's because of the body cast. But he soon learned to pull himself along the floor with his upper body. He would reach his arms in front of him and pull himself forward. His legs, body cast and all, would follow. It took him a while to get the hang of it, and the progress was slow, but Mike perfected the physical skill much like anyone else learns an athletic skill. Soon Mike McCarrick could zip all over his house.

By the time he was eleven months old, Mike mastered the skill of pulling himself to a standing position. Once in that position he would try to wiggle to get around the furniture. But he was unable to move or step because the bar between his legs kept him from moving.

Mrs. McCarrick thought that if Mike were in braces he would be able to walk. "I just thought, if he had the right equipment he could do it."

Barbara McCarrick asked the doctors about giving Mike braces. But the doctors felt that Mike should be in a body cast until he was three or four. More surgery was necessary and Mike would soon outgrow the braces. But Barb and Dick McCarrick kept pestering the doctors. They felt that Mike could do it if he was just given the chance. Finally the doctors relented.

Mike's position in these braces (which extended from his chest to his feet) was odd. Because his hips were locked (due to the congenital defect), Mike was bent forward at the waist and his hips were thrust backward. Once in these braces Mike started walking in two weeks with the aid of crutches. Consequently, the doctors performed surgery when Mike was thirteen months old to reposition his hips so he could stand up properly and use the crutches more effectively.

Free of the leg cast and given better designed braces and understanding how to use the crutches, little Mike took off. He leaned against the back band of the brace for support while standing. He taught himself how to use his waist muscles to help move his legs in a swinging fashion with the help of his crutches. In other words, he would first move one leg forward, shift his weight to that foot, and then swing the other one forward. It wasn't graceful, and it wasn't fast. But it worked.

At fifteen months Mike wasn't very tall. [He was so short he could walk under a table.] According to his parents he looked unreal. Since his hips were locked as he walked, he had poor

balance, and fell frequently—sometimes forward, sometimes backward. His head had more bumps than an armadillo's back, so the
doctors fitted Mike with a hockey helmet. He used it for two years
to protect his head.

From ages three to five Mike was just like any other preschooler. "His friends weren't aware that Mike had a defect," the
McCarricks said. "He'd do anything his friends asked. He'd
swing, using sliding boards, and play Tarzan. If Mike got caught
or stuck somewhere, they'd push and pull him through."

One time Mike's mother found him and his friends doing
something which almost gave her gray hair. The McCarricks live
near a mountain runoff which, in the spring, is filled with running
water. The kids had hung a rope across the streambed. Mrs.
McCarrick heard all the squeals and noise coming from the
streambed and wondered what was going on. She walked over to
the bed and there was Mike swinging out across the water with his
crutches hanging on his arms and his braces on his legs. Now that
kind of daredevil behavior is typical of kids and, of course, quite
dangerous. But it was doubly dangerous for four-year-old Mike.
His braces made his lower body extremely heavy and he hadn't
learned to swim yet. If the rope had given way, or Mike had lost
his grip, he would have fallen into the river and probably
drowned. There was just no way that he could have stayed afloat.

Mrs. McCarrick points out that she's not overprotective with
Mike. "I'm just like any other mother with a child who doesn't
have a handicap. When you find other kids doing crazy things they
shouldn't be doing it scares you. You run out and make them quit.
I'm the same way with Mike."

As a preschooler Mike's active lifestyle also caused some other
problems. He often mounted horse swings in the park and rode on
motorcycles. Whenever he assumed a stride position, the separat-
ing of his legs would cause his braces to bend or pop. This meant a
trip back to Denver to be outfitted once more. It also meant a
couple of days in a wheelchair until his braces were fixed or new
ones made.

When Mike would be confined to the wheelchair because of the
necessity for readjusting braces or repairing them, he was a holy
terror. He learned to do what any other active kid would do when

given a wheelchair. He popped wheelies. He raced other kids on bicycles and did some pretty fantastic feats. Today he can go the entire length of a hall just popping wheelies.

With all the trips to Denver, Mike got to be a favorite with the staff. The doctors, nurses, and physical therapists were fascinated with his mobility. I guess in some small way he made them reassess therapeutic and rehabilitative procedures in kids like Mike. They were amazed at his physical abilities. They would take pictures of him roller-skating down the hall in the hospital. Since there were many doctors who visited from other countries, Mike also became a celebrity among the resident physicians, showing these doctors what Mike was capable of doing.

If all of this sounds as though being born without the use of your legs is no big deal, don't kid yourself. A life of crutches, braces, and wheelchairs is one of inconvenience, heartache, embarrassment, and frustration.

Mike's braces had a back band, a band which is a double-edged sword. The brace gives him support but also gives him some nasty sores. With each step, or swing of the leg, his back rubs against the metal and leather. The result is abrasions and blisters that have to be attended to daily.

And then there is the illioloop. Since Mike is paralyzed from the waist down he has very little control over his bladder and bowels. Consequently, he uses a baglike device which helps him hold his wastes. And an active lifestyle is not condusive to wearing one of these contraptions. Many times the bag has broken: an understandable occurrence for illioloop wearers, but embarrassing to say the least.

While the physical problems can be handled with encouragement and understanding, the psychological and family pressures take more work.

Right from the start Mr. and Mrs. McCarrick decided that Mike was to be treated no differently from the rest of his brothers and sisters. He would have to pull his own weight and would have the same responsibilities with respect to chores, behavior, sports, and schooling. And he would have to learn to fend for himself. That idea and attitude is easier said than done. As I sat with Mrs. McCarrick during our interview she told me, "It's hard. You see

Mike struggling to make breakfast, walk behind the lawn mower, and take out the trash. You want to help him. After all, struggling to hold the garbage cans and crutches is not easy. But you know what's best for him, so you make him do it."

"His friends, brother, and sisters treat him equal physically. By the time the other kids on his block figured out Mike was a little different they, like most kids, had already spent half their lives being mad and fighting with each other. So he's been treated on an equal basis. They aren't about to give in just because he's got something wrong with him. It still makes my other son Rick mad if I insist he do a household chore that Mike was supposed to have done. This is good. It makes Mike independent and accountable."

And as we talked I knew that what Mrs. McCarrick was saying was not idle chatter. Mike was busy making breakfast for himself and casually asking his mother and me whether we wanted anything to eat.

The reaction of some people has also been tough. Some kids have called him a "crippled creep." Mike told me, "That really hurt, but I got used to it." Mrs. McCarrick added, "We've worked pretty hard with Mike on this. One time Mike got mad at his cousin and called her a zit face. I reminded Mike how he hated to be called names. I also pointed out that most kids call you names about the thing they see first. And with Mike they don't have to look for a little pimple. Once I saw Mike stare long and hard at a lady who was obese, and I said, 'See, there you are staring and you tell me you don't like everybody staring at you.' People are just naturally like that."

But Mike retorted, "It still hurts . . . the stares hurt."

Self-consciousness hasn't always been a problem for Mike. His mother relates, "I remember when he came home from preschool. He was four, and he told me not one other kid in that whole class wore braces and crutches. He was amazed. I think that the children were fascinated by all his equipment. So they probably asked him a million questions. I feel that was the first time it registered with Mike that he had a handicap."

When Mike got to school his active ways continued. He climbed trees, jumped off the roof into the yard (which meant broken braces), and rode Crazy Cars—those plastic high-wheeled devices little kids ride. But he also wanted to ride a skateboard and a bicycle! So when Mike was ten he pestered his parents for a skateboard for Christmas. At first the McCarricks were against it. "We're not going to spend money on a skateboard," they said. "You'll never be able to use it." But Mike insisted. So on Christmas, 1975, Mike found a skateboard under the Christmas tree. This one had a wide board. A board wide enough for Mike to sit on. But there was another problem. Mike wasn't going to use this board simply as a downhill racer. Instead he pushed himself with his bare hands across the flat pavements of Longmont. Some days he would go in the house with his hands bleeding, but he didn't stop. He'd just go out for some more. So as an aid his parents bought him heavy-duty gloves—which Mike wore to shreds.

Not satisfied with this mundane activity, Mike started to build ramps for more fun and excitement. Eventually he designed a ramp about twelve inches high, which he approaches at breakneck speed under his own power. The board then hits the ramp and takes off for a brief flight in the air.

It's the same thing with Mike's "bicycle." Designed by a friend of the family, it's really a three-wheeled vehicle made up of two inverted bicycle frames. The decision to go with this occurred after Mike wore out three Crazy Cars in six weeks.

The inverted bicycle allows for more stability and strength. It permits him to pedal the bike with his hands and the front wheel is free. He turns to the left by not turning the left crank and by turning the right, causing the bike to make the proper adjustments. This contraption is the rage of the neighborhood. When I visited Mike, however, it was being dismantled for repairs; a young neighbor had wrecked it.

Being a physical young man, Mike's interests have turned to sports. He's learned to swim by using his powerful arm and shoulder muscles to pull him. But because he doesn't wear his braces in the pool, when Mike wants to get out of the water and dive, someone has to carry him to the board, and place him at the proper spot.

When skiing, Mike has special skis on his ski poles. These act as crutches and a source of support that permit him to do downhill skiing.

But his most astounding physical feats are his competition in football, soccer, and baseball. In soccer Mike is the goalie, where he uses his crutches to advantage. He stops the ball with his crutches and "kicks" the ball with it. He's even mastered the skill of holding the crutch and allowing the ball to roll right up the crutch to his arm.

His baseball technique is also unique. When he bats he hits left-handed. He supports his weight on his right crutch and swings his bat with his left arm. When he hits fairly he has someone else run for him, or he uses the bat as a crutch as he runs around the base pads.

While fielding the ball other adjustments must be made. Normally he plays with two crutches and holds the mitt in his left hand. When the ball comes to him in the air Mike drops his left crutch and catches the ball in his hand. He then throws the ball into the air, drops his glove, recatches the ball in his left and throws it to the appropriate infielder.

But his most outstanding physical feat, as far as I'm concerned, is that Mike played seventh grade intramural football—not touch or flag—but real tackle football. When Mike first approached coach Bill Ciochetti about this the coach was hesitant: "I was concerned about his injuring himself, but when I checked with his doctor he told me his only concern was about the other kids hurting themselves on Mike's leg braces. Fortunately this didn't turn out to be a problem."

Ciochetti puts Mike at center "since the center doesn't have to run as much." At the center, Mike used one crutch for support. He also held the other crutch in that same hand. He then leaned over the ball in the customary position, snapped the ball crisply and then blocked charging foes. On defense he played linebacker.

His teammates and opponents showed him no special favors. He hit the dust just like any other football player. And he had to get back up with the aid of his crutches.

Mike played football like everything else he does in life—with hussle and determination. Coach Ciochetti says, "I wish other kids had the desire he has. He's a real go-getter."

Unfortunately, Mike couldn't play when he reached the eighth grade. In seventh grade all his playing was with fellow classmates. Intramurals. But in eighth grade Northeast Junior High plays other schools. The coaches of other schools heard of Mike's desire and playing skills but felt that Mike might get hurt or that his braces might hurt other players. In short, since the other players didn't know Mike, they might be afraid to block or tackle him. Consequently, several schools protested Mike's playing. His coaches suggested that Mike become manager, but he wouldn't have anything to do with that. "It's too much like being water boy."

Mike took this lack of permission to play pretty hard—just as any youngster would. But, according to his mother, it's something he'll have to learn to accept. I'm sure Mike feels some resentment and bitterness over it, but I am equally sure he will get over it. Most kids do.

Unfortunately, his school doesn't have a sport for the fall to complement Mike's abilities. And this has been tough on him.

In physical education classes, however, Mike keeps up with the rest of the crowd. He does practically everything except play basketball. He wrestles, for example. I've coached wrestling and I wondered how he did it. "Simple. I just wait for the guy to come to me. Then I go for his legs and hook him down. I try to do most of the things on the mat." Easier said than done. Of course, Mike does have a few advantages. He wrestles in a relatively lower weight class. Since his leg muscles are poorly developed he carries appreciably less weight. He has one other advantage. His use of crutches and upper body movement has given him fantastic upper muscles for a thirteen-year-old. So he is exceptionally strong for his size, weight, and age.

This combination of upper body strength and lighter legs also has given him another advantage. He is very close to the school record for pull-ups and plans to break it soon.

During my visit to Longmont I drove Mike to school. We chatted about Mike's goals and aspirations; his problems in school, sports, and play. As we drove along he told me he regularly walked to and from school. A four-mile hike—round trip. Like I said, this kid loves activity.

But this love gets him into trouble at times. His halo does slip. Nothing real serious—just typical kid pranks. For example, he likes to trip other kids with one of his crutches. Or deliberately poke someone with them. Some people receive this as antagonism and resentment. Others feel it is simply kids' play. Whatever, I think it's typical of a thirteen-year-old who likes to fool around.

All of this serves to illustrate that Mike is still working through a phenomenal physical handicap. And quite frankly, he cannot do things as quickly and as easily as you and I. He has to consider the pros and cons and whether he can do it or not. You and I might jump right into a game of sports. He has to think for a moment on how he is going to make the proper adjustments. Fortunately, he has become such a physical person that he's able to mesh quite well.

Unfortunately, Mike doesn't excel academically in school. Reading is especially difficult for him. This has presented some problems, obviously, in classwork. No one knows whether his reading difficulty is tied to his birth defect or not. On the other hand, Mike's in the above average classification of mental reasoning in mechanical ability. So his teachers and administrators are not writing him off as a nonlearner. They're just trying to teach him different ways of learning—different ways of carrying information and retaining it.

John Grauberger, principal of Northeast Junior High School where Mike attends, said that he realizes that a good deal of Mike's motivation has been in the area of overcoming physical handicaps. "Mike is handicapped physically and he may be handicapped mentally in terms of certain learning skills. Mike, obviously, chose the area he felt he could develop in. Apparently it has been easier for him to develop the physical than to develop academically. I have very rarely seen him become frustrated in the physical realm. That is surprising. Many times kids who have handicaps such as Mike throw themselves into the mental or academic realm. But Mike did a turnaround. He threw himself into learning how to cope physically. And he's done an excellent job. He really has conquered his physical handicap. Now we must help him academically."

Parents and teachers are now helping Mike in this regard. They want him to overcome some of the psychological aspects of being handicapped, something that for Mike has been very difficult. He knows how to deal with other handicapped people. He's a powerful motivator. He must now be prepared to deal psychologically with the able-bodied population.

"If we can get Mike to start verbalizing his feelings about being handicapped and work with him on directing his energies in a positive manner, he's going to turn into a productive citizen. Simply because he's got lots of good ability. Right now I don't even look at the physical aspects of his handicap. I'm concerned more on how he's reacting to the handicap," said George White, the assistant principal at his school. "I do feel he'll be a success in life. It's just vitally important that we as his teachers understand where we can best channel Mike's abilities and have him develop into a productive citizen. I think Mike can do it. It's just a matter of us all pulling together."

Mike's physical accomplishments have been recognized. He's somewhat of a celebrity in the Colorado region. In 1977 he was named the Colorado Handicap Achiever of the Year and in 1979 the Colorado Easter Seal Poster Boy. He's been photographed with professional football players and the governor of Colorado, to name a few. He's been on local and national TV. "Kid's World," ABC's TV news program for children, did a special on him in the fall of 1979.

But perhaps the award Mike appreciates the most is the plaque with an inscription in leather that says he was the number one ladies' man at Easter Seal's Handicamp—a camp for handicapped children near Georgetown, Colorado.

Of course, all of the above symbolize what is pretty evident when anyone meets him—his indomitable spirit. I casually asked Mike if he ever felt like quitting, and before I could get the words out of my mouth Mike shot back, "Never. No way." His mother added, "Mike's too determined and big-hearted. But he also has soft hands."

"What do you mean, 'soft hands'?" I replied.

"In 1976 he tried to compete in a twenty-mile walkathon. But when he got to seventeen miles he had blisters on his blisters and his crutches were worn down to the nubs. His sister had to drag him out of the race."

Mike had another story: "They made me quit."

In 1978 he went back to another twenty-mile Easter Seal Walkathon and this time made it walking only with his leg braces and crutches. And again this year he competed in a twenty-five-mile bicycle marathon for muscular dystrophy. "The hills are the worst part," says Mike. "My sisters had to tow me up them. But I made it."

Of course, Mike's mother also helped out, by giving him hamburgers along the way and providing him with all the necessary worrying.

Recently Mike has been talking about walking without his braces. The answer is probably somewhere between doubtful and impossible. When the doctors told Mike that his chances of walking were not good, Mike shot back in his upfront, strong-willed manner—"That's a bunch of bull."

But that's Mike. Tell him he can't do it and he will. Tell him it's impossible and he'll figure out a way to make it possible. Challenge him and he'll respond.

Mike feels his mission in life is to show other handicapped people that they can do things if they really want to. "You could get out of that wheelchair and learn to walk if you really wanted to," he told one handicapped friend. And how does he motivate them? "I'll show them that I can do better." Denver Bronco wide receiver Jack Dolbin, the Easter Seal campaign chairman when Mike was chosen their Poster Boy, said, "Overcoming this kind of handicap is not easy. Too many of us fail to realize this. Mike happens to be an outstanding example of courage and accomplishment."

Some people might think that Mike doesn't fit the mold of the other people in this book—that is, he doesn't use a physical activity to help overcome a problem or disability. I disagree. Mike has met the challenge. He has the spirit. Everything, and I mean *everything* he does is a challenge. Getting up off the floor is a challenge. Carrying out the garbage is a challenge. "Walking" to and from school is a challenge.

I realize that many people may have a hard time identifying with Mike. After all, his birth defect is way beyond the imaginations of most of us. We don't like to consider the possibility of trading places with him. Yet one thing is clear: if Mike McCarrick can ski, swim, wrestle, play tackle football, tennis, and soccer, no one has a legitimate excuse not to exercise. NO ONE. Just ask Mike.

Paul Leestma

When Paul Leestma woke up one Friday morning in 1972 with a fever, his mother decided to keep him home. Probably a touch of the flu, she thought. Aspirin and rest. When she took her son's temperature again a few hours later, she became a bit more concerned: 103 degrees. She called their doctor, then took him into his clinic later that morning.

Paul felt a little dizzy as he was putting his shirt back on in the little examination room. His arms felt a little stiff as he buttoned the collar. The doctor was smiling.

"Well, Paul, I can't be sure until I get the results of the blood tests back from the lab, but it looks to me like you might have infectious mono-nucleosis."

"That's just great," thought Paul. He remembered how one of his friends had mono and missed the entire track season. "I hope I don't feel this awful *all* the time," he said to the doctor, more in the form of a question.

"Oh . . . I don't suppose you will. Usually the fever lasts for about a week. Then, you just have to take it easy—get plenty of rest—for about four to six weeks. But let's not rush things. Why don't you come back on Monday?"

"Sure, Doc," said Paul as he hopped off the examination table. And then he added, "What if it's not mono?"

"Well, could be a lot of things," his doctor responded cheerfully. His reassuring manner made Paul feel better already. He thanked the doctor and, reaching for his coat, walked out to the waiting room.

"Mom, Dr. Thomas wants to see you. I'll wait in the car."

On Monday, the fever was the same. Paul still felt pretty lousy, but something else developed which really bothered him. He couldn't raise his arms above his head. When he got to the doctor's office, his physician wasn't smiling.

"Mrs. Leestma," he began, as Paul and his mother sat down in his spacious office. "The tests came back negative, so we can rule out mono. The stiffness in his arms concerns me a little. I think we'd better have Paul admitted to the hospital so we can run a few more tests. I'll call down and have a room ready. I think you'd better take him in right away."

Paul and his mother said little as they drove from the doctor's office. They stopped at their small, frame house in West Paterson, New Jersey, to pick up the necessary robe, slippers, toothbrush, etc. Paul had no idea how long he would be staying, so he also picked up a couple of issues of *Sports Illustrated,* and his math book. In the somewhat unique thinking of a seventeen-year-old, Paul was relieved. He hadn't even begun working on the list of problems that were due Wednesday. Now he had a decent excuse. He smiled at this unexpected solution, then winced as he tried to pull his hat on over his head.

"I wonder what's wrong with my arms?" he thought.

While his mother was giving the admitting secretary the necessary information, Paul passed the time by reading one of the several month-old magazines that always clutter waiting rooms in the medical profession. He was wondering whatever happens to the new issues when a tall, attractive nurse approached pushing a wheelchair.

"Mr. Leestma?" she asked, smiling.

"That's me." Paul remembered all the stories about cute nurses and thought a few days in the hospital might not be so bad after all.

His frivolous daydreaming came to an abrupt halt as the elevator door opened. No one had to tell him that ICU meant Intensive Care Unit. Surely, he thought, there must be a mistake. Or perhaps the route to his room went through the intensive care section. His mind was racing. He had a bundle of questions. He felt dizzy. He was scared.

"Just put your things in that closet, get into your pajamas, and make yourself comfortable. Will you need any help?"

The nurse was pulling the curtains that would provide the privacy she knew most seventeen-year-old boys desired. She also knew what his answer would be.

"Ah . . . no, that's all right," he lied. His arms were really stiff and beginning to hurt, but he wasn't about to ask for help in getting undressed.

"Okay," she smiled. "In case you need anything, just push that button there by your bed. Your mom will be up in just a few minutes."

What Paul thought would be a two- or three-day stay in the hospital turned into fifteen long days. It took a week before the staff of physicians and consultants were able to pinpoint the nature of his illness. During that week, Paul gradually lost the feeling in his arms and chest. His hands and feet tingled constantly, and to his horror, he felt his upper body slowly becoming paralyzed.

The doctors called it Gullian-Barre Syndrome. His doctor told Paul that it is a virus that eats away at the nervous system, resulting in paralysis. It's a lot like polio. With early detection, proper treatment, and a little luck, the paralysis is temporary. Without those, it can lead to spending the rest of your life in an iron lung. Or death. Paul had good reason to be scared.

So how does a seventeen-year-old—rugged, popular, athletic—handle the possibility of lifelong paralysis?

"Sure I was scared. In fact, I was scared to death. I had asked a lot of questions and knew that the virus can paralyze your diaphragm. When that happens, they put you in the iron lung. Well, they were monitoring my lung capacity constantly, and I knew why they were doing it. I watched it go from four and a half liters to two and a half liters. But the funny thing was that even though I knew what could happen, I was still worried about making the track team. I was really looking forward to my senior year of track."

Whether that's typical of teenagers, I'm not sure. I know one thing, however. That's typical of Paul Leestma. The guy is simply not a quitter. Even while in the hospital facing possible paralysis, he was thinking about coming off the final turn in the quarter-mile and heading for the finish.

Finally, the oxygen intake started to increase, and some of the feeling returned to his limbs. While he was not out of the woods, his doctors felt he was substantially improving. They sent him home, but told him he would not be able to return to school for the rest of the year. They also told him to forget about track. He would not be able to run again for a year, at least.

When Paul got home, he was in pretty bad shape. He was in constant pain. His body developed shingles. He was given codeine and Demerol to fight the pain. Consequently, he was groggy most of the time. He was clearheaded enough, however, to decide two things: he would return to school and finish his senior year with his class, and he would run track in the spring. When he told me this, I thought the same thing: too much codeine.

At first, there was little Paul could do about either goal. Eventually, however, he was able to make some progress.

"My body was so weak I was vulnerable to anything. I would sleep sixteen hours a day, then lay around in a groggy stupor for the other eight hours. It was an effort just to sit up, but I started by trying to stand up."

Tossing his covers off him, and fighting for balance, Paul would swing his legs out of bed and work at "rehabilitating" himself. Once in this position, he would struggle to his feet, and stand for thirty seconds before falling back onto his bed, drenched in sweat. After doing this for a few weeks, he graduated to standing and moving his arms up and down. Soon he was able to walk slowly for a few steps.

His doctor was amazed, and gave him clearance to return to

school. The total time missed was only two and a half months, far less than the original prediction. Since he had had a tutor come in twice a week, he wasn't too far behind. Paul returned to school with one thing on his mind: get ready for track season.

Fortunately, his body was in far worse shape than his mind. With a little help and understanding from his teachers, Paul was able to catch up quickly in the classroom. On the track, it was a different story.

"The doctor told me to wait a year before I started running again, but I just didn't believe him. I remember the first time I tried to run. I was feeling pretty good—had been walking a lot better, and even tried to jog a little. So one day I put my running shoes on, and took off for a five-mile run. I made it for a half-mile, then collapsed. I mean I literally collapsed. I couldn't believe it."

Paul picked himself up and walked back to school. He began to wonder if he would really be able to run track in the spring. In the fall, before the disease struck, he used to be able to breeze through a five-mile run, but now he could barely make a half-mile. And he was only jogging.

"But I just kept at it. I couldn't see any sense in just lying around, so I tried to do something everyday. I just wanted to get back into shape. I was in top physical condition before this happened, and that's what I was trying for."

When track season rolled around, Paul felt he was ready. He had been out of the hospital for four months; he had been training for one month. In their first meet, his coach put him in the slow heat of the quarter-mile. He was glad to have a chance to prove himself, even though he had never had to run in a slow heat before. The gun went off, and by the time he rounded the first turn, Paul knew he was out of it. By the time he rounded the final turn, he knew just how *far* out of it he was. He was dead last.

The rest of the season was a battle against the damage done by two and a half months of total inactivity. Once, his coach suggested he try the half-mile. It wasn't his event, but the longer distance might be better than the quick pace of the quarter. The advice proved disastrous.

"By the time I came around the first lap, I don't think anyone thought I would finish. I was dead last and really hurting. My time was a slow 2:43 and I felt like dying."

Occasionally, he would jump in the 100-yard dash, figuring the margin of defeat would be less noticeable. That, too, brought discouragement as he fought to stay ahead of girls who had entered.

Gradually, Paul's time improved and he started passing other runners. He recalls with pride occasions when he would finish ahead of runners from other teams. Their teammates would chide them for being beaten by "a cripple."

I would like to tell you that Paul went on to lead his team to the state championships. Perhaps we could throw in a few medals and trophies, and say he broke the school record in the quarter. I'd like to tell you that, but I can't. Paul never regained his status as the top quarter-miler on his track team. The best he could do was run a sixty-second quarter, not even good enough to place in a meet. While Paul overcame the disabling effects of Gullian-Barre Syndrome, his story doesn't have a Cinderella ending. Yet. For you see, Paul's story doesn't end here.

Paul finally *did* regain his speed and endurance and competed as a top 220 and 440 man in college. His time of 51.0 for the 440 and 22.4 in the 220 were good enough to place him third in each event in the New Jersey State College Championships. His coach at Trenton State approached him after his senior year and suggested he try some distance running.

"He knew that unless a sprinter is world class, there is little point in continuing training. I think he wanted to introduce me to the lifelong activity of road running."

He succeeded. Paul trained for the Charleston 15-Mile Road Race. He worked all summer on developing the endurance necessary for distance running. Along the way, he started to enjoy his long, quiet training runs. He found it much more enjoyable than the grueling interval work he experienced as a quarter-miler.

"I ran in that road race and did fairly well, considering I had only trained for a couple of months. From that point on I was hooked. I increased my training and jumped into every road race I could find."

As his training increased, he toyed with the idea of a marathon. Once, he decided he would just run along with a friend of his in the Jersey Shore Marathon. His only goal was to finish. When he crossed the line in two hours and fifty minutes, he knew what he would be doing the following April. To a distance runner, the Boston Marathon held each April is the World Series, the Super Bowl, and the Stanley Cup all rolled into one event. To qualify for a chance to compete in the run from Hopkinton to Boston, a runner has to have completed a marathon in less than three hours. The Jersey Shore Marathon was Paul's ticket to Boston. Now for some serious training.

The first thing he did was increase his mileage. His daily running schedule resulted in about fifty miles a week of long, slow distance running. That wasn't enough. He jumped to ninety miles a week and tried to get in some speed work once a week. The people around his hometown were used to seeing Paul pounding the pavement all winter. His stride was strong. His pace was deliberate. He had come a long way from finishing dead last in his high school days. With Boston looming in his mind, he found little difficulty in motivating himself to train.

Fate has an unkind way of interrupting the plans of men and women on their way toward a goal, and Paul was not immune. One night, while Paul was working as manager of a local dairy, he noticed a young boy in the store. The boy approached the counter, stuck a small gun at Paul, and demanded the contents of the cash register.

"The gun was small, and the kid was only about sixteen years old, so I didn't take him too seriously."

He grabbed the gun away from the would-be robber with little difficulty, but didn't notice the other boy aiming at him. As he struggled with the first boy and chased him toward the door, four shots greeted him. One hit the ceiling. One tore through his right thigh. The next grazed his face. Another ripped into his chest, an inch above his heart. He fell to the ground, blood rushing from his wounds to form a warm, dark puddle.

"At first, I felt no pain, but I was really scared. I looked down toward my leg and saw my jeans were covered with blood. I saw where the hole was, and I knew it was close to a large artery. So I grabbed one of our plastic bags and wrapped it around my leg like a tourniquet. Then I saw that my shirt was also covered with blood. You can't believe how weird it feels to see a hole in your shirt just above your heart. I just lay back and waited for help."

Fortunately, both a doctor and a nurse were in the store at the time, and they provided emergency treatment. The doctor put Paul into his car and rushed him to the hospital. While slumped in the backseat in the nurse's arms, Paul really began to get frightened.

"The pain set in and I started to cough. All I could think about was all the westerns I had seen where a guy gets shot, coughs a little, then dies. I thought, Oh no, I'm not going to make it."

Even though getting shot twice is serious by anyone's standards, Paul was lucky. No serious damage was done internally by the chest shot. The damage to the thigh was more serious. While the bone wasn't broken, the large quadricep muscle was severely shredded.

The Boston Marathon was just three months away. Naturally Paul's first question was, "When can I start running again?" His physician was rather conservative. He explained to Paul the severity of the leg wound. He told him that since the quadricep was the largest muscle in the leg, it would take time to heal. The final word was less than encouraging: no running for three months!

That just wasn't good enough for Paul Leestma. He still thought he had a chance at Boston. He visited a friend of his who also happened to be a sports podiatrist. He knew he was pushing his luck a bit, but he had to try. He asked his friend for a second opinion. Fortunately, he got his news. He could start running again in three weeks. He could hardly wait.

Three weeks to the day from the night he was shot, Paul laced on a pair of running shoes and started on a three-mile loop. Three miles was far below his regular daily distance, but he knew he had to make up for the three-week layoff. Within three hundred yards he was in trouble. His chest hurt, his wind was short, his wounded leg was on fire. He quickly slowed to a turtle's pace. As he struggled back to his apartment, he checked his watch: thirty-one minutes!

"Damn!" he thought. "That used to be a warm-up in eighteen minutes."

He was discouraged. He was ashamed. He was upset. The question, "Why me?" continually crossed his mind. Things were going so great. His training was progressing rapidly and his confidence had been building. If only he had stayed behind the counter when the robbers entered the store. If only he had seen the other attacker with the gun. If only he had skipped work that night. Now this! And where had it gotten him? They hadn't even caught the kids who put him in this condition. As he unlocked the door to his apartment, he thought of quitting, but only for a moment. By the time he got out of the shower, he was ready to fight again. He decided he was not out for the count yet. Paul Leestma was used to obstacles. He knew only one way to get by them: buckle down and work harder!

Progress was slow. At first, he could do no more than three miles at a time. In fact, there were some days he could not run at all. Time was running out. Boston was just over nine weeks away. Most marathoners were hitting about 90–100 miles a week by then, compared to Paul's 15–20. I can assure you, 15–20 miles a week just isn't enough mileage for a person to complete a marathon. On that type of training schedule, most people wouldn't even finish. It looked hopeless to everyone but Paul. He just kept right on training.

Eight weeks prior to the marathon, Paul had managed to increase his daily runs to four or five miles. His leg was still tight, but it seemed to be coming along well. His confidence was returning as he outlined his plans for the remaining two months. He figured he could get up to eight miles a day within a week or so. Then it would be a race against the calendar to see if he could accumulate enough mileage to give him the base he needed to complete the 26.2-mile "marathon of marathons."

On his way home from work one night, tragedy struck once again. While traveling about 45 mph around a turn, an oncoming car swerved into his lane and hit Paul's car head on. Though both cars were totaled, Paul's small foreign car received the worst damage. So did Paul. He was rushed to the hospital, unconscious. When he awoke, he felt as if he had been dragged behind a moving freight train. His ribs were dislocated. His nose was broken. There were several cuts and bruises covering his body. Worse, a stress fracture on his right femur showed up on the X-rays. Though it was only a thin, hairline mark on the X-ray, it looked as if the Boston would have to wait for another year.

"Up to this point I had always been pretty positive. Even after the shooting, I still thought I could make it in time for Boston. But when I woke up in that hospital bed, I literally gave up. I just didn't think it was feasible. I was depressed and mad, and decided Boston was out of the question."

For the first time, Paul seemed to be defeated by his problems. He felt awful, and didn't even want to think about running. But he had friends, and they were right there at his bedside offering encouragement. One in particular was his fiancée, Jill Case.

"After the accident, he was pretty down. He didn't think he would be able to run in Boston. He didn't even want to talk about running, but we just pestered him about it and told him he'd be out and running in no time. It seemed to bring him back into a more positive frame of mind."

Indeed it did. Once again, his doctor said no running for at least a month. Once again, that advice fell on deaf ears. He was released from the hospital at ten o'clock in the morning. That afternoon, he was running.

"It was awful. While my leg hurt pretty badly, the worst, believe it or not, was my nose. With every step, the jarring sent pain streaking up into my forehead. I thought I was going to die. But I was just glad to be running again."

With only seven weeks remaining, Paul pushed himself unmercifully. Every morning before dawn, he would drag himself out of bed, get dressed, and go out on his training run. It would take a couple of miles before his leg would loosen up, but by then, his head ached from the nose injury. By the time he was finished, he was in agony.

"Most of the time, when I finished my run I would tell myself to quit. I would swear I'd never run again, but the next morning, for some reason, I would roll out of bed and give it another try. I'm not really sure why, except I had this goal to run at Boston."

Finally the day arrived, and Paul was just another face in the crowd of eight thousand-plus runners waiting to get started. Mentally, he thought he was ready. Physically, he was not as sure. When the gun went off, however, he shoved all doubts to the back of his mind and took off on the 2:44 pace he had decided upon earlier.

"I felt pretty good at the start, and for the first few miles, but then my ribs started to hurt. By the time I reached twenty miles they were restricting my breathing. I started to have doubts again about finishing."

But Paul kept running.

"At this point, I think I just got stubborn. I was going to finish no matter what happened. I'd driven all the way up to Boston. I'd taken a week's vacation. I had a lot of people back home that would ask me how I did. The last thing I wanted was to have to say 'I dropped out.' So I just refused to quit."

And here's where the happy ending comes. Paul not only finished, but he managed to get under that magic three-hour mark. His official time was 2:54, only four minutes slower than his "healthy" marathon the previous fall. Physically, he was devastated. Emotionally, he was on top of the world.

"It was great. After what I'd been through, you can't believe how good it felt to see that finish line. For once, I reached a goal."

Paul's story continues. He has since opened up a running supply store in Princeton, New Jersey. Without having to worry about being shot or involved in an auto accident, he ran a 2:44 marathon in seventy-eight degree heat in Washington, D.C. And now he's set his sights on the 1984 Olympics.

I don't like to make predictions, but I'm known for handing out free advice. Given Paul Leestma's past record against seemingly insurmountable odds, when the next challenge rolls around, put your money in his corner.

Bob Abels

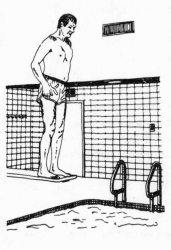

Robert Abels

I want to tell you Bob Abels's story in the worst way, but I'm not sure I can. Bob's got a great story, but I don't think anyone will ever hear the entire thing. I know we will never hear it from Bob. Because he can't talk. The reason he can't talk is that he can't hear. And if that isn't enough of a problem to deal with, Bob can't see either. Yet he is one incredible individual.

I flew to Milwaukee one cold day in December to interview Bob and discovered it's tough talking with him. Tough, but not impossible. After being with Bob, you don't feel like using that word impossible anymore. Just about everything he does is impossible.

I heard about Bob from Anne Kufus, director of services at the Milwaukee YMCA. She told me that they had a guy who regularly came to their Y to swim, dive, and exercise.

"But," she warned, "you're going to have a rough time interviewing him."

She was right. It wasn't until I walked into the lobby of the Y before I thought about how I would "talk" to Bob. I couldn't use my voice because he couldn't hear me. I couldn't use sign language or write him notes because he couldn't see any of it. And how would he answer my questions (assuming I could ask them somehow) since he couldn't talk? I was just about to panic when Anne came to my rescue.

She told me that Bob would extend one of his hands, palm up. I was to grasp it with one of mine and trace the letters of my question on his outstretched palm with one of my fingers. If he could "read" the question, he would nod his head, then reach for an ever-present pad of paper in his shirt pocket. Slowly, almost painstakingly he would place a pencil against the paper and attempt to print his answer.

I tried it and quickly discovered it could take days to interview him in his manner. First, it took a long time just to get one question printed out on his palm, so that he understood it. If you don't believe me, try it sometime with a friend. Second, his written answers, though carefully scratched out on the paper, were almost unintelligible. (See sample on following page.)

Now stop and think about that for a minute. As far as handicaps are concerned, none is particularly attractive. I generally think total loss of movement as being, perhaps, the most devastating. Then I met Bob. Run through yesterday's activities, and tell me how many things you could have done if you were blind, deaf, and unable to talk. What would you do when the phone rang? Maybe you could find it from memory, but what would you do when you picked up the receiver? You couldn't say anything. But wait a minute; how did you even know it rang? You can't hear, remember? Simply living a normal, day-to-day existence is a challenge to Bob Abels, but one that he has met in a remarkable way.

And yet, we may never know how remarkable Bob's story is. In the course of several weeks I put my best detective skills to

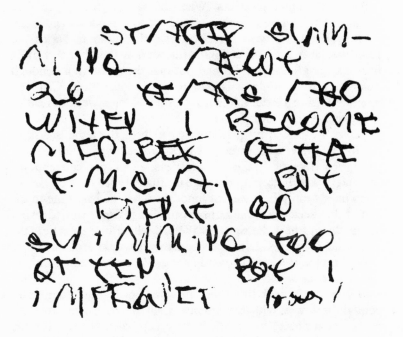

work trying to unravel the details about him. It's not that he's particularly secretive, because he's not. He has extreme difficulty in speaking, and just isn't able to communicate effectively though he tried harder than anyone I've ever interviewed.

Let me give you an idea of what I mean. Anne advised that it would be best if I wrote my questions down and mailed them to her. So, I typed up a list of twenty-seven questions and mailed them off to Milwaukee. When Anne received them, she taped them to Bob's locker at the Y. Remember, I hadn't contacted him yet. How could I? So when he found an envelope containing three pages he rushed up to Anne's office to find out what was going on. Anne wrote in his palm that some guy was writing a book and wanted to include some things about him. Bob smiled and left.

His first stop was the public library where he sought out an old friend, John Huber. John is the director of the Library for the

Blind and is often called upon to transcribe letters into Braille for Milwaukee's blind residents. When he saw the three pages he groaned, but assured Bob they would get to it as soon as possible.

It took about a week for Bob to get the questions back from John, which is no slam at John's fine staff at the library. I did a little checking locally and found out that there just aren't enough volunteers to provide assistance to people like Bob. Can you imagine getting a letter in the mail, then waiting a week to read it? It happens to Bob all the time.

Once Bob got my questions transcribed, the tedious task of typing the answers followed. He uses a special typewriter that has the raised dots of Braille on the keys, but types conventional characters. The bottom of the page is usually typed over on two or three lines simply because he cannot see when he has come to the end of the sheet. Also, the right margin is a bit unorganized. After all, he doesn't hear the signal of the bell telling him he is near the end of the margin. While his typed answers would probably make my old typing teacher roll over in her grave, it represented close to three hours of work!

I was really moved by those answers, not so much with their content as I was with the attempt itself. I noticed he used the exclamation point (!) a lot. At first I was puzzled. Then it hit me. This was his only way of talking, and I think he wanted to make sure I was listening. Just as we raise and lower our voices, Bob was trying to do the same. In a way, Bob was shouting at me.

His answers shed some light on his background and his present activity. But I knew there was a lot between the lines that I needed to know. That's why I hopped a plane to Milwaukee, and even though we didn't get much "talking" done, I wasn't disappointed because I got to see Bob in action.

To watch Bob swim really isn't that spectacular, especially if you are unaware of his handicap. And unless you watch very closely, you just wouldn't notice anything out of the ordinary. In the pool, he would pass for any other tall, well-built man in his late thirties. (I learned later that Bob is closer to being in his early fifties than his late thirties. Obviously, he takes good care of himself.) He gets into the pool with little difficulty and starts swimming a strong overhand crawl stroke. Back and forth. Lap after lap. The tempo of his stroke never changing. His head turning regularly to grab a breath of air. He doesn't appear to labor, but swims smoothly, effortlessly.

I watched for forty minutes and expected him to climb out when he turned over on his back and continued for the backstroke. After forty minutes of that, he rolled over on his stomach and pulled off an energetic butterfly stroke for ten minutes. The guy has amazing endurance! Naturally, I thought that was neat, but the diving was the real treat.

So much of diving depends on sight that it's incredible Bob would even attempt it. I caught myself holding my breath as he approached the two steps leading up to the board—a board that did not have a protective handrail. I was really nervous watching him take those steps up and then out onto the board. Most blind people have a keen sense of hearing and rely on that for guidance. Bob doesn't have that advantage, but he crept out to the very tip of the board. Once he got there, he stood for what seemed an interminable length of time. Then, with a mighty leap, he sailed out over the surface of the water and cleanly entered in a dive that was as well-executed as any I've ever seen.

What intrigued me was the way he just let himself float up to the surface, letting himself drift until he hit the buoyant lane marker. When he found that, he seemed to know exactly where he was. He turned and swam directly back to the edge of the pool where the ladder was. For fifteen or twenty minutes he repeated the process.

To get a feel for the enormity of Bob's accomplishments, try diving with your eyes closed the next time you visit a swimming pool. It's really a scary experience. There is that nagging doubt that you may be diving off into oblivion. Or into an empty pool. Or at least onto another swimmer. Remember, he can't hear someone shout, "Hey, wait a minute; someone's right under the board." But Bob repeats the process over and over and seems to thrive on the thrill.

Frankly, I can't see why someone who is blind needs any more thrills or excitement. It would seem they have enough. Yet Bob faces the challenge of living in modern society on his own, with very little assistance. While many sighted people are afraid to venture out on a city sidewalk after dark, Bob travels all over Milwaukee on foot. And it's always dark for him. He lives alone in an apartment and refuses to be confined by his handicap. And yet his world of silence and darkness never releases its frightening grip. And it never will.

Bob had difficulty communicating the reasons for his handicap, so I snooped around to try and find the answer. It would have helped to have both Dick Tracy and Scotland Yard, for Bob is pretty much alone in this world. His father died when he was a youngster, and his mother passed away several years ago. His brothers and sisters are all deceased, and no one seemed to know of any living relatives. Except for a cousin. Imagine my delight when Mrs. Irma Fowler answered the phone and said, "Yes, I practically raised him when he was young."

She told me that Bob was born a healthy, normal boy, but they began noticing he didn't respond to sounds very well when he was about two years old.

"Some thought he was just slow or something, but I sensed that he just didn't hear very well," said Irma. "When we talked to him, he hardly noticed, unless you looked directly at him."

Soon it was quite obvious that young Bob had a hearing problem, and a local physician suggested it could be corrected with relatively simple surgery. However, Bob's mother had staunch religious beliefs and would not consent to the operation.

By the time he was to enter the sixth grade, Bob was totally deaf. Prior to that, Bob was involved in a backyard accident that affected his vision. As kids are wont to do, Bob and his playmates were throwing stones. Not really at each other, but just throwing them for the fun of it. A sharp stone accidentally struck Bob in the face and he went screaming home to his mother. He was bleeding and unable to see. Try explaining to a four-year-old why he can no longer see. Young Bob was frantic, but within a few days his eyesight returned.

Gradually, however, his eyesight worsened. To this day, no one is sure of the exact cause. It was evident to all that Bob would never be able to see very well again, so plans were made to send him to a workshop for the blind to teach him skills necessary for survival. Up to this point, Bob had attended a special school for the deaf. He had learned to cope with his inability to hear, but his gradually deteriorating vision bothered him. Imagine the anxiety of knowing you are slowly going blind and there is nothing that can be done about it.

While working at the workshop for the blind Bob developed an amazing ability to work with his hands, a facility that is very helpful to him to this day. However, he also developed an allergy that affected his nervous system. Whether or not this caused his blindness is only speclatin, bt Bob blievs th conditions in the workshop contributed to the problem.

"I never had allergies before I started working, then all of a sudden I developed this problem," he wrote.

Then, at the age of twenty-two, Bob woke up one morning to complete blackness. What little vision he had previously enjoyed was gone. For the rest of his life, Bob would have to learn to live without the advantage of hearing, speaking, and now seeing.

Bob's an independent guy, and one of the first things he did after losing his sight was travel to New York City. He had heard of an institute there that helped teach the blind how to get around better, so he hopped on a bus and went to the Big Apple. Now I have good vision and hearing, and I can talk my way out of a lot of jams, but I still have difficulty getting around New York unless I'm with someone who knows the ropes. Maybe I should take Bob along next time, because he got along just fine. No escort. No seeing-eye dog. Just his cane and a lot of courage. He never asked any of his friends for help, but just went and got the training he needed, then returned to Milwaukee. A spokesman at Milwaukee's Services for the Blind who has worked with Bob confirmed this trip and added, "We were all pretty much amazed by it."

Throughout his teenage years and early adult life, Bob was quite active physically. Even though he found certain skilled sports difficult because of his poor vision, he participated in wrestling and track at the school for the deaf. After moving to Milwaukee, Bob began dropping in at the YMCA to lift weights. After ten years of weightlifting he developed quite a strong upper body, but began having chronic low back pain. Still, he felt the need to continue some form of exercise, so he made a visit to the pool. He was immediately hooked.

"Swimming is really enjoyable for me. I feel so fine after a good, long swim. I also find it relieves the unbelievable strain in my muscles as the result of the chronic back pain. When the weather is too bad to go to the pool, I really miss it."

I talked with one of the life guards at the pool when I visited Bob. He told me that Bob is usually quite regular in attendance. In fact, he has been there longer than some of the present workers and he is a far better swimmer than many of the regular members. His physical independence has caused some humorous experiences. Like the time a new locker room attendant was on duty. Bob had just come in to the locker room when the attendant asked him for his card. Naturally, he got no response from Bob. After asking him again, this time in a much louder voice, he realized Bob might be deaf. So he tried sign language, but to no avail. He called upstairs to the main desk to find out what to do. They said, "Oh, that's just Bob Abels. If you want to talk to him, just write in his hand."

So that's exactly what the locker room attendant did. He grabbed a pen, walked over to Bob, and literally tried writing on his hand. Bob pulled his hand back and then almost collapsed with laughter. Soon the attendant realized his mistake and was laughing, too.

Bob's swimming is only a part of his return to normal life. He loves to be around people and entertains lavishly in his apartment.

"Bob is a gourmet cook," says John Huber. "He invites people over to his apartment and treats them to a real great evening. He does the whole thing with cocktails, hors d'oeuvres, and two or three main courses. And he's a real snappy dresser, too." He is able to do all these things because everything in his apartment has Braille labels—the stove, refrigerator, the washing machine. It's set up so that he can do anything, but he doesn't just retreat there to escape the challenge of the outside world.

John Huber told me that Bob regularly stops by the library. One of the things he always does is pull one of the encyclopedias off the shelf and begin to read it. John thinks that Bob has read through at least one entire set of the encyclopedias which are transcribed in Braille. He often comes into the library to ask John to transcribe a new recipe so he can try it to impress his friends. In fact, just before I called John, Bob had come by to have John look up plans for building a special cake-cutting device for the blind. Obviously, if you can't see, it's pretty difficult to cut a cake. So

John and Bob looked up in a resource book and found a special device that looks like spokes coming out from the hub of a wheel. Once he explained the device to Bob, they made calls all over town to try and find the materials so that Bob could build one. Sure enough, Bob gathered all the materials and went home to his workshop and built one.

In addition to entertaining others, Bob loves to attend dances. He regularly visits special dances for the blind held at the Badger Home for the Blind in Milwaukee. His landlord tells me that Bob is just like any other renter. In fact, he's probably better. If he has any problem with plumbing or the electricity, he fixes that himself. He has never had to call for assistance to do anything. Furthermore, Bob is a man about town.

"He has all the bus routes memorized and visits any part of the city he wants," said Huber. "He carries a white cane, and a small sign. When he wants to cross a street, he raises the sign which tells others that he is deaf and blind and would like some assistance."

In answering one of my questions regarding other types of physical activity, Bob's answer really threw me.

"Sometimes a few of my very nice friends take me to the lake in the summer to water-ski."

Now that certainly must have been an exaggeration, I thought. Swimming in a pool is one thing. Even the diving seems pretty courageous for someone who's blind. But being pulled along at 20 to 30 mph behind a boat, not seeing where you're going or when to let go? Not being able to hear instructions? No way! Yet when I checked with Mrs. Fowler, John Huber, and his landlord, all three said, "Sure"—as if such things were commonplace for Bob.

As I sat there by the pool watching Bob, I couldn't help wondering what Bob would like to tell me if he had the freedom of conversation. The typed answers to his questions were adequate, and the attempt at a personal interview was helpful. But these just served to tantalize my curiosity further. I wanted to know what drove this young man to venture out into the cold winter air just to swim in the pool. I wanted to ask him why he dove off into a blackness not knowing what lay ahead—or below. I wanted to ask him why he lived alone instead of at the Badger Home where he would have plenty of people to take care of him whenever he needed help. I wanted to ask him a lot of things, but all I could do was watch. As I watched, I counted the laps and made some quick mental calculations. Bob swam the crawl stroke for over sixty-nine hundred feet, well over a mile. When he flipped over to his backstroke I kept counting. He went over a half-mile. Then came the grueling butterfly stroke. He struggled through about a quarter-mile, then came to a rest at the end of the pool.

I don't think he was aware of me watching him, yet I think I saw the answer to all my questions about Bob as he hung to the edge of the pool for a moment. In that brief span of time, I caught a glimpse of a satisfied grin. That grin seemed to be saying, "Isn't it great to be alive!"

Bob may not be able to see. He may not be able to hear. His mental faculties may be a bit lax due to the disadvantages he faced educationally. But Bob Abels has a lot going for him. He has, perhaps, the best excuse for letting others fight his battles for him. Yet he hasn't learned how to quit. He has faced the ultimate challenge and won.

Jane Tubbs

Jane E Tubbs

The book was finished. My secretary had the manuscript and was typing the final draft. My wife and I were discussing the excitement and satisfaction of another book finished. As we were talking, I heard J. P. McCarthy, a Detroit radio personality say, "Jane Tubbs is my 'Winner of the Day.' Jane—age twenty-three—a fine Open Class—that's top amateur—racquetball player from Costa Mesa, California, will be playing in Michigan this weekend. She was struck down with a stroke ten months ago. Now she's on the comeback trail. Tonight she'll be playing in her first tournament since the stroke. A stroke so devastating that she had to learn to crawl, walk, and run before she could play racquetball once more. Jane Tubbs, I salute you as my winner."

A bell rang inside me. I had a gut

feeling that Jane's story should be in this book. What made it even more appealing was that she was supposed to be playing in Michigan that weekend. I'd promised my wife no more plane trips, so the interview seemed to be convenient. I decided to pursue it.

I rushed to the phone and called the radio station. J. P. had left the studio and would not be back until later that day. No one at the studio, including the sports department, knew where he got the information.

I called our local YMCA to find out if anyone there knew where a racquetball tournament was being held. The local physical director didn't know. I called the city newspaper. A writer friend told me that she saw an AP release a few days earlier on the woman. She said she would try to track it down and call me back. Meanwhile, I called a racquetball friend to see if he could help. He knew nothing. The newspaper friend called back. Not much information, except that the tournament was being held in Lansing.

I called the Lansing Civic Center. The voice said, "No, we do not host any racquetball clubs. No, we don't know who you should contact."

I called the Lansing Chamber of Commerce. No luck. They didn't know anything. But just before I hung up the woman recommended that I call Parks and Recreation. A call to Parks and Recreation was a dead end.

I dialed information and asked for a listing of all the racquetball clubs in Lansing. There were four. I started calling. On my third call I struck paydirt. They were sponsoring a tournament. And yes, Jane Tubbs was going to play at eleven o'clock that evening. I told the director of the meet to have Jane Tubbs call me when she arrived. He said he would. As an afterthought, he said I should contact the Sports Illustrated Racquet Club in Kalamazoo. He thought she was there. He gave me the number. I dialed it. The director told me that Jane Tubbs would be in later that morning and he would tell her to call me.

One hour later Jane called. As we talked I explained why I wanted to interview her. She said, "Sure. I'd be delighted. Flattered." We talked some more. I knew she had a dynamite story.

That evening my wife Beth and I drove to the tournament in

Lansing for an amazing story: a story of a woman who has really accepted the challenge.

Jane Tubbs learned to play racquetball as a freshman at Orange Coast College in California. She learned to play under the tutelage of Barry Wallace—a fantastic coach. As she was learning the indoor game she was introduced to outdoor (three-wall) racquetball through a tournament. The competitive play of the tournament turned her on to the game. She said, "The competition fascinated me. Besides, I like the idea of getting a tan while playing. So I stayed outdoors."

She played outdoors for three years. Her group of competitors were the original outdoor players. They were and are looked upon as the leaders in the sport. It's here that the annual national outdoor tournaments are held. The big boys (and girls) come to prove who's number one in the various racquetball classifications. With this kind of exposure, play, and training, Jane improved steadily. She learned to play quite well, her forte being form and court position.

Soon the outdoor people turned their energy toward indoor competition. In 1977 Jane did likewise. She joined a private club. Because Jane had played indoors at Orange Coast College she had a jump on her friends who also went indoors. She was used to taking the ball off the back wall, and that gave her a decided advantage.

After going indoors the sport became her life. She ate, drank, and slept racquetball. She dropped out of college. She and her friends' skill levels improved. She started to work full-time at the club and began playing in more tournaments. She didn't have the money to travel nationally, but she felt that the competition locally was the best.

With such devotion she started to perfect her racquetball skills and hone her talents. As she saw and felt her skills improve she began to think about the possibility of turning pro.

In December of 1978 Jane decided that she wanted to play in the Fresno St. Patrick's Day tournament. For some reason, she felt that if she did well in this tournament that would be an indication that she should turn professional. She shared this thought with no one except her father, who was an AMF-Voit design engineer in racquetball. He encouraged her to do her best.

With the decision made to use the St. Patrick's tournament as a demarcation point, Jane began to train seriously. Daily, she did one hour of stretching and almost five miles of running on the beach. To improve her strength she did forty-five minutes of weight training. She also spent six hours on the court. Not just playing, but doing drill after drill. She thought deliberately about each shot. Where it was going to be placed. How hard she was going to hit it. She made sure that her form was proper, her style of play deliberate but effective. She did not and still does not believe in any extraneous motion on the court. She was striving to be a pure quality player and would spend hours working on an area that was weak, such as her backhand. She wanted to prove to herself that she had the ability to turn pro.

"I kept constantly thinking about going to Fresno. I wanted to prove something. I'd dropped out of college. I wanted to do something with my life and racquetball was it. My dad knew it, but no one else did," she told me.

Some of her friends were suspicious, however. Because of her intensity of training her friends told her she was going to do well. They thought she was going to win. But Jane told them she only wanted to make a good showing. In reality she was just trying to make it look like it wasn't a big deal. But it was.

All this training and dedication was compounded by the fact that Jane did have some health problems. Three years before (just before she turned twenty-one) she developed seizure activity on the right side of her brain. The misfiring of neurons in the brain would cause her to tremble slightly, bite her tongue, and then sleep.

After a period of tests and experimentation, her neurologist prescribed medication that seemed to control the activity quite well. But every time she wanted to do well in racquetball it would seem to flare up. According to her doctor the increased activity wasn't related to the stress of increased activity and competition. It just seemed to erupt at the wrong times.

Although the seizure activity was reduced by the medication, the effectiveness of it varied greatly. Some days Jane would feel great and other days she'd feel terrible. She and her doctor tried to adjust the medication as best they could, a task which took nearly two years. It was during this time that Jane didn't engage in much tournament activity. She wanted to feel more normal and stronger before going all out.

Then in the fall of 1978 she seemed to be back on a more even keel. She didn't feel perfect, but progress had been made. She decided she was ready to do the necessary training for proper competition. Unfortunately, the seizure activity of the past few years masked the fact that her body was building up for a stroke.

As she was training hard and diligently for the Fresno tournament, Jane noticed some odd symptoms of the impending trouble. First, she didn't feel all that good. She and her doctor felt it was the medication and the seizure activity. He tried readjusting the medication to see if they could reestablish a proper dosage. (The increased exercise may have prompted the need for adjustment in medication.) Second, she experienced feelings of dizziness. Nothing major, and it was somewhat similar to previous dizzy spells, so they both tended to rule that problem out. Third, she occasionally slurred her words. This bothered her, but she tried to forget it.

Then two weeks before the tournament she noticed that the thumb and forefinger of her right hand went numb. Additionally, the right side of her face tingled. All of these symptoms she attributed to being tired. "I just felt that I was training too hard. I tried to ignore it. I kept telling myself I was tired. I couldn't stop; the tournament meant too much to me. I just had to hang in there. In retrospect it was dumb, but that's how I felt," Jane recalled.

She got through the rigorous training regimen in what she thought was pretty good shape, except for those ominous symptoms which she tried to block out. She had five years of playing under her belt and had been exposed to a high level of competition. Moreover, in the past three months she had packed more than seven hundred hours of serious training into her game. She was a rock-solid 145 pounds. Her arms and legs were strong. Her wind was good; her game was in top form. She was now going to Fresno to prove to herself that she had it in her to turn pro.

She knew she was ready for the big weekend—the test of tests. Apparently the officials at the meet surmised that she was ready as well. She was seeded fourth.

On Friday, March 16, Sue Crouse, her best friend, and Jane drove to Fresno for the big tournament. When they arrived Jane found out that she did not have to play until five o'clock on Saturday. That was disappointing and irritating, but Jane had no other choice.

The wait was long. Jane could feel the anticipation and pressure of a big match building. She occupied her time talking to friends and watching other matches. Then on Saturday, Jane started to get ready. She did her customary one hour of stretching prior to her match. She and Sue reviewed strategies. As usual they agreed to provide each other with the moral support they both felt they needed.

At five o'clock Jane walked onto the glass court where hundreds of people could see her. She felt good. She felt as though she was going to do well. "For some reason I had never felt that way before in singles. I just had the confidence that I was going to be able to do it. In the warm-up I felt my volleys were good. I was hitting the ball exceptionally well. Everything was in sync," Jane told me.

At the outset of the game Jane was in top form. But at the seventh point things went awry. Jane recalls, "I killed the ball or something. I turned around to look at the referee. I couldn't hear him saying anything. His lips moved, but there was no sound. I looked at Sue. I couldn't hear what she was yelling. I could read her lips and I knew she wanted me to call a time-out. But there was no sound. All of this happened in an instant. I then went to retrieve the ball, and as I did I didn't feel well. The only thing that flashed through my mind was that I shouldn't faint. I was on a glass court and I didn't want five hundred people to see me collapse. Then I couldn't remember whether I had taken my medication or not. That scared me.

"I walked back toward the wall to get the ball. But I couldn't see it very well. When I got to where I thought the ball was, I bent over and I thought I picked it up with my right hand. I returned to the serving line. As I did, I turned around once more. But I noticed the ball was still on the floor. I then turned, went back, and picked it up with my left hand."

As all this was happening, Jane figured the confusion was due to seizure activity. She also thought she should probably take a time-out but she refused to do so. When she got back to the service line for the second time she felt fine. She could hear everything again and there seemed to be no problem.

She played well the rest of the game and won 15–7. The players then moved on to their second game. Jane knew she had to get off the court quickly. She played hard and well and won the game 15–5. She was pleased. She had won the first two games and therefore the match was over.

Jane got off the court quickly. And as she did Sue came down from the upstairs viewing area, walked over to her and said, "What's wrong with you? What happened to you out there? Why didn't you take a time-out?"

Jane looked at her and tried to say something. But as hard as she tried to speak, no words would come out. She tried to make her mouth say the words. But it wouldn't. She grimaced pretty badly. It scared her.

Sue misread the problem and thought Jane was joking. She started laughing, and told Jane to stop it. "I felt awful. I had this splitting headache on the left side of my head. The headache was maddening. I didn't understand so I went upstairs to get a Coke. I thought maybe food would help. When I got to the counter I tried to ask for a Coke but nothing came out of my mouth. Five times I tried to pronounce the word Coke. But I couldn't get it out. The girl behind the counter was upset. Then scared. She started crying.

"People who were watching me were also confused. They wanted to know what was wrong. One guy came up and asked if I got a rap on the head or something. I felt so strange. I was unable to speak," Jane told me. "Finally, Sue helped me out and spoke for me."

Jane drank some of the Coke. She also started to relax. She thought medication was in order. So she popped a couple of pills.

After her match she was expected to referee the next match. It's standard procedure in racquetball for the winner of the match to referee the next match on the same court. Jane tried to find someone to take this obligation for her. She was unable to talk, had a splitting headache, and didn't feel well. She thought someone else might better shoulder this responsibility. She asked around but there were no volunteers.

In a quandary, Jane went to the two young women who were scheduled to play on her court. She had extreme difficulty speaking. But she told them as best she could that she had tried to get someone to referee for her, but was unable to do so. She explained that she couldn't talk properly, but would give them the score and that would be it. There would be very few additional words said.

Fortunately, there were no problems with the match. It was a definite match and the two racquetballers played their games with a minimum of assistance from Jane. As these games progressed, Jane found out that when she talked slowly and carefully she could get the words out of her mouth. But the headache persisted.

At the conclusion of the match she tried to relax as much as possible. Soon things seemed to be better. She no longer felt sick and the headache subsided somewhat. At 7:30 her next series of games were scheduled. She went to the court and played well. She won the first two games without any problem. During the game the headache persisted but it wasn't nearly so bad as it had been during the five o'clock match.

After the match Jane rested some more. She had one more match at eleven o'clock. She would need all the strength she could muster.

By eleven o'clock Jane felt a lot better. She walked onto the court confident but confused as to why she had had all those problems in the first match. Play started, and before she knew it she was behind 0–8. "I just couldn't believe it. Everything seemed to go wrong. I quickly called a time-out," Jane remembers.

Sue came down and asked Jane what the problem was. She also challenged her to get her act together.

The break and lecture reawakened her. Jane walked back on the court. She recalls, "I was laughing to myself. Zero–eight. Can you believe it? I won the first two matches in two games and here I am down zero–eight. I knew I had to get moving."

And move she did. Jane drew back on all her hard training and experience. She got the serve back and went after her competitor. The rival never had a chance. Jane scored fifteen straight points and won the game.

She went on to win the next game and the match without any problem. She left the court pleased with her comeback. She spoke to her friends for a while and then went to eat.

Jane got back to her room about one o'clock that morning and collapsed into bed. At 2:30 she awoke lying on her back. She tried to turn to her left but couldn't. She found that her right arm fell down behind her and she tried to raise it, but couldn't.

She tried to collect her thoughts. She didn't know if she was sleeping or not. Then she realized she had a terrific headache. She was scared.

Again, Jane says it best: "I looked over at my friend Sue, and she was sound asleep. I called to her. I had to call her three times to awaken her. When Sue awakened I told her that something was seriously wrong with me. I told her to call my parents.

"When Sue left the room to place the call I tried to sit up. I found the only way I could do it was to swing my left leg off the bed. The swinging of my leg down allowed me to swing my upper body up into a sitting position. Successful with that I tried to stand up. And when I did I fell back into the bed. I was scared."

When Sue came back to the room she said Jane's parents advised her to call an ambulance. Jane knew she needed help. Both women were scared and started to cry.

When the ambulance crew came, Jane told them that she thought she'd had a stroke. The paramedics said no. They saw she was able to wiggle her toes and that she could move her ankles.

But Jane persisted. She had worked with stroke patients in a physical therapy class at Orange Coast College and was familiar with their paralysis.

The paramedic crew quickly got her into the ambulance and drove her to the hospital. Enroute Sue asked the crew whether they thought they could get her back to the racquetball court by nine o'clock the next morning. After all, she was scheduled to be in the semifinals. The crew just laughed and said, "We'll see."

They arrived at the emergency room at three in the morning. Her parents had called a neurologist in Newport Beach to get the name of a neurologist in the Fresno area.

At ten o'clock on Saturday morning Jane was assigned to a hospital bed. On Saturday and Sunday the hospital staff ran exhaustive tests on her trying to diagnose her problem. As the doctor examined her he asked her to move her right hand. She couldn't. He asked her to lift her right leg. She couldn't do that either. But she was still able to move her ankle slightly and wiggle her toes. That baffled the doctors. They felt that while a stroke was a possibility, her paralysis could also be due to a severe migraine attack.

During the next couple of days the doctors continued to

observe and conduct more tests. By Wednesday the doctor concluded that the paralysis was, indeed, caused by a stroke.

Jane's mother flew to be at Jane's side during her hospital stay. She provided great emotional support for Jane. While there Jane displayed some of the feistiness that was going to help pull her through. The nurses had wanted Jane to use a bedpan. Her mother wanted her to use a bedpan. But Jane was absolutely against it. Although her arm was in a sling and she was unable to walk she told her mother she was going to use the bathroom and not the bedpan. Everyone discouraged her. Jane responded, "If I have to crawl there I'm going to use the bathroom. I will not use that bedpan. My mother was embarrassed. But somehow with the nurse's help I got to the bathroom and back."

On Wednesday, Jane and her mother flew back home. In characteristic fashion, Jane wouldn't allow anyone to help her off the plane. She was admitted to Hoag Memorial Presbyterian Hospital in Newport Beach. Her neurologist did an angiogram on her and further tests. They found that the clot had formed in her left mid-cerebral artery. Furthermore, one of the reasons she was able to move her ankles and toes was that she had developed excellent collateral circulation around the clot. The clot had been forming for some time, for almost a year, but her body tried to preserve a normal condition by developing extensive new blood vessels to help pick up the function of the affected artery. But eventually the clot grew to such a size that even her body could not maintain this equilibrium.

The reason the clot occurred was not clear. She was young and vigorous. She did, of course, have some serious health problems. But that still didn't explain why she had the stroke. Another confusing fact in Jane's case was that her blood pressure was normal—quite low—before the stroke.

Seven days after being admitted to the Fresno hospital Jane was able to speak pretty well. Her right side—her arm and leg—was paralyzed. The doctors continued to give her additional tests to see if she had any disease or condition that may have helped precipitate the stroke. They found none.

All this time Jane tried to retain her composure. When anyone came to visit her she would smile and laugh. But when they left she would cry and her anger would come out. "I was down. There was nothing for me to do. I was bored," Jane said.

Many doctors examined her. Many gave theories. But that's all they were, theories. One neurologist gave her good encouragement. He told her he thought she would be back one hundred percent. "But only if you work hard," he told her.

Another told her she would never walk back on the racquetball court again. In fact he said, "I don't advise it." That did it. Jane looked at him and concluded that he wasn't an athlete. She shot back, "You don't know what you're talking about. I'm going to be back. I'm going to turn pro." The doctor, realizing Jane was quite upset, wisely chose to make a fast exit.

Jane told me that she really didn't know if the doctor meant it or was trying to motivate her. Whatever his objectives, it did get her moving. She decided to fight back. She was going to come back and play racquetball.

Up till this point Jane had been angry. She said, "I was angry I didn't win the tournament. I was angry I didn't get the trophy. I'd worked hard for months. It was the only thing I had thought about. And now it was taken from me. I was mad. Hostile. I just didn't understand at the time."

But the doctor either knowingly or unknowingly turned her around. Jane made up her mind that she was going to rehabilitate herself. She blitzed the rehabilitation program as she had attacked getting into shape for the Fresno St. Patrick's Day tournament. "My feeling was that I had to come back. I was an athlete. Activity was my life. Racquetball was my life. I could not lead a life without it," Jane said.

Occupational and physical therapy were in order. The therapists started her off with patterning. Jane was unable to walk. So they first had to teach her how to crawl. They taught her how to position her arms and legs properly in a kneeling position. It was just like being a baby all over again. They got her on her knees. They tried to get her to hold that position. She fell many times. They tried to push her over, and she had to fight back.

The physical therapist put Jane through passive exercises. Exercises in which the therapist moved Jane's legs and arms for her. Then they put her in a squat position and asked her to stand up. "That was the hardest thing to do. I just couldn't believe I could not stand up, no matter how hard I tried," she told me.

"As I went through physical therapy and occupational therapy I also looked at the other girls who had had strokes. I noticed that they had a stroke because they had taken the Pill, or they had used hard drugs. These were things I had never taken. And here I was in the same condition. It made me mad, angry, and furious.

"But as I worked with them I noticed something else. They'd just sit there. They had given up. They were totally wiped out. Blasé, I guess, is the word. But I was a physical person. I was not going to let this happen to me. So I fought. For every defeat I felt I had to have a victory. And I tried. Oh, how I tried," Jane continued.

Then one day they got Jane up and started her walking. They told her they were going to put a brace on her leg. She refused. She was afraid her leg would not get stronger. But the physical therapist was adamant. Jane was back-kneeing too much (knee bending backward too far).

Jane got mad. She didn't want a brace. She decided to prove them wrong. When she got home she walked out the front door with her cane. With her arm in a sling, she tried walking from the house to the corner. It was slow-going; she fell several times, scraping her knees, but she got back up. When she got to the corner she dropped the cane. Then she kicked it forward. She limped toward the cane. When she got to it she kicked it again. Each time she reached the cane she would kick it again and walk after it. She'd kick the cane, limp after it, maybe fall down, get up, and then get to the cane and kick it again. She did this from the corner and back to the house forty times.

When she walked she talked to herself as she had on the racquetball court. "I told my leg to raise upward, my knee to bend, my heel to strike the ground, my foot to roll along the sole—along the outer border of the foot—and my toes to push off. I said it over and over again—leg lift, knee bend, heel strike, foot roll, push off with toes," Jane said. She was exhausted by the time she was finished. But she felt it did her some good.

When Jane went back to the physical therapist no one could

believe the progress made in a single day. The physical therapist felt that a leg brace might not be necessary.

Every day Jane spent one hour in occupational therapy, and one hour in physical therapy. At home she worked six hours on her own, concentrating on her legs, deliberately forcing herself to think and talk to her leg and foot about proper movement.

It took Jane two and a half months to get to the point where she could walk fairly comfortably. The mainstays in helping were her parents, Sue, Dr. Smith, and Lew Snyder. Dr. Smith was a psychologist who helped Jane accept what was wrong with her and deal with the frustration. Lew and Jane had gone together before in 1978. But when she started the serious training for Fresno they broke up. After her attack, however, Lew stuck by her side. Each day he would come to Jane's door to see her and encourage her to walk. Even when she didn't want to, Lew kept encouraging and demanding she do it. There were many times she hated the thought of going around the block one more time, but she did it because she knew she had to.

As her walking improved, the physical therapist concentrated on Jane's arm. Even though her arm and shoulder muscles ached when moved, Jane knew she had to do it. The therapist moved her arm through selected movements. The therapist also had Jane work with putty—squeezing and pulling. This activity strengthened her fingers and got them to respond somewhat.

Her parents also worked with her arm patterning movements. They enjoyed it and helped her move her arm properly. Her mother had polio as a youngster so she had some ideas on how to accommodate for the loss of a limb. She showed Jane how to navigate around the house and be self-sufficient. Her mother and dad were a real inspiration and gave plenty of physical and moral support. Jane says, "They were special. They meant everything to me."

Unfortunately, the old friends back at the racquetball club did not provide similar support. They had a hard time accepting Jane after the big event. Up until the stroke Jane was the chief jock, the great Southern California girl. After her injury these athletes deserted her. Jane says, "The day after I got out of the hospital I went back to the club to see my friends. I had my arm in a sling and walked with a cane. I couldn't walk very well. I couldn't talk very well. When I walked in the expressions on their faces were unbelievable. It hurt. I didn't know what to do. From that day on they treated me like an invalid. Fortunately, they did let me play on the court."

That attitude left a mark on Jane. She says, "It was tough to compete in that kind of environment. As long as you're healthy they're with you. When you're on top they're with you. But if you're average or something is wrong, you're down at the bottom of the heap. You're a nobody. You're a failure. That attitude crushed me."

Within six weeks of the cerebrovascular accident, Jane began weight training under the supervision of an experienced coach, Leon Skeie. To complement her walking she also rode her bicycle. Of course she had to learn that skill all over again, too. She rode a ten-speed, and since she couldn't use one arm very well, that in itself was a trick. She had many a fall but stuck to it. Again Lew rode and encouraged her.

Three months after the stroke, Jane began jogging. But the jogging was not easy. Each time she took a step her foot would flop on the ground and hit hard. It was awkward, but she kept trying. Since it was June and hot, she had to run at eleven o'clock in the evening. She started by running two hundred feet. And again Lew was by her side encouraging her and telling her to stick with it. In a matter of months she was up to four miles. She knew the jogging would make her stronger. It would help her get back on the court and she'd be able to show that doctor that he didn't know what he was talking about.

Slowly, ever so slowly, additional progress was made. Jane kept fighting back. She kept pestering the physical therapist to let her go back to the racquetball court. But the therapist thought it was too soon. She felt it might be an emotional and physical setback for Jane; stepping onto the court and not having the skills might be too much of a shock.

But Jane persisted. She wanted to get back to racquetball. Five and a half months after the stroke Jane walked back onto the court. She was scared and knew she wouldn't do well, but she had good moral support. Lew told her, "When you get on the court I want you to laugh. You're going to have problems. Things are not going to be the same. But I want you to laugh no matter what."

That was excellent advice. When Jane got onto the court she found she didn't have the arm strength to throw the ball onto the floor. Furthermore, she had such poor right hand movement that she could not hold the ball properly. As an alternative, she dropped the ball with her left hand and then tried hitting it with the racquet which she held in her left hand. But her concentration was off. She would drop the ball, swing, and miss. Again and again she tried it. Each time she missed. She was frustrated but remembered Lew's admonition to laugh. So she did. After ten minutes of trying she was exhausted, totally fatigued. Jane describes how she felt: "I walked off the court and I laughed. It was my only salvation. But when I got home that night I cried."

Emotionally devastated, she waited to go back on the court again. Fortunately the physical therapist now realized how important it was for Jane to play racquetball again. So she started to work Jane's hand vigorously. In addition to using putty the therapist had her squeeze a racquetball. They had her type on a typewriter in occupational therapy. This, too, strengthened her finger and arm muscles. They wanted her to be able to drop the ball with her right hand.

In two weeks measurable progress was seen. Lew, Sue, and her parents encouraged her to try playing again. She contacted Scott Winters, the club pro, to help her. She knew she had lost everything. The only way she could come back would be to relearn her footwork, swing, form, court position—everything. Scott worked closely with her and showed her some new tips. Gradually some of her skill returned.

The physical aspect of coming back was only part of the problem. When she came back to the club she noticed that she couldn't remember anyone. "I'd see their faces. I'd recognize them. But I couldn't remember their names. That was exceptionally hard on me. They didn't understand. They thought I was cold-shouldering them. They'd say, 'Hi Jane, how are you doing?' and I'd say, 'Oh, fine, how are you?' I guess I seemed distant."

The more she played the more she continued to improve her racquetball abilities. Each time she came to the court, things seemed to be a little easier. She was able to hit the ball with a little more power and accuracy. Soon she improved to the point where she was able to move to the challenge court of the club. This is where the better players sign up to challenge each other. It is highly competitive. Her reassociation with the court members also helped bring her memory back.

But soon she could feel the pressure building. She was finding it increasingly difficult to compete in the Southern California attitude of high competition. Jane recalls, "I lost every single time on the challenge court. And I cried every time. Of course people were amazed that I tried. But it wasn't the same as before. I didn't have the zip I once had. People viewed me as an invalid. They remembered how good I had been. I got a lot of pity which I couldn't handle. I wasn't the same athlete as before. I was a nothing. I was someone who had had a stroke."

Jane's parents felt that California was hindering her progress. She was getting high blood pressure and was exhausted emotionally. Jane and her parents thought it best to leave California for a while. To take a vacation. Her sister lived on a farm in the Midwest. They all thought that it would be a good idea for Jane to spend a few weeks there and get some R and R. So in August Jane went to live with her sister.

One week of living on the farm was therapeutic. Mentally she felt better. More relaxed. And she could move her arm better. The pressure was off.

Jane was anxious to play again, so she visited a local racquetball club. The manager saw her play and was impressed. Believing she had real potential as a teacher, he offered her a job. Unfortunately, Jane was planning on returning to California in a few days. But she told the manager that she would think about it.

When Jane returned to California the pressure returned. The competition was crippling. She decided it would be best to return to the Midwest and start her life all over again. So in late September she left her friends, parents, and the only world she knew to start anew.

On October 1 Jane took her job at the club. She was named program coordinator of the club. Now she was living on her own terms. It was a difficult decision to leave all her loved ones, but she knew it was the best thing for her.

Getting back on the racquetball court as a teacher has been good therapy for her. She still has a long way to go, but her racquetball skills are returning. She's jumping back into life as before. She is establishing new friends and a new way of life. She's also setting some pretty hefty goals. A few of them are:

• She wants to finish college and get a degree in psychology. That will take about two years.

• She wants to play racquetball competitively and improve to the point where she is Open Class. She's realistic, though. She feels pro competition will never be a reality because she doesn't have the moves she once had.

• She'd like to manage a club in the future. She likes the business aspect of it.

• She would like to talk to other people about strokes. She wants to speak to hospital groups, young people, old people, telling them what a stroke is. That it can happen to anyone, young, old, male, or female. Recently she's been given that opportunity and she's taking it.

• She is cultivating a personality that is warm and caring. She didn't say that, but it came through loud and clear. She makes it a point to be caring of others. It's a special quality few of us have, or take the time to nurture as Jane has.

After the interview my wife and I stayed to watch Jane play. She competed in the Class C level. Her serve was excellent. I could just visualize what she must have been like in early 1979, before the stroke. In fact, after her first two serves I was so impressed I thought the match would be a piece of cake. When her service is broken, however, or when the play is furious, she has some problems, being unable to get around the court as fast as she wanted to. I detected some real frustration because of this. But I noticed she wouldn't let it get her down. I also noticed why she is where she is in only ten months. When down 2–6 she came back and tied the game. When down 6–9 she came back and tied it again. And when the game was at seventeen all her concentration was unbelievable. She talked to herself, the ball, and the racquet. And in a matter of seconds she put the game away 21–17.

Yes, J. P., you were right. Jane Tubbs is the "Winner of the Day" and certainly a winner at life.

Epilogue

I hope these people have challenged you. I hope they've shown you there is only one excuse not to live well—that is, you choose not to. That is the only legitimate excuse. Rationalizations such as the weather, how you feel, your busy schedule, etc., are not valid.

From now on, when your good intentions falter, as mine do, think of these stories. When you think you have a good excuse, as I do at times, think of these eighteen amazing people.

• Too old: Reread Hulda Crooks and Millie Smith. Here are two people who are well past seventy-five and can walk and run most people half their age under the table.

• Too heavy: Review the stories of Chris Stutzmann and Ginny Murling. Ginny lost a whole person and then some. Yet she still weighs more than two hundred pounds and logs over six miles a day.

• Too sick: Examine the stories of Deanna McKenzie with multiple sclerosis, Steve McKanic with a diseased heart, Susan Guild and Bob Gilley with cancer, or Jane Tubbs with a cerebrovascular disease. If they can exercise, in spite of these significant diseases, you certainly can.

• Too depressed: Go over the stories of Elizabeth Andersson or Dave Roberts. These two people reached the depths of depression yet they came back.

• Physically unable: Reconsider the stories of Mike McCarrick, Billy Haughton, and Lori Markle. They either lost or were born without adequate legs. Yet they exercise with an intensity that is truly amazing.

• Life too rough: Look at Paul Leestma, Mike Levine, Bob Abels, or Randy Nelson. They have real excuses not to exercise. But they have not permitted their afflictions to hold them down.

And of course, these people are only a partial list of the amazing people who grace this land. They are not unique. They are not stars. There are many, many more. Unfortunately, I could only tell a few. But one thing is clear. They all have drive, feistiness, and spunk.

Hulda Crooks, the eighty-three-year-old wonder from Loma Linda, who climbed Mt. Whitney eighteen times in the past eighteen years, told me that I should look at a rose bush to understand more about life and how these people respond to challenges. "On the stalk of a rose bush you'll find thorns and prickles. Thorns grow deep into the stalk. Into the heartwood. A thorn is a stunted branch. It cannot be pushed off. Blindness, a loss of a limb, or a dreaded disease are all thorns. We cannot push them off. We must learn to live with them. A thorn serves a purpose. They help to mold our characters and make us more understanding of others.

"Prickles, on the other hand, do not grow into the stem. These are things which you can push off if you want to. A prickle can hurt. It can make the blood run, but it can be pushed off. It does not grow into the stalk. Prickles are irritations, hurts, and disappointments in life. But don't let them get you down."

Life is full of challenges. Some are prickles and some are

thorns. Most of us, however, make prickles into thorns. We tend to focus on the trivia of life. We let the wrong things destroy us. Think of Hulda. Push off the prickles. Live with enthusiasm and joy.

In reality, I was only a chronicler of these people. I did not walk in their shoes for a lifetime. I could only tell the story as I viewed it, and as it was told to me. To compound the problem, in these biographies I only told one small part of their lives—their affliction, their dedication to exercise, and their refusal to quit. But, as their stories began to unfold, I felt that their attitude about life shone through.

The cynic in the crowd might say that I made these stories too dramatic—that these people are unreal in this modern world. Let me assure you that these stories are true. These people have been beaten and battered, but not defeated. They have faced some of the harshest realities of life. They have been to the brink but have continued to struggle and fight back. And in doing so they have succeeded.

Some had and have significant disease. By the time this book is published some may have died—their diseases are that catastrophic. But one thing is clear. Despite these significant ailments, they have lived life on a positive note. These challenged people have not wallowed in self-pity. They all feel that to best manage their disease they must maintain a bright and sunny mental attitude that will help pull them through. Many have read Norman Cousins's account of how he laughed himself back to good health after suffering from a supposedly fatal illness. These people accepted the challenge. The challenge to do their best in spite of hardship, and to get the most out of life.

Most of you reading this book do not have significant heart disease, cancer, multiple sclerosis, blindness, cerebrovascular disease, a loss of a limb, arthritis, or whatever. You don't have such a challenge. But you do have a challenge of living in modern-day America. Science and technology have brought us to the point where we must go out of our way to exercise. We must force ourselves to take time for relaxation and time to select and prepare good food. To live well in America is a counter-culture action. The modern-day American faces a challenge. And that challenge is to overcome an unhealthful way of living.

I would like to reiterate that these individuals are more than afflicted or handicapped people. They are human beings. The physical is only one aspect of their personalities. They are positive, warm, caring people who have a strong desire to help others. They think that exercise is important, but so is their intellectual and spiritual development. I think that attitude is important.

There are people today who make their active lifestyle their religion. I have a good friend who is like that. He's a fitness fanatic. He honestly thinks that exercise is going to solve all of his mental, physical, and spiritual problems and hangups. I don't. I think the exercise may help him feel better, but he cannot run away from his problems. He needs more.

One prestigious running newspaper states on its masthead that "running is the key to life." I don't buy that. Running is only one part of a person's total life. In fact, an obsession with exercise can be destructive.

My biography on Elizabeth and Tom Andersson reflects that concern. Tom was negatively addicted to running. *Everything* in his life revolved around it. His job, avocation, leisure time, reading, and eventually even his love life focused on it. In the process his marriage and relationship with his children were destroyed. His wife, on the other hand, saw this negativism and approached her running in a more relaxed manner. Her running was positive and fulfilling. That is the approach that I prefer.

While exercise was an important part of these peoples' return to a normal, healthy life, it was only part of it. All had other interests and activities. They were pursuing life, not exercise. I think we need to remember that. We sometimes forget the big picture and turn a positive into a negative. The big story, as far as I'm concerned, is not that each chose to exercise, but that each chose to live, and live well.

Their biographies were not intended to make you feel guilty about exercising or show you that exercise is the key to life. Instead they show you that you take time to do the things you want to do.

Don't let this book lead you into negative addiction. If it does I have failed in my mission to tell the stories. These are stories which are supposed to encourage, support, and motivate—make your exercise a positive, rewarding experience. Don't make it punitive and destructive. Everyone in this book saw the value and importance of exercise in his or her life. But it was only one aspect of it. They also saw that the ideal person is one who personifies the ideal of a sound mind, body, and spirit.

About the Authors

Charles T. Kuntzleman is a consultant to the National YMCA's Nationwide Cardiovascular Health Program and to Phillips Petroleum Company's Operation Lifestyle Program. He is the author of over a dozen books on health and fitness, and has developed three National YMCA Fitness Programs. He has conducted over a hundred workshops across the United States and Canada. He received his doctorate from Temple University.

Lyn Cryderman is a writer/photographer who lives on a small farm in Michigan. A former high school and college coach and teacher, he has written several articles for trade and professional journals. He holds an M.A. in English Literature from Eastern Michigan University. This is his first book.